5090057:

C000259391

The Road to Dunkirk

The Road to Dunkirk

The British Expeditionary Force
and the Battle of the Ypres–Comines Canal, 1940

Charles More

Frontline Books, London

In memory of

Major C. S. Hedley MC

Captain R. W. Thorne MBE

The Road to Dunkirk: The British Expeditionary Force
and the Battle of the Ypres–Comines Canal, 1940

First published in 2013 by Frontline Books,
an imprint of Pen & Sword Books Ltd,
47 Church Street, Barnsley, S. Yorkshire, S70 2AS
www.frontline-books.com

Copyright © Charles More, 2013

The right of Charles More to be identified as the author of this work has been asserted
by him in accordance with the Copyright, Designs and Patents Act 1988.

ISBN: 978-1-84832-733-7

CIP data records for this title are available from the British Library

For more information on our books, please visit
www.frontline-books.com, email info@frontline-books.com
or write to us at the above address.

Typeset in 10/13.75 point Minion Light by Wordsense Ltd, Edinburgh
Printed and bound by CPI Group (UK) Ltd, Croydon, CR0 4YY [TBC]

Contents

Illustrations

Plates

Maps

Abbreviations, Conventions and Glossary

Abbreviations

BA-MA Freiburg	Bundesarchiv Militaerarchiv, Freiburg
BEF	British Expeditionary Force
CAB	cabinet
CCMA	corps commander medium artillery
CGS	Chief of General Staff
C-in-C	commander-in-chief
CIGS	Chief of the Imperial General Staff
CO	commanding officer
CP	counter preparation
CRA	commander royal artillery
DCLI	The Duke of Cornwall's Light Infantry
DCM	Distinguished Conduct Medal (other ranks; equivalent to the DSO)
DF	defensive fire
DLI	The Durham Light Infantry
DLM	Division Légère Mécanique
DR	dispatch rider
DSO	Distinguished Service Order (officers – major and above; for leadership and/or gallantry)
FDL	forward defence locality
GF	gunfire
GHQ	general headquarters (from 25 May 1940 used to refer to advanced general headquarters)
GOC	general officer commanding
GSO1	general staff officer 1
HE	high explosive

HQ	headquarters
HQMA	headquarters medium artillery
HQRA	headquarters royal artillery
ID	infanterie-division
IO	intelligence officer
IR	infanterie-regiment
IWM	Imperial War Museum
LHCMA	Liddell Hart Centre for Military Archives
MA	medium artillery
MC	Military Cross (officers – majors and below; for gallantry)
MG	machine gun
MM	Military Medal (other ranks; equivalent to the Military Cross)
MT	motor transport
NAAFI	Navy, Army and Airforce Institutes
NCO	non-commissioned officer
NW	northwest
OKH	Oberkommando des Heeres
OP	observation post
RA	Royal Artillery
RAF	Royal Air Force
RAMC	Royal Army Medical Corps
RAP	regimental aid post
RASC	Royal Army Service Corps
RE	Royal Engineers
RSF	The Royal Scots Fusiliers
RSM	regimental sergeant-major
RT	radio transmitters
TNA	The National Archives
VC	Victoria Cross (all ranks – supreme award for gallantry)
WO	War Office

Conventions

Artillery regiments	Field artillery regiments are usually referred to in this book as, for example, '9th Field'; medium artillery regiments are similarly abbreviated; Field engineer companies are referred to by their full title, e.g. '245th Field Company'.
Place names	British usage of the time has been adopted for place and river names, which means more often the French than the Flemish name. Thus it is Escaut rather than Scheldt, Courtrai rather than Kortrijk, etc.
Quotations	The wording of quotations has not been altered (except that dots signify omissions) but a few silent adjustments have been made for ease of reading. Thus the British army habit of capitalising proper names has been dropped, some less obvious abbreviations have been expanded and misspellings corrected (Ploegsteert, for instance, has almost as many spellings as there are war diaries). In German war diaries the German convention of writing IR as JR, etc. has been reversed.
Regimental names	British regimental names have been abbreviated by the familiar abbreviations for individual counties: e.g, Warwicks (The Royal Warwickshire Regiment), Ox & Bucks (The Oxfordshire & Buckinghamshire Light Infantry).
Time	Expressed throughout in the 24-hour clock, unless given otherwise in quotations.
Umlauts	Umlauts have been replaced by an 'e' after the letter concerned: for example, *Vortraege.*

Glossary

Adjutant	Person with an important role in charge of battalion operations; the position is usually occupied by a middle-ranking officer.
Army	A headquarters formation, usually commanding between two and four corps and some ancillary formations. The BEF was, in organisational terms, an army.

Battalion	Its composition is discussed in Chapter 1. Comprises about 800 officers and men at full strength.
Bombardier	Artillery equivalent of corporal.
Brigade	Usually three battalions with anti-tank support.
Corps	A headquarters formation, usually commanding between two and four divisions with medium artillery regiments and (British army) machine-gun battalions.
Division	Usually three brigades (regiments in the German army) of three battalions each, plus field artillery regiments and engineer companies.
Guns/Howitzers	The technical military distinction is that howitzers have a higher potential angle of fire than guns. However, 'gun' is also the term in common use for any artillery piece, including howitzers. Here 'howitzer' has been used if there is some specific reason for distinguishing the type of weapon, but where all the artillery pieces involved in an action are being described then 'gun' is used indiscriminately. The British described howitzers by muzzle diameter (e.g. 6-inch) and guns by weight of shell fired (e.g. 18-pounder).
Infanterie-Regiment	The German regiment was equivalent to a British brigade in strength and, unlike the British army regular brigades, the battalions in German regiments came from the same geographical area (as, frequently, did the regiments in divisions). German battalions were, therefore, designated simply by their number in the regiment followed by the latter's number, e.g. III/17.
Lance-Sergeant	Acting sergeant.
Medical facilities	A casualty would move successively through the regimental aid post, advanced dressing station, main dressing station, casualty clearing station to, if appropriate, a general field hospital.
Officer ranks	The British had more commissioned officers in a battalion, and up to the level of brigade/ infanterie-regiment equivalent ranks were higher in the British army than the German. Thus majors often commanded companies (German *Hauptmann* – captain), lieutenant-

	colonels commanded battalions (German *Major*) and brigadiers commanded brigades (German *Oberst* – colonel – commanded the equivalent, an infanterie-regiment). The Germans appear, therefore, to have been lightly officered, but it should be born in mind that their NCO ranks included trainee officers (*see* Chapter 1). At the start of the Battle of the Ypres–Comines Canal several of the British battalions involved were commanded by majors because of previous casualties.
Tanks	The British tanks referred to in this book were either light tanks (6-ton Vickers tanks armed with machine guns and intended for reconnaissance and anti-personnel operations) or else infantry tanks, which were more heavily armoured but slower.
Time zones	No information has been found as to which time zone the British army used, so it has been assumed that it must have been the same as the French, that is, West European Summer Time. The Germans used Central European Summer Time, one hour ahead.
Tommy gun	The British nickname for the German *maschinenpistole* (submachine gun).

Acknowledgements

Numerous people have helped me with this book and I would particularly like to thank the following: Benjamin Haas of Recherchedienst Haas; Sheelagh Neuling of Anglo-German Translation Services; Suzanne Richards; Andy Cocks; staff of the Imperial War Museum, the National Army Museum and The National Archives; David Baynham of the Royal Regiment of Fusiliers (Royal Warwickshire) Museum; staff of the Royal Green Jackets (Rifles) Museum and Green Howards Museum; Martin Brown for the maps; Joanna Chisholm; and Stephen Chumbley of Frontline Books. I also owe a particular debt to two anonymous referees, one for Frontline Books and one who made some extremely useful comments on an earlier draft of the book.

My wife, as always, provided invaluable support.

Photographs

Plate 1: by courtesy of the Green Howards Museum
Plates 2 and 8: Imperial War Museum
Plates 3 and 4 (trans. German orders; both reproductions) The National Archives, WO 167/29/7, 24 May, Appendix 13
Plate 9: The National Archives, WO 167/831, 28 May
Plate 12: with permission of the Royal Green Jackets (Rifles) Museum, Winchester

Other plates: © Charles More

Prologue

O N 4 JUNE 1940 THE last troops were evacuated from Dunkirk. The campaign, which had begun with the German invasion of the Low Countries on 10 May, was a humiliating defeat for the two allies, Britain and France. For France, Dunkirk was just one of a catalogue of disasters that culminated in the signing of an armistice with Germany two-and-a-half weeks later. For Britain, however, the evacuation also contained the seeds of hope. Some 224,000 men – the bulk of the British Expeditionary Force (BEF) – had returned to form the nucleus of the much larger British army, which was to fight the battles of the years ahead.

That the troops came back seems remarkable – so remarkable that the evacuation has sometimes been called a miracle. On 20 May the German Army Group A, having broken through the French defences on the Meuse a week earlier, had reached the Channel coast at Abbeville. It had cut off a mass of British, French and Belgian troops, who were simultaneously being pressed from the east by German Army Group B. There was little effective co-ordination between the Allied armies; parts of the Belgian and French forces had already been defeated; and many of the Allied tanks had been lost. The Germans had air superiority. Nonetheless not only the British but about 140,000 French troops were evacuated.

To many historians, the critical factor in their escape was the German 'Halt Order' of 23 May, which limited Army Group A's offensive operations along what had become the BEF's southwestern front. And there is little doubt that the Halt Order was of critical importance. During the three days it lasted the British were able to move three divisions, in order to establish a defence line of sorts along the threatened front.

However, while this was happening, Army Group B continued its pressure from the east. By 26 May, having defeated the Belgians in a battle along the river Lys, it was poised to attack the BEF. The subsequent battle, which started in earnest on the 27th and lasted for two days, was the Battle of the Ypres–Comines Canal. Had it not been fought, and fought successfully, by the British, then the four divisions of the BEF that were helping the French to garrison the salient around Lille would have been trapped south of the river Lys. Yet as late as 25 May Lord Gort, the commander of the BEF, was planning to use the troops who fought in the battle to attack southwards. His decision to direct them northwards to defend the canal was, therefore, also critical – perhaps as critical as the Halt Order – to the BEF.

Little has been written about this battle. The official historian, L. F. Ellis, devoted about six pages of his volume to it and acknowledged its importance, but some of the authors writing about the Dunkirk campaign say practically nothing about the Battle of the Ypres–Comines Canal. Indeed it is so little known that some books refer to it as the Battle of Wytschaete. It was sometimes called that in the war diaries of the units involved, but its official British army name is the Battle of the Ypres–Comines Canal, and that is how it is named in the battle honours of regiments engaged in it. Locally, too, it is almost unknown – or at least not mentioned in museums and their literature – in and around Ypres. Not surprisingly, attention there is directed towards the great battles of the First World War. The battle is, however, remembered in Comines, the small Belgian town about six miles south of Ypres, where it is known simply as the Battle of the Canal and where a memorial exists to the British who participated.[1]

If the battle was so important, why is it so little remembered? This raises complex questions about the writing of history, both the history of the campaign of May–June 1940 and the wider history of the British army in the Second World War. In such writing there are perhaps two dominant narratives. One is what might be called 'drum and trumpet' history. It focuses on acts of heroism, of self-sacrifice, of gallant last stands and successful victories. It is right and proper that these should be written about. Bravery should be remembered, and so should the Allied victories of the Second World War, a war that every sensible person believes was fought for a good cause. Such history, however, does not help much in analysing other questions in which historians are interested: for example, what were the strengths and weaknesses of a country's military forces; and what were the underlying reasons for those strengths and weaknesses?

Here there is another narrative, which is more critical of the British army. Perhaps the best exemplar of this approach is David French's *Raising Churchill's Army*, an important book which concludes that, eventually, the British army in the Second World War became a competent and effective army, if not an outstanding one. But the course of getting there, according to French, was a slow and painful one, and the British army of 1940 was still an inchoate and badly trained force.[2]

The Battle of the Ypres–Comines Canal does not fit easily into either of these narratives, and so it is hardly surprising that it is not prominent in most accounts of the campaign of May–June 1940. Of course during the fighting there were many courageous actions and many awards deservedly won. But the battle did not contain the drama of the counterattack at Arras of 21 May (in which British tanks temporarily shook several German divisions) or the self-sacrifice of 145 Brigade's defence of Cassel. So both of these, although smaller in scale than Ypres–Comines, embody more obvious stories of heroism and are better known. Nor, however, does the Ypres–Comines battle bear out a narrative in which the British army was barely competent in 1940.

Unlike many other actions in the campaign when the Germans had tanks and the British did not, or had very few, Ypres–Comines was fought between forces that were roughly equal in qualitative terms. It was basically an infantry and artillery battle, not a matter of tanks against infantry. Indeed unlike the usual perception of the fighting in 1940, only the British had tanks, although not very many. The Germans started with about twice the strength of the British in numerical terms, but the mismatch was reduced during the battle as reinforcements were fed in. And the initial differential in strength was not extreme given that the British were defending. So it was an action between two roughly comparable adversaries, and a close study of it suggests that the British units engaged had considerable fighting skills.

The Road to Dunkirk, therefore, has two aims. One is to demonstrate the importance of this battle to the success of the Dunkirk evacuation – and to pay tribute to the men of the BEF who fought and often died at Ypres–Comines. The other is to suggest that historians need to rethink the abilities of the British army of 1940 and the achievements of those who supplied it and trained it. The book starts with a description of that army and of its adversary the German army, and follows with an outline of the campaign up to 25 May 1940. The next chapter discusses the critical decision that Gort took on 25 May to send his reserve divisions, 5th and 50th, north rather than using them to attack southwards as had been planned. New light is cast on why he made that decision. The succeeding chapters outline the battle itself, ending with an account of the evacuation from Dunkirk from the point of view of the units involved in the battle.

I. Armies

I N MAY 1940, AS the Allied and German armies made their preparations, each side was roughly equal in numbers. The German army in the west had 135 divisions. The French had 117 and the British thirteen, three of which were understrength labour divisions. Yet Britain's population was larger than that of France. Why was the BEF so small?[1]

Historically Britain had relied on the Royal Navy for defence. Compared with Germany and France its army had always been limited in size, relying on volunteering rather than conscription. After its huge expansion during the First World War, the old pattern reasserted itself. This seemed doubly appropriate in the 1920s and early 1930s because of the collective security provided – it was hoped – by the League of Nations and the Locarno Treaty. This was also a period when international disarmament was an active topic of discussion.[2]

As the 1930s advanced, the high hopes for disarmament faded. First Japan's aggression in Manchuria in 1931, and then – much nearer to home – the rise of Adolf Hitler, turned the pacific horizons of the 1920s into war clouds. By 1935 Britain was set on a course of steady rearmament. But there was now a new competitor for military expenditure – the Royal Air Force (RAF). It was particularly attractive because even those sceptical of the effectiveness of collective security were seduced by the notion that bombing would render land warfare out of date. Hence the RAF's emphasis on strategic bombing. Spending on the army was, therefore, slow to rise, although by 1938 it amounted to 2 per cent of national income, not much less as a proportion than total military expenditure in Britain today. Behind this expenditure lay a series of debates that attempted to define the role of the army in a future war.[3]

In 1934, when the rise of Hitler began to sound alarm bells, Britain had no formal alliance with France, although there was a general assumption that the French would be allies in the event of a war with Germany. If this occurred, the

I

role of the other services, and Britain's overall part in the alliance, seemed clear: the Navy would blockade Germany, the RAF attack it, and Britain would provide financial support for the alliance as it had in the First World War. The army was to be equipped for a limited continental role, but what that actually would be was not specified and this 'continental commitment' was actually downgraded in 1937.

However, 1938 was to see both the Anschluss with Austria, and Hitler's aggressive support of the Sudeten Germans, which led in September to the Munich Agreement and Germany thereby gaining control of Czechoslovakia's former borderlands. In spite of Munich and Neville Chamberlain's famous 1938 statement about 'peace for our time', one result was an increased wariness about Germany's intentions. By January 1939 it was also clear that the French would expect some assistance from British land forces in the event of a German attack.

In February 1939 the continental commitment was reinstated, and Hitler's takeover in March of the rump of the Czech lands – Slovakia becoming a German client state – led to a raft of measures in Britain. Financial constraints on rearmament were loosened still further, limited conscription was introduced and the territorial army greatly enlarged. Britain and France also guaranteed Poland's independence. The stage was set for 3 September, when Britain declared war on Germany after the latter's invasion of Poland.[4]

In spite of the army's rapid expansion, the core of the BEF was still provided by the prewar regular army battalions. There were forty-nine of these deployed in the ten fully equipped infantry divisions,* out of a total of eighty-seven.[5] Although the British army is always known by its regiments – whether famous names such as the Grenadier Guards or county regiments such as The Royal Warwickshire Regiment and the splendidly named Duke of Cornwall's Light Infantry (DCLI) – the system did not bring the units within a regiment together in a fighting capacity. Regiments existed for reasons of sentiment, recruitment and administration. Since the late nineteenth century county regiments had had two regular battalions, which had little knowledge of each other and did not serve together, except occasionally in wartime. A battalion – about 800 soldiers in 1940 – was the unit to which infantrymen owed allegiance.

David French has many criticisms of the training of these prewar battalions. Some of these points were also made at the time by one of the BEF's most perceptive generals, Alan Brooke, commander of II Corps. In early November 1939, when his corps consisted mainly of regulars, he wrote: 'We still require months of training

---

* Divisions usually had three brigades, each with three battalions; 5th Division only had two brigades, one having been detached for operations in Norway.

with the necessary facilities, such as artillery and anti-tank ranges, before this Corps can be considered as fit for war' – a view he was to reiterate.[6]

Brooke's comments were echoed from a very different perspective by my late father-in-law, Robert (Bob) Thorne, who had joined one such county battalion, the 1st Battalion of the East Lancashire Regiment, as a private in early 1933, during the depths of the Depression. By the outbreak of war he was a sergeant. He was not himself at Dunkirk, but was one of the 140,000 or so British troops who were south of the Somme and were evacuated from the western French ports in June. Subsequently he was commissioned and seconded to a newly formed tank regiment, seeing active service in it as an acting major from soon after D-day until the end of the war. He had, therefore, observed the prewar British army from the grass roots, and in his subsequent career as a tank officer gained a wider perspective. About twenty years ago I talked to him extensively about his army experiences.

He, too, was critical of the higher formation and combined arms training undertaken in the prewar army. In such training:

> it was very difficult to whistle up a lot of enthusiasm for chasing around the moors of Catterick playing soldiers, as it were, because it was very unrealistic. There was no live ammunition fired anyway. You never saw such a thing as a field gun for example, as the artillery support had to be imagined because it never actually appeared at any time.

He contrasted this with post-Dunkirk training, where 'we used to train troops to advance along a line where you fired on either side of them. Real fire down on either side of them . . .' Apart from the absence of live ammunition and artillery, other misleading aspects in his view included a complete lack of training involving air support, and simplistic assumptions about the use of tanks: 'The tanks were brought into the exercises to finish it off . . . It was assumed that by bringing the tanks in they could roll over everything there was.' He was critical also of the lack of training in anti-tank gunnery.[7]

Thorne was, however, much more positive about the basic elements of an individual soldier's training – musketry (learning how to shoot), map-reading, marching and the other basics – which he thought were well done in the prewar period. Training in small-group infantry tactics – 'minor tactics' – was also thorough:

> In the attack, for instance, the idea would be that part of the platoon would use their weapons to produce fire to keep the enemies' heads down whilst the other half moved . . . And you move as fast as possible with as much cover

as possible. You had to learn to use sort of every bit of natural [cover], every fold in the ground, and that sort of thing as cover from enemy fire.

His views were more optimistic than French's who was critical even of training in this very important department of the soldier's job. Bob Thorne also thought that the quality of the average regular private and of the non-commissioned officers – who were recruited from the ranks – was remarkably good. Again, there are differing views, and it may be that his perspective was influenced by the fact that he joined in the depths of the Depression, when even high-quality men found it difficult to get a job anywhere else and would be more tempted to join the army.[8]

Thorne was less sanguine about the quality of some of the officers, believing that: 'There were far too many officers who were not up to their jobs.' He pointed out, however, that in the period from around the end of 1936 to the outbreak of war a number of unsatisfactory officers in his battalion were quietly persuaded to leave. So clearly some attempt was made to improve officer quality. The promotion of efficient non-commissioned officers such as himself in the early part of the war was another aspect of this, even though it was also necessary because of the army's rapid enlargement.[9]

If regulars still comprised the larger part of the BEF, the territorial battalions were a major component. Since 1907 county regiments had had battalions of territorials attached, and in 1939 the territorials had formed the basis for a massive expansion of the army. As a result, five of the BEF's fully equipped divisions had just fifteen regular but thirty territorial infantry battalions between them. Since until only a few months before war broke out they were part-time soldiers, territorial training was much inferior to that of the regulars. There was little time for individual or tactical training in their regular training sessions, so their four weekend camps per year and fortnightly annual camp tended to be devoted to this. Combined arms training was more or less non-existent. Furthermore the territorial army had hugely expanded just before the war to accommodate the influx of new recruits when conscription was introduced in April 1939, diluting each battalion's military skills even further. Perhaps not surprisingly as a regular, Thorne was critical of the territorials as 'very much novice soldiers'.[10]

It is not known how far these weaknesses were rectified by training within the BEF during the winter of 1939/40, but historians have expressed scepticism about the effectiveness of such training. The comment by Henry Pownall, the BEF's chief of staff, in October 1939 that digging defences on the French frontier was 'all excellent training for the troops, much more so than if we had stayed in back areas practising battles' has been noted as an example of a retrograde British attitude. But Pownall's comment should be seen in the context of another one he made shortly afterwards – that the French were not digging any defences at all on that part of the front. Once the defences were dug he was certainly aware of the need for training, commenting in January that, as more British divisions came in, there was only limited space provided for them: therefore, 'can we please have a training area south of Amiens?'[11]

In order to put a little flesh on what is, so far as the BEF is concerned, essentially anecdotal evidence, three war diaries were searched for information on training. One was 5th Division's, whose commanding officer Harold Franklyn was well known for his attention to training. In December 1939, soon after the division arrived, there was movement practice, but this only applied to the HQ (headquarters). The war diary noted in January that a field-firing range had been allocated to the division and was used in the first two weeks of the month for practice on all sorts of small arms, including small mortars, grenade throwing and anti-tank rifles. In February 1940 training exercises were set for 15 Infantry Brigade – this formation was later withdrawn for service in Norway; in March for 17 Brigade; and in April for 13 Brigade. Unfortunately 13 Brigade's diary, the second one consulted, did not record any details of its training, although clearly there were some exercises unrecorded by the division: for example, one on 2 March involving 'defence against enemy air born attack'.

Later in April 1940 plans were underway for the entire division to move to the Picquigny area southwest of Amiens – presumably the training area that Pownall had requested in January – for six weeks of training. On 9 May this was about to start, but on 10 May Hitler put an end to 5th Division's plans. It is not known how many divisions went through their six weeks of training, but given the time available it cannot have been many, if any at all.[12]

The very absence of evidence here shows that there was not much opportunity for higher formation training or for combined arms training with the artillery. This could only take place, except for paper exercises, in a large-scale training area, which the BEF did not have until it was too late. However one battalion war diary suggested that at battalion level there was considerable activity. This diary belonged to the 1/7th Royal Warwickshire Regiment (1/7th Warwicks), a territorial formation attached to 143 Brigade of 48th Division. The 1/7th was not chosen wholly by chance, since it played an important part in the Battle of the Ypres–Comines Canal. So its experience may not be typical, but if it was it suggests that battalions took training seriously.

A few extracts over a period give some idea of activities after the battalion's arrival in France in early January. On the 25th and 26th of that month companies practised attack schemes; on the 30th 'fighting patrols and small attack schemes'; and on the 31st 'attacks on houses and imaginary pillboxes'. The last entry shows that practice without a proper training ground had some limitations. During February the battalion spent much of its energies on working parties to assist the Royal Engineers, presumably in constructing defences. A number of exercises were fitted in between these. On 12 February, for example, there was range firing; on the 13th firing of the 2-inch company mortars; and on the 15th a battalion attack scheme that included the Bren carriers.* Also on the 12th the intelligence section was on a brigade scheme that involved the use of wireless; and on 21 and 22 February companies practised the use of assault boats. On one occasion 'night patrol practice' were going on 'as usual'.[13]

Similarly in March a lot of time was expended in providing working parties for an ammunition field park company in order to unload a number of trains. But along with this went a battalion exercise in taking up a defensive position, several days of platoon training, some route marching, a night exercise involving HQ and one rifle company, and firing on ranges. In addition a number of exercises, or 'schemes', were carried out under brigade auspices: a battalion attack exercise; withdrawal by night; and reconnaissance and 'fighting patrol' work at night. In April there was a cryptically entitled 'Corps manning exercise' in which 143 Brigade was to put in a counterattack; this involved two fourteen-mile marches in between the attack, for which the intelligence section had laid out tapes overnight. The routine training continued, with fewer working parties to interrupt it, and on 25–26 April there was a brigade exercise to practise taking up a defensive position and a subsequent withdrawal, which included marching thirty miles in two days. It was a prescient exercise given what was to come.[14]

If the 1/7th Warwicks is anything to go by, battalion training was not only thorough but also involved a number of exercises that would be of real practical value in the battles ahead, even though that could not have been known at the time. Furthermore their war diary showed that a number of these exercises involved their brigade, 143, in one form or another, although only one seems to have involved I Corps to which 48th Division was attached. It can be speculated from the scattered comments reported earlier that not all of the training was realistic. The lack of any mention of artillery or tanks also suggests a paucity of inter-arms training, although

---

* Small tracked vehicles that are described on p. 8.

that cannot be stated definitively. Clearly there is room for a more systematic survey of the BEF's training.

Whatever the state of training, historians have also pointed to other systemic weaknesses in the prewar British army, which carried over into the BEF. The British army had always had a tendency to hierarchy and an emphasis on detailed orders, which were expected to be strictly followed. Hierarchy and detailed orders would not have mattered so much – and could have advantages in terms of co-ordination – if communications had ensured that orders were relayed quickly. But the BEF still relied largely on cable networks, even though battlefield radios originated in the First World War. Once the BEF was forced to retreat and had moved off established cable routes, easy communication broke down, and it relied increasingly on liaison officers to carry messages. This lack of rapid communication could also hinder artillery support for the infantry; by comparison German units tended to have more firepower under the direct control of the unit commander. The total artillery support available to the BEF was substantial, but it was all under the ultimate control of divisions and corps, although in practice this was often delegated. How far slowness of communication and lack of liaison with the artillery were problems will be explored as the narrative unfolds.[15]

How far did the BEF's equipment compensate for weaknesses in training and communications? Plenty of critics, then and later, have portrayed the army's equipment as deficient too. But recently David Edgerton has argued that this was not the case, and that the BEF had good claims to be the first fully mechanised army in the world.[16]

As with the German army, some of the basic infantry weapons of the British army were of First World War vintage. These were the Lee-Enfield .303 rifles and the Vickers heavy machine guns. The latter were placed in separate machine-gun battalions, each with forty-eight guns. There was roughly one per division, although they were technically under the control of a corps.* The merits of this arrangement can be contested. The German army did not follow it, keeping its heavy machine guns in its infantry battalions. But there was little complaint about the equipment itself, elderly though it was in design. Both the Vickers and the Lee-Enfield were reliable and efficient weapons, although the rifle had the basic limitation that it could only fire at the pace of the man pulling the trigger.

Infantry battalions also had the newer Bren light machine gun. The lessons of the First World War about the importance of giving the infantry firepower had been

---

* A corps usually contained two or three divisions.

reasonably well attended to here. Each rifle company in a battalion had nine Brens, light and reliable weapons. In addition, and unique to the British army, the HQ company deployed a reconnaissance platoon consisting of ten Bren gun carriers. The Bren carrier was a small tracked vehicle with a three-man crew – and a Bren. It was lightly armoured, but its mobility gave it the ability to reinforce beleaguered positions rapidly.

Possession of the Bren carrier was one area where British infantry battalions were markedly superior to the Germans. Otherwise, in terms of firepower, the German battalions had the edge. Their light machine guns (MG), the MG 34, had a much higher rate of fire than the Bren. (As a partial compensation the Lee-Enfield could be fired more quickly than the German K98k rifle.) It is unclear how far the heavier versions of the MG 34s, with more ammunition and a larger tripod, were in use, and certainly some units still had the standard First World War heavy machine gun, the MG 08/15, the equivalent of the Vickers.

Some personnel carried lighter automatic weapons still, *maschinenpistolen* (variously called machine pistols, machine carbines, or submachine guns), although again it is unclear how many of these were deployed in 1940. British war diaries made frequent reference to their use by the Germans, usually calling them 'Tommy guns'. Very importantly, the Germans had six 8-cm medium mortars per battalion as opposed to the two 3-inch mortars of British battalions. In view of the impact mortars had in the First World War, the British army's lack of attention to them in the interwar period seems distinctly odd. The problems entailed in carrying large amounts of heavy mortar ammunition up to the battle zone may be one reason, although this is only conjecture. The British medium mortars were frequently in use when battle commenced, but the little 2-inch mortars issued to companies do not feature much in the war diaries viewed for this book. Finally, each German *Regiment* – the equivalent of a British brigade – had some light artillery attached to it as well as anti-tank guns. Brigades in the BEF only had the latter.[17]

Within a British battalion, there was a battalion HQ and an associated HQ company. Collectively these two formations were the home of signals, heavy mortars, the carrier platoon, an anti-aircraft platoon with some more Brens, medical personnel and stretcher-bearers, drivers and mechanics, miscellaneous administrative and supply personnel and cooks. They contained around 260 officers and men. The other constituents of a battalion were four identical rifle companies. On the establishment laid down in 1938, each had three platoons, and each of these had three sections containing just eight men, two of them manning a Bren. Thus the rifle sections and, therefore, the rifle companies were remarkably thin in numbers. This presumably reflected a concern with mobility, which obsessed some army thinkers between the wars.[18]

In April 1940 the establishment of each rifle section was increased by three, which enlarged a rifle company from around 100 to 130. Shortly afterwards no less than eleven officers were added to the battalion establishment. By May 1940 British battalions at full strength, therefore, had 757 men and thirty-three officers. The increase in the number of officers allowed all the platoons formerly commanded by an NCO (non-commissioned officer) to have an officer instead. Whether swapping an experienced NCO for a young 2nd lieutenant was a gain is a moot point. Potentially there were far more of the latter, while senior NCOs were a rare and, therefore, precious commodity, needed to form the nucleus of the new battalions constantly being raised. Bob Thorne, for example, was promoted to captain after Dunkirk and posted to the new 8th Battalion of the East Lancashires, which eventually became an armoured regiment.[19]

The most important change was in the number of riflemen. It seems that the intention here was not to increase the basic size of the squad, but to allow for spare men to cover losses. To check that the increase was carried through, the personnel lists in fifteen battalions were researched for this book.

By the time the German attack began, practically all battalions had close to their correct number of 'other ranks', and the growth in numbers seems to have begun before establishments technically increased. The only exception was the Inniskillings, which was up to full strength by the beginning of May 1940 but subsequently lost about a quarter of its men. Similarly there were between twenty-nine and thirty-three officers in all the battalions except one – the 2nd Sherwood Foresters, where there were only twenty-four.[20]

Of course all this does have one corollary, which is that a fair number of the men and officers in each battalion were new and relatively untrained. And in total the number of troops in a new-style, large battalion was still forty or so below the number in a German battalion of 1940. The difference is accounted for largely by the increased numbers the Germans had to serve their mortars and heavy machine guns. When account is taken of the machine-gun battalions in the British army, the numbers become more even.

The artillery was a vital component of the British army. By providing a powerful incentive for the enemy to remain in their trenches or dugouts, it allowed attacking infantry to manoeuvre and eventually take enemy positions; in defence it broke up the momentum of enemy attacks by forcing the attackers to take shelter. In other words its role was seen as neutralisation of the enemy, rather than primarily as a killing machine, although of course it became one of the main means by which casualties were inflicted. Its other essential task was counter-battery work, that is, neutralising the enemy's artillery.

The total volume of British artillery deployed was far below German levels since the BEF was much smaller. Allowing for this, the Royal Artillery was reasonably well equipped in material terms by 1940, although most guns were not new. At corps and army level there were a total of seventeen heavy and medium regiments, each with sixteen guns.[*] Whether their official nomenclature was medium or heavy, these were big guns, the shells weighing 56 pounds and upwards. The guns themselves were all First World War vintage, but they had been fitted with pneumatic tyres so they could be towed by a gun tractor.[†]

By 1939 regular field artillery regiments were equipped with the 18/25-pounder – the chassis of the old First World War 18-pounder 'retubed' with a barrel firing 25-pound shells and, again, fitted with pneumatic tyres. These were effective enough weapons, and the standard allocation was three regiments, or seventy-two guns, per division. There were also a number of field regiments allocated to corps or held in reserve at army level. Some territorial artillery regiments still had the 18-pounder, fitted with pneumatic tyres. It had a shorter range and threw a lighter shell. A few field regiments were equipped with 4.5-inch howitzers; at least one battery of these was in action at Ypres–Comines. Divisions also had an anti-tank regiment with forty-eight guns and one or more anti-aircraft regiments, but these formations did not play a major role in the Ypres–Comines battle.[21]

The Royal Artillery had evolved a sophisticated command and control mechanism, which later in the war would bring down the concentrated fire of every field regiment attached to a division within thirty minutes or so. However, there have been suggestions that training was inadequate, and, as has been seen, there was undoubtedly a deficiency in all-arms training so other units might not have understood how to work with the artillery. There was also the danger, usual with the British army, of everything being too centralised and, therefore, slower to respond in practice than in theory. Again how far these criticisms were justified is best judged by the actual experience in battle.[22]

Artillery and air support for ground troops were substitutes, not totally different in kind. Of course aircraft can range far more widely than artillery. But unless air support is available in overwhelming quantity – as for example was Allied air

---

[*] Some of these were allocated to corps, some kept in army reserve.

[†] One of the types used, the 60-pounder, is on display in the Imperial War Museum in its First World War guise with iron-shod wheels.

support in Normandy in 1944 – it is unlikely to play a critical role. There is plenty of evidence that the pervasiveness of the German Air Force in 1940 had a considerable nuisance value. And undoubtedly at one point, during the Meuse crossings, it played a major role. Whether it was so important at other times has been questioned. Thus the lack of any coherent doctrine of close air support for British ground forces was not necessarily a major disadvantage if adequate artillery support was available. This is not to defend the RAF's obsession with strategic bombing in 1940. At that time, when night bombing was hopelessly inaccurate and bomb loads were small, it was a lamentable policy. As Brooke wrote with some bitterness on 28 January, when the policy was to start bombing the German homeland if the Germans attacked in the west: 'To contemplate bombing the Ruhr at a time when the Germans are using their combined army and air force in one mighty uniform attempt to crush the French and British forces to clear their way into France, is in my mind sheer folly.'[23] In that sentence he foresaw correctly that the German attack would be concentrated, and that they would focus their entire air efforts when they attacked on support for their ground forces. Yet on the very date, 15 May, when the Germans were breaking out from the Meuse crossings westwards, the RAF launched an attack on the Ruhr.

There were extremely brave efforts made on the battlefronts as well. The crews of outclassed Battle and Blenheim light bombers carried out almost suicidal attacks on German troops at the Meuse crossings and elsewhere, and on 14 May some forty of seventy-one aircraft carrying out such raids were lost. But these very high loss rates meant that future efforts had to be scaled down.[24]

Whatever one's views about the RAF's strategic bombing policy, the relevant point is that, although a coherent doctrine of air support for ground troops would have been helpful, it was not essential as long as there was adequate artillery support. The artillery's effectiveness would have been enhanced by air observation, but unfortunately this was not developed in a satisfactory way – the Lysander aircraft designated for it proving too vulnerable. At Ypres–Comines this was not to prove a major problem since the British possessed high ground behind the battlefield for artillery observation.[25]

The German army may have had effective air support but, apart from the elite units, it was largely a horse-drawn army. The British army, in contrast, was almost fully motorised. There were some limits. There was not a place for every infantryman on a lorry, and at the beginning of the war a large number of civilian vehicles had to be requisitioned. These were not necessarily in good repair, and army fitters would have been unused to them. Viscount Montgomery in his memoirs recalled 'the countryside of France . . . strewn with broken-down vehicles' when his division, the

3rd, moved up to its concentration area near the French frontier in autumn 1939. It is possible to make too much of this. The bulk of the vehicle park seems to have worked well. *The Story of the RASC* (Royal Army Service Corps), the nearest thing to its official history, noted that during the campaign 3.7 per cent of all vehicles had to be sent to a base repair depot for heavy repairs. This is not a high proportion and, correspondingly, references in war diaries to breakdowns are scarce.[26]

The mechanisation of the artillery was probably the single most important achievement, since it was the teams of horses plodding along with their guns that did more than anything else to hold up an army's progress. The regular field artillery was equipped with Guy 'Quads' – four-wheel-drive gun 'tractors' as they were called, although in appearance they were like an orthodox, though rather short, truck. The territorials had six-wheel Morris Commercials for their 18-pounders, and there were some other types in use. The medium artillery was largely equipped with six-wheel Scammel Pioneers.[27]

While the artillerymen could ride on their vehicles, the infantry might still have had to march. Each rifle company had four fifteen-hundredweight (three-quarters of a ton) trucks, so equipment, Bren guns and so on could be loaded onto vehicles. There was more transport available at battalion level, each battalion possessing about fifty vehicles in all plus Bren carriers and motorcycles for dispatch riders.

When rapid movement of infantry was needed, the BEF had the power to provide it. The instruments were the troop-carrying companies, under army or corps control. By the time of the German attack there were nine of these. Each consisted of three sections, each section having thirty-three three-ton lorries. A section could carry a battalion, at about twenty men per lorry.* Furthermore the BEF also had motor transport companies, which had four sections, and were intended to carry either troops or stores and water. Each troop-carrying company had the capacity to carry a brigade, so the nine companies could transport three divisions. The motor transport companies provided further capacity. There were also numerous Royal Army Service Corps (RASC) units to ferry supplies from railway unloading points – trains remaining the standard means of long-distance transport – to unit dumps.[28]

In total the BEF, with its ten infantry, one armoured and three labour divisions, had about 68,000 vehicles. The French army, with 117 divisions, possessed 300,000 vehicles, a much lower ratio of vehicles to troops. And the German army, with 135 divisions in the west, had just 120,000 trucks, although presumably other vehicles

---

* Remember that a significant number of the 790 troops in a battalion would travel by its own transport – company trucks, the battalion's own supply trucks and Bren carriers.

such as staff cars should be added to the German total. Even so, the contrast in levels of mechanisation is striking.[29]

Set in the context of prewar attitudes, the fact that the BEF was as large and well equipped as it was by 1940 was actually fairly remarkable. But the significant achievements of army rearmament were not much consolation in view of the size and quality of the German army.[30]

Among the provisions of the Versailles Treaty after the First World War were limitations in the German army's size and composition. Historically the German Empire, and before it Prussia, had had a large conscript army. It was organised and trained by an efficient corps of permanent commissioned and NCOs, at the apex of which were the general staff, responsible for the victories of Prussia in its wars with Austria and France in the 1860s and early 1870s. The general staff were responsible, too, for the Schlieffen Plan, by which Germany nearly conquered France in 1914. The Versailles Treaty had swept away Germany's mass army and staff apparatus, limiting the country to a professional army of 100,000, no air force and no general staff.[31]

Well before Hitler came to power, senior German military figures had started to prepare for the rearmament which, they hoped, would come one day. Whatever the treaty requirements, there was in practice a general staff, and from 1933 specific plans were made for rearmament including a substantial increase in the size of the army. As a result, when Hitler finally gave the go-ahead in March 1935, enlargement could take place relatively easily on the basis of reintroduced conscription. With France and Britain reluctant to act against Germany, the only constraints on the military's size were financial and economic. These were real, but to Hitler the military always took priority. By 1939 Germany had more than two million soldiers and a similarly enlarged air force.[32]

This German army was one designed for attack rather than defence. To the French and British, one lesson of the First World War was that defence trumped attack. In both the memories of numerous unsuccessful and costly offensives were deeply ingrained, manifested in France in the defensive mentality of the Maginot Line. Offensives were not always unsuccessful, however. In the spring of 1918 the Germans had achieved a series of spectacular breakthroughs on the Western Front, although ultimately they lacked the mobility and the reserves to achieve complete victory. Then the Allies in their turn achieved a series of breakthroughs starting with the Battle of Amiens on 8 August, and culminating in the German request for an armistice. Success was achieved by a combination of massive but short artillery bombardments (which demoralised the defenders but did not churn up the ground too much), support for the attack from numerous light machine guns and mortars pushed up into the front line, and flexibility so that attacks infiltrated the weakest points rather than simply hammered at the strongest. Tanks were a relatively minor factor.[33]

German military thinkers drew the conclusion that, with the assistance of much faster tanks than were available in the First World War, the attack was not necessarily at a disadvantage. And historically the German army and its predecessors, for example, in the Austro-Prussian and Franco-Prussian wars of the 1860 and 1870s, had favoured attack over defence. It had been the logic, too, behind the German actions of 1914, based on the Schlieffen Plan of a few years earlier. The possibility of war with Russia led to Germany mounting an attack on Russia's ally, France, with the intention of knocking it out of the war at once. In spite of the failure of the Schlieffen Plan and Germany's defeat in the First World War, the rump German army of the 1920s did not lose faith with the offensive, which would now be carried out even more rapidly with the aid of tanks and aircraft. But the word *blitzkrieg*, now so associated with this type of attack, was actually only used occasionally in Germany before the war. Its popularisation seems to have been due to an article in *Time* magazine about the campaign in Poland in 1939, after which it became ubiquitous in the English language. After the triumphs of 1940, it became popular in Germany too – only for the Germans to become disenchanted with the term after they became bogged down in Russia in 1941.[34]

After the *blitzkrieg* of 1940, the tendency within the Allies was to stress the modernity and dynamism of the German army compared with their own armies. And certainly the elite formations of the German army were well equipped. These were the ten panzer (tank) divisions and the six motorised infantry divisions, which were designed to operate with the panzers. Tanks and motorised infantry were vital to the attack of Army Group A, but they were barely in evidence during the Battle of the Ypres–Comines Canal. It was the standard infantry divisions of the German army that fought here and, in general, on the rest of Army Group B's front. These were not motorised, nor did all of them have a great depth of experience.

The 100,000 strong army of the Versailles Treaty had just 4,000 officers. No doubt many First World War veterans were subsequently added to that number as rearmament progressed, but even so Hitler's rapidly expanding army only had a thin layer of experienced officers to carry out its training. As a result training for many units was limited – often lasting only two to three months. Of the German army's apparently impressive 157 divisions, only seventy-seven – including the panzer and motorised ones – were considered to have a full combat capability. Many of their infantry weapons, such as the rifles and heavy machine guns, dated back to the First World War, although as with the British army the quality of these was adequate. And with the exception of the elite divisions already mentioned, most of the German army was horse-drawn. An ordinary infantry division had about 900 motor vehicles, some of which would be staff cars and other small vehicles, and more than 5,000 horses. The infantry marched, as infantry always had done, and horses drew the supply wagons and much of the artillery. As one historian put it, the German army was semi-modern.[35]

It would be wrong to focus too much on the defects and weaknesses of the German army. Even the average infantry division and its associated artillery were a formidable fighting unit. Contrary to the widespread British view that the Germans were overcontrolled, German military training stressed flexibility and individual autonomy within the framework of orders that set objectives rather than prescribing detailed methods. This was an *Auftragstaktik* ('mission-orientated') command system. And although not all the German army was trained to the highest pitch, the long period between the Polish campaign, which had revealed many deficiencies, and the attack in the west was used for intensive training at all levels, but especially of officers. This built on the thorough training given to young officers, which included a period serving with the troops as NCOs. These cadets joined the cadre of experienced NCOs, who had also undergone specialised training.[36] Here there were distinct differences with the British army, whose officers were trained separately and whose NCOs did not undergo dedicated training.

Finally, at the level of small-group infantry tactics, the Germans had probably done most to assimilate the lessons of the First World War, stressing infiltration by small groups and the lavish use of small arms and machine-gun fire to suppress enemy movement. In addition, the Germans used their air force as mobile artillery in close support of the ground troops.[37]

The British army's relatively high equipment levels would be no compensation against such an enemy if its commanders were no good. Later in his career, when he was Chief of the Imperial General Staff (CIGS), Alan Brooke was wont to lament the dearth of good British generals. He attributed this to the loss of the best leaders when young men in the First World War. Yet Germany, although losing a higher proportion of young men, still produced a large number of competent generals in the Second World War. Although one needs certain basic qualities to command successfully, generals are surely made not born. The difference between Britain and

Germany was that the latter had a far larger cadre of trained young officers at the beginning of the First World War. Enough of them survived to form the nucleus of the interwar army, oversee its expansion under Hitler, and become generals in the Second World War. In addition German training at higher levels was probably better.

Germany's best-known generals were also relatively youthful. Generals in modern warfare do not usually ride long distances or command on the battlefield as they did in Wellington's day, but conducting a battle, even in an office, must be a punishing affair. It does not sit well with advancing age. Relative youth might be important for other reasons. Anyone between their mid-forties and mid-fifties would have started the First World War at a fairly junior level. They would have experienced modern warfare on the ground. Since future generals are likely to be high achievers, they would then most likely have been promoted rapidly, but have still been young enough to remain in roles that kept them in close contact with the front line. This was important because many of the key lessons in fighting the Second World War were learned in the trenches of the First: the vital importance of firepower, and the need for speed of decision and movement. They were lessons that relatively junior officers had learned at first hand and may have absorbed better than those who were more senior.

Gerd von Rundstedt, who was sixty-three when the Second World War began, was by a long way the oldest of Germany's active generals. Fedor von Bock, the chief of Army Group B, which fought the campaign in central Belgium and northern France, was fifty-eight. The generals of subordinate formations were usually in their early fifties or late forties. Walther von Reichenau, the commander of Sixth Army, which was directly involved in Ypres–Comines, was fifty-four at the outbreak of war; Hermann Hoth and Erwin Rommel, corps and divisional commanders respectively in the fast-moving panzer attack in the south, were both forty-eight.[38]

British generals were probably slightly older when direct comparisons between those in similar positions are made, but not much. Leslie Hore-Belisha, the war minister until the end of 1939, was unpopular in the army but he had made some positive reforms. One of these was to insist on a clear-out of elderly generals. The senior ranks in 1937 were still dominated by those who had served in the Boer War, but they had gone by 1939. Nevertheless the average age of British divisional generals in that year was still 52.5 years.[39] Those in more senior positions were not all that much older, however. Brooke was fifty-six and John Dill, his fellow corps commander in the first months of the war, was fifty-seven. John Gort, the BEF's C-in-C, was fifty-three – much the same age as Reichenau, who was at a roughly comparable level. The best-known British divisional general, Bernard Montgomery of 3rd Division, was fifty-one; Harold Franklyn of 5th Division was fifty-three; Harold Alexander of 1st Division, later to achieve eminence as C-in-C in the Middle Eastern and Italian theatres, was only forty-seven. Montgomery and Alexander were peripherally involved at Ypres–Comines; Franklyn centrally. At brigade levels some commanders were quite youthful: Miles Dempsey of 13 Brigade was forty-three. The most important thing about this age range is that, as with the German commanders, all those named above would been relatively junior officers in the early years of the First World War.

By contrast, many of the French generals were distinctly elderly. The two most senior French commanders, Maurice Gamelin and Alphonse Georges, were sixty-six and sixty-five respectively. Gaston Billotte and Georges Blanchard, commanders respectively of an army group and an army, were not much younger, at sixty-four and sixty-two. John Smyth, a British brigadier who visited a number of French corps and divisional HQs, thought that most of the commanders 'appeared far too old for their jobs'. The significant difference in the age of commanders, therefore, seems to have been between the French on the one hand, and the German and British on the other, although a bigger sample of all nationalities would be needed to state that as a definitive proposition.[40]

The elderly French commanders were a sharp contrast to the 53-year-old John (Jack), Viscount Gort, C-in-C of the BEF. Gort's First World War record was one of astonishing bravery. He was awarded the Military Cross (MC) and the Distinguished Service Order (DSO) with two bars, and in September 1918, when commanding the 1st Battalion the Grenadier Guards, the Victoria Cross. Gort rose rapidly in the interwar army and by 1938 was CIGS. Hore-Belisha had appointed him as a reformer, although, like most military men, Gort came to dislike and distrust the war minister. In spite of the breakdown in their relations, Gort had a good claim to become C-in-C of the BEF when it was formed, because of his fighting record and the generally high reputation he had won in the interwar period.

At the time and subsequently, Gort has had critics and admirers. The arrangement of his command post, which was split off from general headquarters (GHQ) when the Germans attacked, was one subject of criticism. The official historian pointed to flaws in the passing of intelligence both from the front upwards, and vice versa, as a result of Gort's arrangements. In fairness to Gort, he was faced with the difficult task of running the entire BEF (which had a vast base organisation set up to service what was intended to be a much larger army) as well as of commanding the fighting forces themselves when active hostilities broke out. The split of GHQ and the command post was intended to bring him nearer to the fighting.[41]

More seriously, Gort has been criticised both for his lack of strategic grasp and his obsession with detail. Brooke had a low opinion of him. Comparing Dill with Gort in November 1939 he wrote: 'I do wish he was C-in-C instead of Gort, he has twice the vision and ten times the ability. Gort's brain has lately been compared with that of a glorified boy scout! Perhaps unkind, but there is a great deal of truth in it.'

There are other views of Gort, though. On 17 May 1940, as the situation deteriorated almost hourly, Henry Pownall, his chief of staff, described Gort as, 'quite splendid, not at all rattled, rather enjoying himself, with a fine grasp of the operation as a whole'. As things continued to get ever worse Gort did become anxious, but no one has suggested that his anxieties rattled his nerves or impaired his judgement. Major Archdale, a liaison officer with the French armies in the north, reported on the 26th that, in contrast to the French: 'The atmosphere at General Headquarters could hardly be better – there was no sign of frayed nerves, and the staff were barely ruffled.' Meanwhile Gort's personal bravery and imperturbability remained intact. Captain Robert Tong recalled one incident at Renaix, where the command post was then located, when during an air raid he had taken refuge under a table while making a phone call. A pair of boots 'suddenly appeared from a chair and placed themselves firmly in the middle of my back. I was brought to my senses by hearing the chief's voice say: "I always find it less inconvenient to telephone in a sitting or standing position." '[42]

Pownall himself had played an important part in the short fighting life of the BEF. He had been a gunner during the First World War, earning an MC and a DSO. He distinguished himself by his administrative skills at the Committee of Imperial Defence in the 1930s and gained rapid promotion. Pownall, who was fifty-one at the outbreak of war, was calm and efficient. He may not have been an outstanding leader, but he never really got an opportunity to demonstrate this and as chief of staff it was not his job. Those who served closely with him in 1939–40 spoke highly of his imperturbability, his ability to think ahead and his well-ordered mind. Robert Tong, from a relatively junior perspective, perceived him as 'a little remote, very courteous and considerate and always ready to listen. He brought with him an air of calm professionalism into situations that to many seemed chaotic and indeed desperate'. Given the immense strain on Gort in his dual role, it is a tribute to Pownall that he was able to absorb part of this strain and carry out the multifarious roles of a chief of staff.[43]

Brooke, the commander of II Corps and responsible for overall control of the Ypres–Comines battle, was universally acknowledged to have the positive qualities credited to Pownall and, many think, was also one of the outstanding leaders among

British Second World War generals. Like Pownall, Brooke was an artilleryman by training and had won rapid promotion between the wars – suggesting that the British army could identify real talent when it had to. From the end of 1941 he was CIGS, in which position he was one of the few with the moral courage and authority to prevent Winston Churchill's madder schemes getting off the ground. His dynamism was captured by the novelist Anthony Powell, who described:

> . . . the hurricane-like imminence of a thickset general, wearing enormous horn-rimmed spectacles. He had just burst from a flagged staff-car almost before it had drawn up by the kerb. Now he tore up the steps of the building at the charge, exploding through the inner door into the hall. An extraordinary current of physical energy, almost of electricity, suddenly pervaded the place . . . This was the CIGS.[44]

In the early days of the BEF both Gort and Pownall thought Brooke too pessimistic. Many of Brooke's forebodings turned out to be prescient, however, and his apparent pessimism could be put down to his habit of saying bluntly what others were thinking. Once battle commenced, Brooke appeared rock-like to his subordinates, although privately fearing the worst. His actions, and his pervasive presence, during the Ypres–Comines battle will be related in due course.[45]

For many years Brooke's role in Britain's war effort was underrated, partly because Churchill's enormous ego, manifested in his multivolumed *Second World War*, minimised the importance of practically everyone save himself.[46] Arthur Bryant's two-volume work on Brooke, a mixture of Brooke's diary extracts, reminiscences by Brooke and linking commentary by Bryant, was published in the 1950s.[47] Although it sold widely it seems to have faded from the consciousness of the average historian, and Brooke was again consigned to the shadows. Recently Alex Danchev and Dan Todman's edition of his diaries, and Andrew Roberts' *Masters and Commanders*, have helped to redress the situation.[48]

Harold Franklyn, the 5th Division commander directly responsible for Ypres–Comines, remains almost unrecorded. As late as 2009 he did not have a Wikipedia entry, although he has since acquired one. If Ypres–Comines is a forgotten battle, then Franklyn is a forgotten general. Franklyn started his army career in the Green Howards and was a staff officer throughout the First World War. He admitted in his brief memoir that his consequent lack of experience in command could have been a serious defect when he commanded a division in war.[49] However even as a staff officer he had managed to acquire an MC, a DSO and six mentions in dispatches. For most of the 1930s he served in the West Indies and the Sudan, but had returned to command 5th Division in 1938 as the BEF expanded. Once active hostilities broke out, Franklyn probably gained more experience of leading a division in combat, even before the Ypres–Comines battle, than any other BEF divisional commander. He organised the counterattack at Arras on 21 May and then took charge of the defence around Arras. Both are discussed in Chapter 3.

We know little about Franklyn personally. He was never one of Brooke's close friends, who were called by their first names or nicknames in Brooke's diary, although Brooke thought he was a 'more attractive type of individual than Montgomery' – not that this was very difficult. Other occasional references to him in the diaries, both before and after May 1940, suggest that Brooke also thought he was professionally competent. Quite unusually for Brooke, there were no criticisms of Franklyn in the diaries and several words of praise. Miles Dempsey, later to command the British Second Army in Normandy in 1944–5 and one of Franklyn's brigadiers in 1940, noted that 'he gave a feeling of great confidence to those below him'. From a more junior level there is the testimony of Patrick Turnbull, who as a 'motor contact officer' took messages to Franklyn during the defence of the Arras salient. He described Franklyn as possessing 'an unruffled Olympian calm, comforting in the extreme under the circumstances'. On 23 May, when Turnbull arrived at Franklyn's headquarters, the latter felt that Turnbull must have had 'a very unpleasant trip' ('this was no exaggeration', wrote Turnbull) and told one of his staff to give Turnbull and his driver a glass of brandy. Franklyn was thoughtful enough to reflect in his memoir that he did experience anxiety, but that he believed 'a commander . . . must do his best not to show signs of the tension which he is inevitably undergoing'; although in spite of Dempsey's tribute he thought that sometimes he failed altogether to conceal his own tension.[50]

To summarise the strengths and weaknesses of the BEF: in physical equipment it was unquestionably well equipped for its size and more mobile than any other army in 1940. The German army, however, contained more panzer and motorised infantry divisions than the entire strength of the BEF, so the latter's qualities must be seen in perspective. Nevertheless comparing like with like, the BEF's equipment was generally adequate and in several cases superior. The major defects were the insufficiency of heavy mortars and the paucity of effective radio communication. The other question marks over the BEF lie in the quality and amount of its training, both within battalions and that involving different formations, and in its alleged tendency to be too hierarchical and slow moving. Finally, many new generals had been appointed in the late 1930s: they would only be tested by performance in action.

What was the intended task of the BEF as it built up its strength during the winter of 1939–40? Gort's remit was first of all to 'co-operate with our Allies in the defeat of the common enemy'. To ensure a unified policy, he was under the command of the French commander-in-chief (C-in-C) Northeast Theatre of Operations and was enjoined to 'carry out loyally' any instructions issued by that commander. But if an order 'appears to imperil the British Field Force', the French and British governments had agreed that Gort could 'appeal to the British government'.[51]

Over the next few months Gort and Pownall listened while the French elaborated a plan. This was the period that became known as the Phoney or Bore War. The French, culpably in many people's view, had no plans for attack even though Poland was being overrun in the first weeks of September. But the French and subsequently also the British inaction against the German army had some rationale. The German economy was considered to be dangerously dependent on imports, particularly of oil and food. A strict blockade would, it was hoped, weaken Germany to a point where Hitler could not continue the war. In the circumstances a defensive military stance seemed a reasonable option.

French policy, however, also owed a great deal to their belief, born of bitter First World War experience, that defence would prevail over attack. The British tended to follow the French lead, partly because of their own First World War experience, and partly because of a failure to analyse and draw lessons from the successful offensives they had mounted in the last months of the war. So far as there was analysis, in the early 1930s, it tended to focus on the importance of mobility in order to convert a 'break-in' of the enemy lines to a 'breakthrough'. This bore some fruit in the importance attached to infantry and artillery mobility, but there was no development of a coherent offensive doctrine involving tanks such as the Germans had.[52] So the British accepted with very little questioning the French plans.

The French plans, therefore, were solely concerned with what actions they and the BEF would take in the event of a German attack on France. The French assumed that a German attack would come, as it had in the First World War, through central Belgium. Most of France's northeastern frontier was protected by the Maginot Line. To get to the Sedan sector running along the central stretch of the Meuse, German forces would have to pass through the hilly and wooded Ardennes in southeast Belgium. With poor roads, this was considered to be virtually impassable to tanks. Since the Germans were expected to attack with tanks, it was ruled out as a likely target and was lightly defended. That left the plains of central Belgium, which led directly to northwest France.[53]

An attack through Belgium would draw it into the war. It had remained resolutely neutral before 1939 and continued that stance into 1940. There were, it is true, some exchanges of information with France and Britain, but these were unofficial and were not approved by all Belgians in high military or political office. Basically the Belgians were terrified of exciting German antagonism by appearing to waver in their policy of neutrality. As a result the French plans were drawn up on the basis of incomplete knowledge. By the spring of 1940 the Allies had a reasonable grasp of the likely Belgian response to a German attack, but lacked accurate knowledge of the state of Belgian defences.[54]

In spite of this the French supreme commander, Gamelin, devised a plan that involved the Allies advancing into Belgium as the Germans attacked. This was Plan D, for an advance to a line running more or less south from Antwerp to Givet, where the Meuse flowed into Belgium. The Belgians themselves planned to hold out in front of this position for some time. They would then withdraw and position themselves on the northern sector of the Antwerp–Givet line. The British would be on their right, along the river Dyle from Wavre to Louvain. So to the British this became the 'Dyle Line'. The French would then extend the line south to join the Meuse at Namur and along it farther south to Givet. The rationale for Plan D was that a large proportion of Belgium, an industrialised country with valuable economic potential from the Allied point of view, would be defended, while the Germans would be unable to use the country for air bases to attack Britain and northern France.[55]

However, Gamelin added an extra ingredient to Plan D. It was thought likely that, if Germany invaded Belgium, it would also invade Holland. Gamelin stationed the French Seventh Army on the far left of the Allied forces, with the intention of moving into Holland in the event of a German attack. Seventh Army, originally intended as a central reserve, was a relatively mobile force compared with much of the French army. Gamelin's idea in changing its role was that it would link up with Dutch forces and allow them to continue fighting as part of a unified Allied formation. The basic ideas of Plan D were accepted by the British. Pownall was extremely positive: 'If we can bring it off neatly [it] will be an excellent move.' He had some reservations about the commitment of Seventh Army on the far left but did not make much of it in his diary. Even Brooke seems to have been happy about the advance to the Dyle, in spite of his usual caution.[56]

The British seem initially to have had confidence in both Gamelin and his immediate subordinate and the commander of the French armies of the northeast, Alphonse Georges, to whom Gort was accountable. Unfortunately, relations between Georges and Gamelin were poor. In 1935 the latter had been preferred to Georges as supreme commander, largely for political reasons. Georges was unhappy over Seventh Army's new role but felt himself unable to intercede about it with Gamelin. Then in January 1940 Gamelin reorganised the command structure – it seems with the main aim of reducing Georges' authority. Intelligence, supply and transport functions were moved away from Georges' HQ, leading to significant liaison problems. Pownall regarded it as a 'clownish arrangement' and reflected that: 'It's a pity the French get so infernally ambitious and internecine when they get up to high places,' although he excepted Georges from these strictures. Later on he made another extended diary entry that was critical of Gamelin.[57]

Pownall's comments, after his and other senior British commanders' willing acceptance of the French plans, signals a growing tendency to have doubts about French military effectiveness. Brooke was even more critical than Pownall. This could not be attributed to typical English insularity. Brooke – in fact Anglo-Irish – was born in France and lived there for much of his childhood and youth. As a result he spoke French fluently. In his postwar reminiscences, he reflected on a ceremony held on 5 November 1939 to mark the anniversary of the first German request for an armistice in 1918: 'I can still see [the French guard of honour] now. Men unshaven, horses ungroomed, clothes and saddlery that did not fit . . . What shocked me most, however, was the look in the men's faces, disgruntled and insubordinate looks.' At the time Brooke only put in his diary: 'I could not help wondering whether the French are still a firm enough nation to again take their part in seeing the war through.' But in January he wrote more explicitly in it about his 'feeling of depression as to the lack of real finish in the French army . . . I only hope that they still possess the same fighting qualities which they showed in the last war.' He contrasted them unfavourably with the 'utter efficiency' of the Germans. He also criticised the French reliance on the Maginot Line and the psychology it engendered: 'a sense of false security . . . a feeling of sitting behind an impregnable iron fence'. In a prescient passage he then wrote: 'Should the fence perchance be broken then French fighting spirit be brought down crumbling with it.'[58]

The intention of the Germans was to break the fence decisively, not by attacking the Maginot Line itself but by going for the weakest part of the French defences. The early plans of the army high command (Oberkommando des Heeres, or OKH) had been for an attack through central Belgium into northern France, but it was realised that this was unlikely to achieve a rapid breakthrough. While it was the route that the Schlieffen Plan had prescribed, critics of the OKH plans pointed out that the French would be expecting just such an attack. And a long-drawn-out fight was thought to be dangerous for Germany because her economy was vulnerable to Allied blockade. Hitler too was dissatisfied with the initial ideas. The German generals Erich von Manstein and Heinz Guderian can probably take most of the credit for the plan that was eventually developed, which Hitler then enthusiastically adopted. The result was Fall Gelb (literally Case Yellow, although it is sometimes translated as Plan Yellow).[59]

Case Yellow had all the characteristics of a classic German army manoeuvre. The *Schwerpunkt* (centre of gravity) of the attack was moved to the central Meuse around Sedan. This involved a lengthy approach through the Ardennes, a risky route because of the poor roads. But the Germans were sure their tanks could get through, and anyway risk was an almost inevitable part of attacks that aimed for rapid victory. Once through the Ardennes, the attack had to cross the Meuse, not heavily defended at this point but nonetheless a considerable obstacle. The attack would then push rapidly westwards, well behind the Allies' front line, until it reached the Channel coast at the mouth of the Somme. This was the manoeuvre to which, subsequently, the name 'Sickle Cut' was given. The term probably originated with Churchill but was so evocative that it was subsequently adopted by German historians. The overall plan still called for an attack to be launched into central Belgium, as well as one into Holland. The attack on Belgium would be heavy enough to persuade the Allies initially that it was the *Schwerpunkt*. The Germans were fairly sure that the Allies would simultaneously advance into Belgium. So if all went well Case Yellow would result in the Allies moving northeast, away from the main German forces, which, having come through the Ardennes, were poised to cut through the Allies' rear. A classic encirclement would result, thus achieving a modern Cannae – the battle in 216 BC in which Hannibal encircled and destroyed the Roman army.[60]

2. Case Yellow

10–24 May 1940

O N 10 MAY 1940 German armies invaded Holland, Belgium and Luxembourg. Case Yellow had begun. It was, Brooke wrote in his diary, 'a most glorious spring day with all nature looking quite its best'. But presciently he also wrote, as the British advanced into Belgium: 'We were taking the first step towards what must become one of the greatest battles in history.'[1]

The German advance had two main thrusts. Army Group A, with a high proportion of panzer and motorised divisions, was to attack through northern Luxembourg and southern Belgium – the Ardennes – and cross the Meuse. Army Group B consisted largely of marching infantry with horse-drawn transport. Its initial task was to knock out the Dutch and Belgian forces, with the help of paratroop and glider troops who would seize frontier defences and bridges and disrupt enemy communications. Even before the German attack started at 0535, the Belgian government had asked for Allied help. Granting such help was a formality, since the Allied Plan D called for them to advance into Belgium anyway.

In spite of the lack of prior liaison with the Belgian armed forces, the advance went smoothly. British light mechanised units were up to the Dyle by the evening of the 10th, with the remainder following over the next few days. At the same time the French Seventh Army was advancing on the BEF's left into Holland. This was the French supreme commander, Gamelin's, extension of Plan D. It was to prove a serious mistake. The Dutch forces had retreated away from the French and were unable to link up with them. Seventh Army itself soon retreated again and was then moved south – losing many of its tanks through wear and tear in transit. Most critically, with Seventh Army stranded in the north, the French had no reserves to stem the German advance if they crossed the Meuse.[2]

Negating the French generals' confidence in the barriers imposed by the Ardennes roads to tanks, forward units of Army Group A reached the Meuse by 12 May. There were a growing number of reports on their progress from Allied reconnaissance aircraft, but their own preconceptions prevented the French from understanding the speed of the German advance on this front. The initial violence of Army Group B's attack was also a distraction, since it reinforced the idea that the main German thrust would be in the north. On the first morning paratroop and glider assault teams seized bridges and airfields in Holland as well as bridges across the Albert Canal, Belgium's first line of defence. This first morning also saw the famous glider assault on Fort Eben-Emael, a key component of Belgian defences lying at the junction of the Albert Canal and the lower reaches of the Meuse, near where it becomes the Maas and flows into Holland.[3]

It was much farther south – some seventy miles south of the BEF – that Army Group A achieved its shattering breakthrough. The Meuse was crossed in several places on the 13th, and by 15 May the Germans had broken through the French defences. Now that the Meuse had been crossed and the French line broken, the German realised that conditions were ripe for the ideal outcome of their plan – an advance due west to the Channel coast.

As this happened Army Group B, having broken through the first Belgian line of defence, encountered British and French forces farther north. The British seem to have resisted successfully. There are differing accounts of the French fortunes, and this stage of the battle for France still lacks a definitive English-language history. Julian Jackson states that the French fell back on the 16th because they were in an increasingly exposed salient, as a result of the German breakthrough on the Meuse. They had fought a tank battle against the Germans – called either the Battle of Hannut or the Battle of the Gembloux Gap – with some success on 12 and 13 May, and then continued to hold this line with infantry and artillery. Billotte, 'co-ordinating' the northern group of armies on behalf of Georges, was slow to respond to the dangers of the salient but finally did so under pressure from Gort, and ordered a general retreat. The British official history has a more pessimistic interpretation, suggesting that a 5,000-yard gap was torn in the French line on the 15th, and as a result the French First Army retired and the right wing of the BEF had to fall back on the night of 15/16 May. The French then began a more general withdrawal, and the British – following Billotte's orders – retired with them. The Belgians seem to have been holding firm at this point, but were thrown off balance by the withdrawal of the main British forces on the night of 16/17 May. An accident to the British liaison officer with Belgian HQ compounded the problem by preventing the news of the British withdrawal from reaching the Belgians in time.[4]

The withdrawal took the British all the way back to the Escaut – the French name for the Scheldt – fifty miles west. Only six days earlier they had crossed it

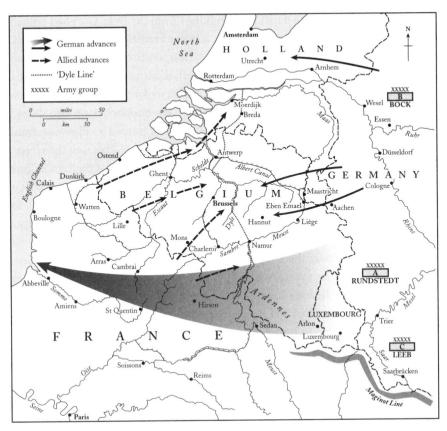

MAP 1: *German & Allied Operation plans, May 1940.*

on their way to the Dyle. Now, like the Duke of York's men, they marched back again. By the 19th most units were on the Escaut. Gort had kept much of his force in reserve behind the front line, which reduced the distance they had to move when they retraced their steps. Ironically, an advance to the Escaut rather than to the northern Meuse and the Dyle had been one of the options considered when Gamelin was formulating his plans. From the British and French point of view, it would have given more time for defensive preparation. More importantly it would not have involved Seventh Army's fruitless chase into southern Holland and would have made reinforcement of the Meuse front farther south much easier.

However all this is hypothetical. The reality was what counted, and the reality was grim. The German southern attack by Army Group A had not so far directly affected the BEF, although its destabilising effect on the whole French front had been one factor in Billotte's decision to withdraw from the Dyle. Gort had limited information, but it was now apparent that a major breakthrough was under way, which threatened his southern flank. By the 16th, units of Army Group A had reached the line Guise–La Fère. On the 17th Gort, at his command post at Renaix (in Flemish, Ronse), about twenty miles east of Lille, took action, forming a scratch force – Macforce, commanded by Major-General Mason-Macfarlane – to defend the BEF's right rear to the south of Lille. On 18 May he formed another one, from units stationed in the Arras area, to defend the town of Arras. This was 'Petreforce', commanded by Major-General Roderic Petre. In the early hours of the 19th Billotte had visited Gort and told him the latest situation. His explanation left Gort even less confident that the gap to the south would be closed, as did his whole demeanour. In the car over to Renaix, Billotte had repeated again and again: '*Je suis crève de fatigue – et contre ces Panzers je ne peux rien faire*'.[5]

Having opened badly, the 19th continued to be a day of fears and alarms. There were rumours of the complete collapse of French First Army, detailed by Pownall in his diary. In light of the rumours and of the continued progress of German panzer forces towards the sea, Gort and Pownall drew up preliminary contingency plans. The British would have to turn back on themselves like a hairpin to form a flank facing southwest, and thus ensure that there was a corridor running to the sea at Dunkirk. Pownall's diary specifically mentioned the possibility of evacuation, although he was not very hopeful of its practicability. On the phone to the War Office, he spoke of 'the way our minds were running' to the director of military operations, Major-General R. H. Dewing. Dewing was 'singularly stupid and unhelpful', but nonetheless the War Office initiated discussions with the Admiralty on the practicalities of evacuation.[6]

Meanwhile on the Escaut the 20th was a day of relative peace for the British, with only probing attacks by German forces. On the following day, 21 May, however, Army Group B had closed up and started a major attack. It was successfully resisted and the Germans achieved only one lodgement on the west bank of the river. The situation in the south was very different.

As Gort was forming his scratch forces to guard his southwestern flank, Army Group A continued to move rapidly west towards the coast, against little resistance. Billotte's writ did not run this far south, and on the 17th Georges had ordered British and French troops to garrison the Canal du Nord between Douai and Péronne. But most of the French troops never arrived. The defence of the entire territory between the canal and the sea rested on two British territorial divisions, undertrained and understrength and with minimal artillery support, which had been sent out to France in the spring for labour duties and further training. On 19 May the Germans had crossed the Canal du Nord and on the 20th had driven rapidly westwards. Not surprisingly the British forces were blown away, although a German war diary recorded British units 'defending [themselves] stubbornly'. But with no resistance at all on much of the sector, the German advance continued at a rapid pace. The leading units reached the sea at Abbeville on the evening of the 20th.[7]

In ten days, Army Group A's mechanised divisions had achieved an extraordinary breakthrough. Their achievement was the German army's revenge for the failure twenty-five years earlier of the Schlieffen Plan. The underlying principles behind each attack were similar, although the main axis of attack was different. The Schlieffen Plan had foundered on the inability of marching troops and horse-drawn supply to maintain the pace of advance, while the tanks and motorised infantry of Army Group A had overcome this lack of mobility.

The success of Case Yellow confronted the Allies with a set of appalling dilemmas. The entire northern group of troops were now cut off, both from the Maginot Line on France's northeastern frontier and from the remaining French troops to the south of the Somme. This northern group consisted of three armies: at the northern end, the Belgians, who were being driven back by units of Army Group B; to the south of them, the main British forces, also facing Army Group B on the Escaut; and, at the southeastern end of of the pocket, the French First Army.* In spite of the fears expressed on the 19th, it had fallen back in fairly good order and occupied a semicircle roughly on the line Maulde–Condé–Valenciennes–Douai. The Arras garrison and some thinly scattered British units formed a salient to the southwest of the French, sticking out into the main line of Army Group A's advance. Indeed, one German panzer division, the 7th, had been attacking Arras all day on 20 May without success. This was the division commanded by Rommel, soon to become famous for his exploits in North Africa. Rommel had been in the forefront of the advance over the Meuse but was now held up by the Arras defences.[8]

Gort and the BEF shared in these dilemmas and had other, more specific, ones. One was that the BEF's lines of communications had now been cut. There was no immediate threat to supplies as the British had substantial dumps, but within a short period food and ammunition would start to run short, and in fact the BEF went onto half rations on 23 May. More immediate was the threat to the entire

---

* See Map 2 (p. 41) for Allied positions at a slightly later date.

British rear. From La Bassée southeast of Lille through to the coast was now open to German attack as soon as the panzer units regrouped and turned north. As Allied defences along this line solidified it became known as the Canal Line, running fifty miles northwest from La Bassée along a series of canals to Gravelines, ten miles west of Dunkirk. The prevalence of canals in northern France and Belgium can be confusing. The Canal Line had no connection with the Ypres–Comines Canal, which was twenty-five miles farther east. For the moment the Canal Line was the focus of attention.[9]

So far Gort had formed scratch forces to protect the BEF's southern flank – although in practice the French First Army continued to do this – and to defend Arras. Now he had to construct a new line of defence facing roughly southwest, capable of resisting panzer forces.

The task was, of course, impossible. Most British troops were facing east and had to remain facing east against sustained German pressure. So any such line of defence was going to be hopelessly thin. But that did not stop Gort trying, and it did not stop the small, scratch units he formed mounting heroic and sometimes astonishingly successful defensive actions. At the same time Gort was organising a larger-scale action on the Arras front, with the intention not just of defending but also of attacking the Germans.

The defence of the Canal Line is thoroughly covered in most books about Dunkirk so it will be treated here only briefly, in order to put events elsewhere in context. On 20 May Gort formed 'Polforce', initially with a brigade of 50th Division, some Royal Engineer (RE) units, and one battery of field guns. Polforce's writ ran from Carvin, a few miles southeast of La Bassée, to Aire-sur-la-Lys – twenty-eight miles, or one field gun every two-and-one-third miles. Other units were subsequently added but the line was also extended a further seventeen miles – to Saint-Momelin, just north of St Omer.[10]

German troops closed up to the Canal Line at St Omer on the night of 22/23 May. Single guns defended a number of bridges in the St Omer area, in some cases holding the line successfully for several hours on the 23rd. In one case – Saint-Momelin itself – the defenders held out until the 25th, when French troops relieved them. By the evening of the 23rd, however, German troops had crossed the canals from south of Saint-Momelin to Robecq. The defenders had fallen back in front of Hazebrouck. The situation on the Canal Line, or the new line established behind it, seemed extremely serious. But then, for two days, enemy pressure slackened. To understand why it is necessary to go south, to Arras.[11]

The Arras action had its origins when, as part of his measures to strengthen his defences on the BEF's southern front, Gort ordered two divisions to move south. The 5th moved on 18 May to Seclin, a few miles south of Lille. The 50th advanced on the 19th to Vimy Ridge, just north of Arras and famous as the site of the successful attack by the Canadian Corps in April 1917. The next day Gort ordered 5th Division and 1 Tank Brigade to join 50th Division, and he gave Franklyn, commander of 5th Division, orders for an attack.[12]

Gort's orders had been framed in the light of one overriding preoccupation. This was the fear that he would be cut off from the south – which by the evening of the 20th he was – and, therefore, that the bulk of the BEF would have to retire northwards towards the sea. A limited action at Arras would relieve pressure there and thus help to protect the BEF's southern flank, while also interfering with German movement eastwards. But Gort's essentially defensive intentions were not to the liking of Churchill, who had been informed of them on 19 May. Churchill and the War Cabinet wanted a decisive move south to block the German advance and link up with the French. In practice the War Cabinet's idea was fanciful. The line of defence they indicated had already been breached by German forces while the bulk of the BEF was committed to the east against Army Group B. Gort convinced Ironside, the CIGS, who had arrived on the 20th bearing the War Cabinet's instructions, that he could not mount a large-scale attack. The French would have to bear most of the responsibility for closing the gap. However, the 5th and 50th Divisions' planned action would at least be a step in the right direction.[13]

Franklyn, however, was not told of these potentially wider implications by Gort – an omission for which the latter was implicitly criticised by the official historian. Thus Franklyn formulated his plans along the lines of his existing instruction: to 'support the garrison in Arras and to block the roads south of Arras', and to 'occupy the line of the Scarpe [a river] on the east of Arras'. Although the Arras action is usually called a counterattack, in conception it was only a limited one, concerned more with clearing the area around Arras than anything more. For the purposes of the attack, the two divisions and 1 Tank Brigade were put under Franklyn's command and became 'Frankforce'. This was, however, rather different from the scratch forces formed so far, which consisted of any odd units in the vicinity.

With two divisions and a brigade of tanks, Franklyn became the equivalent of a corps commander, although 5th and 50th divisions only had two infantry brigades each, not the usual three. Franklyn's plan was optimistic in the light of the actual German strength, which included an entire panzer division in the immediate vicinity. Only one infantry brigade of 50th Division was actually deployed in the attack, together with the tank brigade – itself depleted in strength. But Franklyn had to fulfil his instruction to support the garrison in Arras and to occupy the Scarpe for more than ten miles east of Arras. Two of Frankforce's infantry brigades were actually engaged in this, while the other was in reserve. The Scarpe forces also relieved French light tanks, which then strengthened the British attack by operating on its right flank. The attacking forces themselves were commanded by 50th Division's Giffard Martel.[14]

In spite of its limited strength, the operation on 21 May achieved temporary tactical success. Sweeping round to the west of Arras, advanced forces reached Wancourt, lying to the southeast of the town and a distance of around fifteen miles on the semicircular route taken. Although most of the British tanks, quaintly named Matildas, were slow and armed with no more than a machine gun, they were heavily armoured and initially rolled through the German lines. By nightfall, however, opposition had stiffened and the British troops and tanks were forced to withdraw. They had been fortunate in that they at first met infantry armed with light anti-tank guns, which could not stop the heavier Matildas. However the Germans were also fortunate in that Rommel, of all German commanders the one who tended to operate nearest the battle zone and be the most decisive in action, was on hand to organise the defence.[15]

The operation's limited tactical impact was outweighed by its larger effect on German thinking. Rommel's 7th Panzer Division, which bore the brunt of the attack, claimed that five British divisions were involved. As a result the attack aroused all sorts of fears. The German 6th Panzer Division, farther to the west, was about to start moving north but instead remained in a defensive position all day on 21 May. Even when the German forces to the west of Arras began a general move north on the 22nd, strong elements were left behind in case of further Allied attacks. These included 10th Panzer Division, whose initial target had been Dunkirk. The German reaction showed the power of a limited but vigorous thrust to disturb an enemy, by posing a threat that appeared much greater than it actually was. Their reaction was magnified, however, by a combination of inter-force politics and higher command nervousness. Rommel may have been aware that the British attack was not as strong as he claimed, but to have apparently beaten off five divisions obviously reflected well on him. Neighbouring corps-level German formations had actually dismissed the attack as a relatively small affair. But Hitler and Rundstedt, the Army Group A commander, were both expecting an Allied counterattack. They, therefore, read more into the Arras counterattack than it warranted and were inclined to accept Rommel's propaganda about its size.[16]

The action at Arras, therefore, had a significant impact on the immediate movements of the German army after its breakthrough to the coast. As a result of the delay, German units took some time to close up to the Canal Line, thereby allowing a scratch defence to be arranged as described above. But even after they had closed up, and while the BEF was still extremely vulnerable, German units ceased to press forwards so vigorously on the Canal Line front. Their inaction was a result of the famous Halt Order given by Army Group A. The extent of Hitler's responsibility for this has been the stuff of debate ever since. Here, only the outlines will be sketched.

The Halt Order is shorthand for a series of instructions to units of Army Group A not to advance beyond the Canal Line. The first was issued by Rundstedt to Fourth Army, responsible for the panzer divisions that formed the cutting edge of the German attack, at 1800 on 23 May. Fourth Army passed the order onto subordinate units, calling for a halt and 'closing up' – in effect consolidation – during the 24th. Then on the morning of 24 May, Hitler visited Rundstedt's HQ near Charleville–Mézières in the French Ardennes. According to the Army Group's war diary, the Führer agreed with the view that the main attack on the BEF and the French forces with them in the pocket should be made by Army Group B. The mobile forces should be halted on the Canal Line to form a 'stop'. This would conserve them for future operations against the remaining French forces to the south, and also leave plenty of space for the Luftwaffe to attack the trapped British and French troops. Subsequent to Hitler's visit, Rundstedt issued another order emphasising the earlier one. So was Hitler or Rundstedt really the prime mover behind the extension of the Halt Order, and what lay behind the sequence of events?[17]

After the war German generals, notably Guderian, who in 1940 was the commander of XIX Corps in which were Fourth Army's leading panzer divisions, were quick to condemn Hitler for the order. For generals such as Guderian it was convenient to put the blame on someone who was reviled for all sorts of other reasons. There is an obvious flaw in their argument, however, in that Rundstedt issued the original instruction. On the other hand, those who support the emphasis on Hitler's ultimate responsibility can point out that during the night of 23/24 May OKH had been planning to override Rundstedt, by the simple expedient of removing control of the panzers from him and giving it to Army Group B. When Hitler learned of this decision during his visit to Rundstedt's headquarters, however, he immediately reversed it, thus giving weight to his support of the Halt Order. Nevertheless, Rundstedt clearly bears considerable responsibility. His motives are fairly clear. The main one was to allow the panzer divisions to rest and refit.

They had suffered significant losses, either through combat or breakdown. And in Rundstedt's eyes Army Group A's next task was to attack the substantial French – and some British – forces still lying to his south. Its main task in the north was over and mopping up could be left to Army Group B. He also, of course, had to have some regard to the possibility of counterattack, whether from the south or north. Hence the emphasis on closing up – bringing up infantry and artillery to form a solid line. Here the significance of the Arras counterattack, and the state of nerves it engendered in Army Group A, are apparent. Whether or not it was responsible for tipping the balance in Rundstedt's mind in favour of a pause we cannot know. He was undoubtedly nervous even without Arras. On 16 May he had temporarily halted the panzer forces' headlong advance because: 'This southern flank is just an invitation for an enemy attack.'[18]

Similarly Arras is likely to have influenced Hitler, whose motivations – as always – have attracted the most speculation. It seems clear that allowing the British forces to escape was not, as is sometimes said, a piece of sportsmanship by him, in the mistaken belief that Britain would make peace. The OKH Chief of Staff Halder, in his diary, suggested that Hitler had a political motive. By allowing the remaining Allied forces to be driven back by Army Group B, with Army Group A forming a stop line, surrender would take place in France and hence more fighting in Flanders would be avoided. The implication is the Hitler wished to conciliate Flemish nationalism. This, however, sounds like a typical piece of *post-hoc* rationalisation by Hitler, who was adept at putting the best face on something he felt constrained to do for other reasons. It is more likely that Hitler was influenced by Hermann Göring into slowing down the panzer forces' advance, so the Luftwaffe would have full scope for its activities. This is an explanation frequently advanced, and there is probably something in it. However it is likely that the main reason in Hitler's mind, as in Rundstedt's, was a mixture of concern over the possibilities of Allied counterattack and a desire to conserve his tank forces. Like some of his generals, Hitler was nervous during the advance. Halder acidly commented to his diary on 17 May: 'The Führer . . . mistrusts his own success: he's afraid to take risks; he'd really like us to stop now. His excuse is anxiety about our left flank.' Hitler had, therefore, endorsed Rundstedt's earlier Halt Order of the 16 May.[19]

This pervasive nervousness about Allied counterattack is reinforced by the fact that between the 22nd and the 26th Boulogne and Calais were invested and reduced, at a significant cost to the panzer divisions in time and material, rather than simply being bypassed, as the Germans had done to other towns such as Arras in their initial advance. The attacks on Boulogne and Calais are usually discussed in the context of whether their defence held up the Germans on the way to Dunkirk. But they also illuminate German thinking on the possible dangers to their flanks. Ellis cited a German war diary that specifically referred to the continuing threat to the flanks of the German attack posed by the failure to take Boulogne and Calais. Concern over this meant that the Halt Order did not apply to the attacks on these two towns.[20]

Finally Karl-Heinz Frieser has suggested one other factor behind Hitler's stubborn support for the Halt Order in spite of protests by OKH. He believed that Hitler deliberately humiliated Walther von Brauchitsch, the commander of the German Army who had planned to negate Rundstedt's original order of the 23rd by stripping him of the panzer divisions. Hitler did this to emphasise his own supremacy.[21]

The Halt Order was finally lifted by Rundstedt – to whom Hitler had left the final decision – on 26 May. But in the substantial respite it had brought, the British improved their defences on the Canal Line. On the 24th and 25th the scratch forces between Saint-Momelin and the sea were relieved by French troops and retired towards Dunkirk. To the south, where from just south of Saint-Momelin to Robecq the scattered British defenders had fallen back, the line bulged dangerously inwards. By the 23rd, however, withdrawal and shortening of the main front to the east had enabled 2nd, 44th and 48th divisions to be freed. Overnight they were making their way to the relief of Polforce and the Canal Line or, where it had been breached, to new defensive positions around Cassel and Hazebrouck, and by the 24th they were getting into position. The Halt Order did not completely preclude German forces attacking in the meantime, but they made only minor gains.[22]

At the same time other German units had been moving northwards along the coast after the temporary pause caused by German anxiety over the implications of the Arras attack. Their advance restarted on the 22nd. Units of 2nd Panzer Division reached Boulogne by mid-afternoon. Scratch French forces and two British battalions defended the town. Most of the British troops were subsequently evacuated, although a few, with the French, fought on until the 25th. In Calais, a largely British force of three battalions and a tank regiment fought from the 23rd until they surrendered on the 26th, having resisted two German panzer divisions. By this time – in fact as early as the 22nd – any personnel who were not of military value were being evacuated from Dunkirk on Gort's orders.[23]

Meanwhile on both the main BEF front – the eastern front – and around Arras German attacks continued. On the eastern front, British troops pulled back from the Escaut during the night of the 22nd/23rd, returning to the Franco-Belgian frontier. This was the line from which they had moved less then two weeks earlier, on 10 May, in order to advance into Belgium. Not a natural line of defence, it at least had the benefit of fortifications, which the BEF had spent all winter laboriously constructing. The frontier line was relatively quiet on the 23rd and 24th, but on the left of the BEF the situation was becoming serious. Until then the British had been in touch with the Belgian army, so there had been a continuous Allied line extending more or less to the sea. On the afternoon of the 24th, however, Army Group B opened another offensive against the Belgians, driving them back in a northerly direction. By nightfall contact between the British and the Belgians was being lost, and so, as the Canal Line gap was being plugged, another gap was opening on the BEF's left.[24]

Thinking at Army Group B gets very little attention in accounts of the campaign. Yet Bock, its commander, was one of the most senior German generals. His personal diary, written up soon after the events it recorded, gives a valuable insight into German decision-making, and it can be supplemented by other sources from the Army Group.[25]

Bock's task was not easy, because with a relatively weak force, compared with Army Group A, he had a number of targets. He had to neutralise and if possible knock out the Belgian army. He was also attacking the British and French around Lille, and with the Halt Order this became the main attack on the Allied forces in the northern sector. Finally a successful attack on the Belgian army would open up the possibility of moving westwards and driving a wedge between the Allied forces around Lille and the coast. However on the night of 23/24 May Bock thought he had been given control of the panzers and that he could carry on their northeastwards drive into the Allies and cut off the Lille salient that way. At that stage Bock seems to have believed that the other main direction of attack would be a 'vigorous advance to the north-northwest at the junction between 6th and 4th Armies ...' The junction was at the outer, eastern, edge of the salient, and it seems likely that this attack was intended to pin the Allied forces in position while the panzers cut them off. Bock had no time for Rundstedt's halt and thought the panzers should keep going.[26]

As already related, Hitler stymied much of this plan by forbidding the transfer of Fourth Army, which controlled the panzers, to Army Group B, and supporting Rundstedt's Halt Order. But soon afterwards, Army Group B's offensive against the Belgians opened and quickly achieved considerable success. As a result Bock rethought his priorities, with results that will be described in the next chapter.

Back on the southern flank, at Arras, the retirement of the counterattacking forces in the evening of 21 May had been followed by German attacks from the south. By the 23rd they were across the river Scarpe both to the west and east of Arras, thus threatening to cut off the British-held salient, of which the town itself formed the tip. Up to the evening of that day Gort had resolved to hold the town to 'the last man and the last round'. But this condemned the substantial forces in the Arras salient to almost certain annihilation for no other purpose than absorbing the attacking power of a small fraction of the total German force. Clearly a better place for them was northeast of the Canal Line, the effective southwestern line of defence for the BEF. Gort therefore had second thoughts, and 5th and 50th Divisions, plus the Arras garrison, pulled back during the night of 23rd/24th.[27]

The Arras counterattack had momentous consequences. Subsequently, however, Arras was a wasting asset for the British. Continued resistance there on 22 and 23 May made little or no difference to the Halt Order, which was actually confirmed after the town had been evacuated. So Gort's decision to pull out was correct and might, in fact, have been taken earlier.

While Frankforce was defending Arras, the French and British were concerting a plan to bridge the gap between their forces north of Army Group A's corridor to the sea, and the – mainly French – forces to the south. The idea of bridging the gap had been mooted as early as the 20th by General Maxime Weygand, the new French supreme commander. It was a fairly obvious move; indeed the first, and last, order that Gamelin had issued, on the 19th, said much the same thing. Weygand had had a brilliant First World War career as a staff officer to General Ferdinand Foch. He had retired in 1935 at the age of sixty-eight, so on his return was even older than the other French generals. Originally bought back to command the French forces in the Levant, his semi-legendary status made Paul Reynaud, the French prime minister, decide that he was the right man to replace Gamelin, who was clearly useless.[28]

As recounted earlier, the War Cabinet had themselves urged Gort to undertake a major attack on Army Group A from the north but he had convinced Edmund ('Tiny') Ironside,* the CIGS, that he was not in a position to do so. The limited Arras operations had then followed on the 21st. Weygand appeared to share Churchill's desire for a decisive attack, and at a series of meetings at Ypres, also on the 21st, he outlined a plan. Units of both the BEF and the French First Army would strike south while other French forces south of the Somme would attack northwards to meet them. Unfortunately Gort did not hear of Weygand's arrival at Ypres – a telegram

---

* Ironside was 6 ft 4 in tall and built in proportion.

seems to have got lost – and the plan was initially agreed between Weygand, the Belgians and Billotte. When Gort was finally tracked down and arrived at Ypres, Weygand had departed. Gort agreed to join an offensive if the British line in Belgium was shortened by withdrawal to their old positions on the French frontier. By freeing units this would enable him to strengthen the scratch defences on the Canal Line. This manoeuvre was agreed and later carried out, but Gort also asked for a general shortening of the Allied line, to be achieved by a Belgian withdrawal to the Yser. This would result in a reasonably straight defensive line running roughly northwest from the vicinity of Valenciennes. Belgian uncertainty as to their future movements meant there was no firm agreement on this point.[29]

By dint of pulling 5th and 50th Divisions out of Arras, the British had a striking force for an attack south. In the meantime, however, plenty of other things had gone wrong. Billotte had been seriously injured in a car accident after he left the Ypres conference and died two days later. In purely military terms this was not much of a loss, but Blanchard, his temporary and then permanent replacement, was little, if any, better and for several days had to carry out two jobs at once – running First Army and also 'co-ordinating' it, the Belgians and the BEF. In these circumstances an elaboration of Weygand's and Churchill's offensive ideas, concerted between them and the French prime minister Reynaud in a meeting on 22 May, was not much help. Ellis reproduced a message from Churchill and an order from Weygand, both of which resulted from this meeting. The two communications more or less reversed the normal procedure in which a prime minister might exhort and a general give precise instructions. Churchill's message was terse, concrete and totally impracticable. Weygand's order was rambling, vague and equally impracticable. And on the same day a more concrete operation order from Georges made barely a reference to the mooted attack.[30]

By 23 May Georges had recognised the significance of the planned attack and there were the beginnings of a more organised French plan. However this was abruptly put on hold during a confused episode in which Weygand appears to have either mistaken Gort's withdrawal from the Arras salient on the night of 23rd/24th as the British reneging on their agreement, or else to have lost his own nerve about the ability of the French south of the Somme to attack northwards. In a message to Churchill Reynaud, presumably echoing Weygand, accused Gort of withdrawing twenty-five miles northwards, when the actual distance of the withdrawal was fifteen miles. Reynaud then claimed that Weygand was 'compelled to give up his attempt to close the breach'. In reality the commander of the forces to the south of the Germans, General Besson, seems to have decided that he could not mount an attack, adducing various reasons. Weygand accepted his views and transferred the blame for the failure to launch a two-pronged offensive to the British. As Julian Jackson, an author both knowledgeable about and sympathetic to the French perspective, stated: 'The alacrity with which [Weygand] dropped his plan suggests that Gort had offered him the alibi he needed.' However, although the attack from the south was dropped, Weygand authorised Blanchard to continue planning for the thrust in the opposite direction, from the Allied troops to the north of the German breakthrough, if an attack was thought possible. The stage seemed set for a much-delayed attempt to cut off the German forces pouring through the gap.[31]

3.   Decision

25 MAY 1940

O N 18 MAY 1940 Lieutenant-Colonel G. H. Gilmore, CO of 5th Division's 2nd Cameronians, joined a mass of troops at London's Victoria Station. Gilmore was returning to France from leave, which had started on the 8th – bad timing in the light of subsequent events. Leave trains had stopped running as a result of the emergency following the German attack, stymieing his attempts to return earlier. On the 18th, however, the trains had restarted in order to return men to France.

With the BEF's lines of communication running through Normandy, Gilmore landed at Cherbourg. But by then the Germans were near to cutting off the BEF from the Normandy ports, and Gilmore seemed to be stuck. With Lieutenant-Colonel Tod of the 2nd Royal Scots Fusiliers (RSF), also in 5th Division, he managed to persuade the commander of a motor torpedo boat to take them up the coast. After an eventful journey involving two separate attacks by German aircraft they landed at Dunkirk. They had another difficult journey south before they finally caught up with the division, now in the Seclin area after its defence of Arras.[1]

Almost immediately, Gilmore set off to travel another twenty miles or so in order to reconnoitre the ground for the planned attack towards the south. One thrust was to have been across the Canal de la Sensée between Douai and Valenciennes. The canal describes a large loop, curving to the south, and Gilmore left an account of the site where his battalion was expecting to attack. Between the Allied and the German positions were the canal and a river, flowing within a wide swampy area with higher ground on the German side. It was 'an excellent defensive position. A piece of ground which, had you been reconnoitring for an attack exercise, you would not have considered for one minute.' The British had no bridging equipment and Gilmore suspected that the French artillery and infantry, who were meant to support him, were heading away from the site of the impending attack. His mind went back to a frontal attack on Guillamont he had been ordered to make in 1916 as a junior

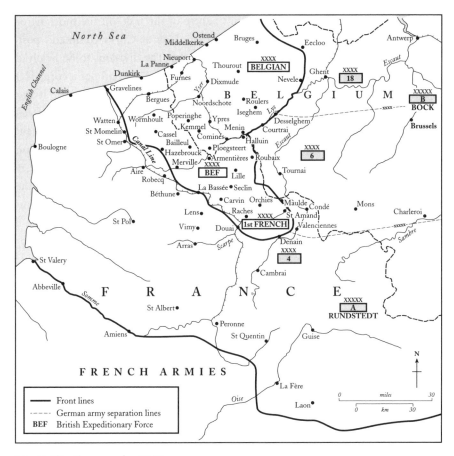

MAP 2: *Situation, morning 25 May.*

officer on the Somme (fortunately it had later been cancelled): 'I knew then, that the task allotted was a suicide one . . . and this I felt was a similar forlorn hope.'[2]

Gilmore's suspicions of the French were paralleled by French suspicions of the British, with allegations that the British were already planning to retreat. In his postwar memoirs Weygand clears Gort of some of these allegations concerning the latter's absence from the Ypres conference and the withdrawal from Arras. But he still leaves the impression that Gort was extremely lukewarm about the whole idea of a southern offensive. Mentioning the visit of Major Fauvelle, one of Blanchard's staff officers, to GHQ on the morning of 25 May, he reported – without comment – Fauvelle's statement that 'the British seemed to be concerned above all about the preparations for their re-embarkation'.[3]

In reality, and in spite of the difficult nature of the task, on the morning of 25 May planning for the attack dominated thinking at Gort's command post, now at Prémesques between Armentières and Lille.* The divisions to be involved in the attack south were 5th and 50th, as at Arras, and Gort had put a corps HQ in charge. This was III Corps, commanded by General Sir Ronald Adam. It was originally to have taken over 2nd, 44th and 48th divisions, which had been freed by the shortening of the British eastern front as it was pulled back from the Escaut to the French frontier. They had now moved south and were getting into position on the Canal Line, hitherto defended by scratch forces. But for the time being they were put under the command of Major-General 'Rusty' Eastwood, who was on the staff of GHQ. So whereas the Arras counterattack four days earlier had been put under Franklyn, a divisional commander, the new attack was thought to merit a separate corps command, while the Canal Line, a vital defensive position, was put under a temporary commander. All this suggests that Gort attached considerable importance to the operation.[4]

Adam was an old friend of Brooke's and in 1941 became the army's adjutant-general, in charge of personnel, in which role Danchev and Todman described him as outstanding. His French counterpart, General René Altmayer, was the brother of General Robert Altmayer, who commanded a corps south of the Somme. René Altmayer was one of a number of French generals who were rather easily discouraged. A French liaison officer reported just before the Arras offensive that Altmayer 'tired out and thoroughly disheartened . . . wept slightly'. However, he seems to have recovered enough to be ready to co-operate with Adam in this latest attack. Three French divisions and 200 tanks were to join the two British divisions, and the attack was due to begin on the evening of the 26th.[5]

At this point an element of mystery enters into the events of 25 May. What exactly did Gort and Pownall expect the attack to achieve? John Dill, the erstwhile commander of I Corps, probably the only general in the British army whom Brooke looked up to, and now vice-CIGS, arrived at GHQ about 0700 to find out what was happening and report back to the War Cabinet. He reported to Churchill that: 'There is NO blinking the seriousness of situation in northern area.' After briefly outlining the plan of attack, he cautioned that in the circumstances it could not be important. However at that point Blanchard arrived at GHQ. In what must have been his most active intervention during his period of command, he informed Gort

---

* At 0300 that morning the command post changed its name to Advanced GHQ. From then on diaries refer to it simply as 'GHQ' although in fact the administrative element of GHQ was elsewhere. I will emulate that practice and also refer to the ex-command post as GHQ.

and Dill that the offensive was to be an altogether bigger affair and *was* to include an attack from the south, as well as the thrust from the north in which the British were involved. As Ellis drily observed, the fact that Weygand had already 'felt compelled to give up his attempt to close the breach does not seem to have been made known, yet, to General Blanchard'.[6]

It must have been this misunderstanding that led Gort and, presumably, Pownall to put the whole idea of retirement towards Dunkirk on the back burner, briefly, in favour of a more radical plan – to move the whole BEF south. One of the puzzles of the day is that this is known only indirectly, but the evidence is persuasive. The main sources are the diaries of Brooke and Montgomery, and the war diary of 1st Division. Brooke went to the command post early on 25 May because he had received information in the early hours of that morning that German penetration through the Belgian front was growing rapidly and that there was little Belgian resistance to it. Brooke concluded that the Germans were preparing an attack 'intended to push right through to our left rear' – in other words from Belgium to the Canal Line. If successful this would cut the BEF off from the sea. Brooke obtained reinforcements – a machine-gun battalion and an infantry brigade – although apparently not without considerable difficulty. He then recorded in his diary: 'I was informed that the "Rush for the Sea" plan was abandoned [that is, the Dunkirk plan]. Thank God for it, I have always hated this plan. The new plan is to break through to join the French forces south of the German penetration. It might be possible, but I should doubt it.' Montgomery's diary stated that Brooke visited him at 1600 hours 'with outline idea on how BEF might abandon the Belgians and fight its way through to join the French'.[7]

Taken by themselves the diaries are limited as evidence, if persuasive enough because Brooke was hardly likely to have misunderstood Gort. There is, however, further supporting evidence that seems previously to have gone unnoticed in 1st Division's diary for 25 May. It reported what Michael Barker, commander of I Corps, told his audience at a divisional conference. Barker was – no doubt like Brooke – passing on what he had heard at GHQ:

> 5 and 50 Divisions were likely to be launched southward in an attempt to drive the way through the gap and join hands with the French. The Northern Divisions (ex Escaut) [i.e. I and II Corps] would swing round, pivoting on S.E. of Lille and form a sort of rearguard as a prelude to following up through the corridor formed by the 5th and 50th (3 French Divs. co-operating).[8]

GHQ's war diary did not mention the idea, but that is hardly surprising because it would only have shown up in operational orders if it had been more developed. Nor was there any reference in Pownall's diary, although this may be because it was written up later when the plan had been reversed. One can only suppose that, in a desperate situation, Gort for a few hours thought that he saw an opportunity for a decisive attack, rather than the piecemeal defence and limited counterattack, which was all the BEF had contributed so far. But the very existence of the plan, sketchy and short-lived as it was, is important. It gives the definitive lie to French insinuations that Gort had decided to desert them, via Dunkirk, before the decision was actually announced.

Brooke's comments are also interesting. There was perhaps an element of *schadenfreude* in his comment about the abandonment of the 'Rush to the Sea', because, when the Dunkirk idea was first evolved as a precautionary measure on 19 May, he had preferred a line of retreat that ran up to the coast much farther east and included as possible ports Zeebrugge and Ostend. But by the 25th his own plan was history because the BEF had already come back too far. Dunkirk was now the only option on the northern French coast. It seems contradictory to criticise the Dunkirk plan while at the same time wresting reinforcements from Gort in order to protect II Corps' own left flank, which linked it with the Belgians and thence the sea. The diary entry suggested that even a general as rational as Brooke was feeling the strain.[9]

While Brooke was visiting his divisional commanders in the afternoon of 25 May, other commanders who were to be involved in the southern attack were preparing for it. 50th Division's war diary recorded that Martel, their commander, visited GHQ, subsequently holding a divisional conference and outlining a 'probable move south for offensive action'. The commander of 5th Division's 13 Brigade spent the afternoon with his battalion commanders 'recceing an attack with the French on the Canal de la Sensée'.[10] As well as Gilmore, there were the COs of the 2nd Wiltshire Regiment (Wiltshires) and the 2nd Royal Inniskilling Fusiliers (Inniskillings). Company second-in-commands and guides from the latter, as well as its CO, went to the river Scarpe, the general area of the attack, as advance guard to the battalion. The commander of 5th Division's artillery, Brigadier J. R. Barry, set up an advanced HQ southeast of Douai and reconnaissance parties from his field regiments went out to meet him. However, most of the men in 50th and 5th Divisions were able to enjoy a much-needed day of rest.[11]

Until mid-afternoon at least, preparations for the operation were also going forwards at GHQ. The most striking testimony comes from Major O. A. Archdale, liaison officer to the French First Group of Armies, who was at GHQ arranging liaison duties for the attack. Archdale noted that at 1500 he 'was told that Winston Churchill had sent instructions to fight south, and that the C-in-C was determined now to do that with or without the French'. In fact on 25 May Churchill seems to have been mainly preoccupied with the defence of Calais and there is no evidence that he knew of the idea for a complete shift of direction for the whole BEF. Indeed he had already accepted, in a message to Ironside the CIGS, that Gort might have to fight his way out via Dunkirk. So the wholesale shift of the BEF southwards must have been Gort's own idea.[12]

Then at some stage in the next three hours Gort changed his mind. 5th Division was not to be used for the southerly attack, but was instead to be sent north. 50th Division would soon follow it. Even now, there is a lack of agreement as to the reasons for this decision. Yet it was one of the most important of the war.

To understand why the decision was made, it is necessary to be certain of when it was agreed. Ellis stated that it was taken at 1800 and this was no doubt based on the GHQ war diary, which said the same thing. But the war diary is likely to be recording the actual promulgation of the decision, the point at which Pownall, as chief of staff, started drafting orders. Gort might have actually made up his mind somewhat earlier. Archdale's diary, again, comes to the rescue. At 1730 Pownall explained that Archdale would have to go to Georges' headquarters at La Ferté-sous-Jouarre so that the position could be explained to Georges. Archdale then proceeded to meet Gort, and takes up the story:[13]

> The C-in-C was sitting at his table very silent, and looking rather bewildered and bitter. I felt most strongly that he was wishing that he could take an active physical part in the battle: that it was irking him terribly to be forced to sit there with nothing but weary Allies all round him: weary in body but oh! so terribly weary in mind.
>
> He said that he had had a raw deal from the Allies; not only had their army continually pleaded that it was too tired to fight, and their staff work broken down, but from start to finish there had been no direction or information from the High Command. 'Why' – he asked – 'did they retreat to the Escaut when they knew of the great gap in the middle – why not retreat south and preserve a front and lines of communication?'
>
> The CGS [Pownall] asked me whether I knew what the situation was. I replied that I did, but that I would like to hear it from him. He gave me this rapid appreciation.

Belgians hard pressed at Courtrai: one Brigade and Machine Gun Battalion, the only available reserves, were being sent to their support.* 5th and 50th Divisions were going to do the attack South on 26th, but this could never be anything but a 'sortie' by a beleaguered garrison, and for success MUST be met by a French attack from the South. If the enemy were to break through on the Belgian front, instant help would be demanded and for obvious reasons would have to be given: in that case the attack planned for 26th could not take place as 5th and 50th divisions were the only units available either for the attack or for Belgian support. In the latter case there would have to be a retirement to the line – Gravelines – Bethune – Armentières – Comines – Ypres – the sea.[14]

Archdale represented Pownall's intervention as immediately succeeding Gort's anguished comments, although it is not clear whether the three men were in the same room at the same time. Lieutenant-Colonel Templer, who had reported to Pownall before Archdale and had to pass through Gort's room to get to Pownall's, recorded Gort as alone at that point. Templer was so apprehensive at the thought of meeting Gort again on his return that he left through Pownall's window. Whether Gort was alone or not when he spoke to Archdale, Pownall's conversation with Archdale suggests strongly that Gort, either by himself or with Pownall, had already come to the view that the attack south would very probably have to be called off. However the final decision had clearly not yet been made and, therefore, must have been taken between 1730 and 1800.[15]

J. R. Colville in his biography of Gort listed the influences that led Gort to change his mind. Adam had rung up with the news that Altmayer could provide only one division for the attack. 50th Division, one of those assigned to the attack, had had to provide two battalions to support French troops at Carvin on the southern front. Brooke was still concerned about his left flank. The British tank force was now very small, and the attack south would bring the attackers face to face with the main German tank divisions. The colonel of the 12th Royal Lancers, a reconnaissance regiment, reported that the Belgians had no fighting spirit left. Finally Montgomery's 3rd Division had captured some enemy plans that showed the strength of the assault that Bock of Army Group B was about to launch between Ypres and Comines. Alternatively, and according to the official history, the

---

* These were the reinforcements assigned to Brooke; it would be more accurate to say that they were protecting the BEF's left from the consequences of a Belgian collapse.

reason was much simpler: Gort told Pownall that 'he had a "hunch" that calamity threatened in the northeast and only instant action could avert it.'[16]

So there is a formidable list of possible factors that persuaded Gort to change his mind, and most of these crop up in other accounts, although not necessarily together. One reason for this, of course, is that many authors writing about the campaign have taken much of their information from another secondary source – as is inevitable, especially in more wide-ranging accounts. It is necessary, therefore, to look carefully at the primary source material.

One of the reasons assigned by Colville can be dealt with quickly. 50th Division did not have its battalions detached until the 26th so this could not have been a factor in Gort's decision.[17] For another – the telephone call from General Adam indicating that French support for the British would be much weaker than expected – no primary source evidence has been found. According to Colville, Adam had spent the morning with Altmayer, discovered that the latter could offer no more than one division, and 'at once telephoned to Gort'. Therefore Gort apparently had forewarning. But then in the afternoon: 'Hardly had Archdale left when Adam rang up with the news that Altmayer could only provide one division for the attack.' The implication, although it is not absolutely clear, is that Adam gave Gort the same news twice. Colville thanked Adam in his acknowledgments so presumably the latter told him about the call or calls. But the story as told not only appears to rely on Adam's memory some thirty years after the event, but also begs the question as to how Adam could know that Archdale had just left Gort, when Adam was at the other end of a telephone line.[18]

Gort's own dispatches actually suggest that he did not know of the reduction in Altmayer's offer until later. He stated that the possibility of an attack was not altogether precluded by the British withdrawal from it, since the French were still planning to attack with three divisions and the 'Cavalry Corps' (not cavalry but light tanks), although he admitted that British non-participation rendered a French attack unlikely. It is true that Gort's dispatches are not always reliable: for example, immediately afterwards he stated that he ordered 50th Division to join II Corps, followed by 5th, whereas the sequence was the other way round. So the timing and influence of Adam's phone call or calls must remain an open question, although it may be that there is an answer in some source yet to be found.[19]

Both Brooke's concern about the Belgian situation, and the small size of the remaining British tank force, were not new news. Most of the tanks had been lost in the Arras counterattack four days earlier, while Brooke had been making his concerns known since the early morning. This is not to deny either as factors in Gort's reasoning. But if he had considered them critical he would already have called the attack off, let alone have toyed with the more grandiose plan of moving the whole BEF south. However the fact that at around midday Brooke had been assigned the brigade – 143rd – which constituted the BEF's only significant reserve must have influenced Gort. There is no direct record of its transfer, but at 1305 a message from II Corps ordered it to report to the corps HQ. A machine-gun battalion – the 4th Gordons – was also transferred from I to II Corps and constituted another loss of GHQ's potential reserves. Almost as soon as Gort had decided to stake all on an attack southwards, he saw his ability to concentrate his forces in that direction beginning to dissipate.[20]

What a number of authors have considered critical is the capture of German plans to which Colville alluded. This resulted from the quick thinking and courage of Sergeant R. S. Burford of the 1/7th Middlesex, a territorial machine-gun battalion. The credit for tracking down Sergeant Burford some thirty years after the events, and uncovering the full story, must go to Gregory Blaxland, from whose book much of the next paragraph has been taken.[21]

Burford was attached to 4th Division, stationed on the flank of II Corps at the point where the river Lys runs roughly east–west. He was patrolling on the north side of the river on 25 May – at what time is not known although morning seems most likely. The area should theoretically have been in Belgian hands, but 4th Division, like Brooke himself, was uncertain about the Belgians and feared that its flank was exposed. This was correct. Burford entered a village between Comines and Menin where some Germans had been seen. His Bren group came under fire and then a 'big blue car came up the street, containing two German officers'. Burford emptied his .38 revolver at the car, which crashed. One officer jumped out and fled, the other remained in the car, wounded or dead. It must have been one of the few instances in the war when revolver fire actually inflicted any damage on the enemy. In this case the damage was momentous. Burford retrieved a briefcase in the car containing maps, documents and a bootjack. He returned, with a wounded man from his Bren group, and deposited the briefcase at the HQ of 3rd Division. The 1/7th Middlesex had only just been transferred to 4th Division and perhaps Burford assumed he was still under 3rd.[22]

The chapter of accidents and coincidences continued. Brooke was visiting 3rd Division, partly to talk over Gort's idea for a breakthrough to the south. The story is best continued in Brooke's own words, taken from the 'notes on his memoirs' he wrote subsequently. The extracts are taken as published in Arthur Bryant's account of Brooke's wartime career:

He [Montgomery] had his HQ in a small villa and, as I walked through the dining-room to the drawing-room he was in, I noticed that his staff were very busy with some papers round the dining-room table. After seeing Monty and on walking back through the dining-room, by way of making conversation I said to them: 'You seem to be very busy round that table.' Whereupon one of them replied: 'Oh! yes, we have some most interesting documents here.'[23]

Montgomery's staff informed him about Sergeant Burford's exploits, and Brooke told them to give him the briefcase (he called it a wallet). One member of the staff knew some German and may have been able to give Brooke an idea of the documents' potential importance. Montgomery's diary extract about this visit has already been noted. Brooke departed for GHQ and again takes up the story:

As I drove along towards GHQ [General Headquarters] I remembered the papers which Meinertzhagen had planted on the Turks for Allenby . . . I wondered if the Germans were up to some such trick and then remembered the boot-jack in the wallet. I thought it was highly unlikely that the Germans would have thought of placing a boot-jack in the wallet, whilst on the other hand, it was highly probable that a German staff officer might have tight boots requiring a jack to pull them off.[24]

Meinertzhagen, in spite of his Germanic name, was a British officer engaged in the First World War Palestine campaign against the Turks. According to his own account, he had ridden towards the Turkish lines, pretended to be wounded, and dropped falsified British plans, which then deceived the Turks. Brooke seems to be implying that the Germans would not have had the imagination to make false papers more realistic by adding the flourish of the bootjack.[25]

Brooke arrived at GHQ and handed the briefcase over to Pat Whitefoord, the senior intelligence officer. Brooke then proceeded to attend a GHQ conference and 'as soon as the conference was over got hold of Whitefoord to find out what he made of the German documents'. Whitefoord had only had time to glance at them, but knew that they gave orders to one corps to direct an attack on the Ypres–Comines front. 'I told Whitefoord to give full details to Gort, and told him personally of the important part.'[26] Whitefoord later told Blaxland that he believed that the documents 'were important in convincing Gort that the forebodings of Brooke, with which he had so often been inflicted, were in this case genuine'.[27]

The English translation of these plans – in fact, a set of orders to units of German Sixth Army – is rather confusingly filed in the Advanced GHQ papers for 24 May, the date on the orders and evidently when Sixth Army staff had completed them, late at night, as the time of 2330 indicates. The internal evidence of the documents seems to bear out the sequence of events noted by Brooke. Perhaps after Whitefoord had been handed the orders he had started to translate them in full. There is a suggestion near the top of the second page of the full translation, where there is a crossed-out sentence, that he ran out of time; maybe he then hastily made the handwritten summary which is also in the file, presumably for Brooke to show Gort. It can be speculated that when GHQ pulled out of Premesques on 27 May and made for the Channel coast, documents were crammed into boxes willy-nilly. And perhaps some War Office clerk in England, sorting everything out and seeing the date of the 24th,* filed the orders under that date, although, from the British point of view, the 25th would be more appropriate.[28]

At this stage it would be useful to work out the actual sequence of events on the afternoon of the 25th. Montgomery's diary stated that Brooke was at 3rd Division at 1600, but it is not known when he left or whether he went anywhere after visiting 3rd Division and before arriving at GHQ. Brooke's memoir described how when he arrived at GHQ he gave the document to Whitefoord, attended a conference, then got the gist of the plan from Whitefoord and told Gort about it.

There is, however, a problem. It is not possible to square this scenario with Gort reaching his decision *after* being informed of the captured plan. According to Brooke's diary, rather than his later memoir, he attended a conference at GHQ at 1900: 'I found the atmosphere entirely changed, and was at once presented with 5th Div. to hold Ypres–Comines Canal.' Unless he had attended another conference at GHQ, which he did not mention in his diary, only an hour or two before this one, then discussed the captured plan with Gort before 1800, Gort cannot have known about the plan before making his decision.[29]

But there is no hint anywhere of an earlier conference, and it is virtually impossible to fit into the known timings. Templer's and Archdale's testimonies indicate that Gort and Pownall were engaged, or alone, from some time before 1730 to some time after it. Since Brooke did not leave Montgomery's headquarters before 1600, there is far too little time for him to have done everything he had to do if the

* For photographs of the first pages of the full translation and handwritten summary see the plate section.

German orders were indeed transmitted to Gort in time to influence his decision. Brooke would have had to drive some miles to GHQ, attend a conference during which Whitefoord translated part of the orders and wrote a summary of them, and then see Gort, all within less than an hour and a half.

Furthermore there is a small but important omission in the published version of Brooke's memoir. As already related, Brooke according to the memoir arrived at GHQ, handed the briefcase over to Whitefoord, and 'then proceeded to attend a GHQ conference'. What Brooke then wrote, which is absent from Bryant's version, is 'about which I wrote the following' – and he then extracted a section from his diary beginning 'I found the atmosphere . . .' which is reproduced above. In other words, when he wrote his memoir, admittedly some years after the event, he remembered only the one conference, at 1900, at which he was immediately presented with 5th Division.[30]

It seems quite clear that Gort had changed his mind before he saw the captured orders. Sergeant Burford's courage and quick thinking were still important, however. The other document captured was the German Army Order of Battle as of 1 May 1940 and, although a few pages were missing, '. . . it gave the War Office for the first time an authoritative picture of the German army'.[31]

It is also possible that the capture of the orders influenced Gort when, the next day, he sent 50th Division north to defend Ypres itself. This was perhaps what Brooke meant when he wrote in his memoir: 'From now on I had less difficulty in obtaining reinforcements for this front.' But it is not the impression given by Bryant, nor by Ellis who wrote: 'The second of the captured documents [i.e. the orders] was of even more immediate importance to Lord Gort and General Brooke.'

Any reservations Brooke himself may have had about the significance of the orders to Gort's original decision seem to have been lost on subsequent historians. Most have followed the inference in Ellis' statement, which is that they were crucial in changing Gort's mind. Interestingly, a belief in the importance of the orders' capture was current well before the idea was popularised by Ellis and Bryant. An article in the *Daily Mirror* of 8 August 1945 revealed the story and claimed that it 'robbed the German High Command of the chance of trapping the British Expeditionary Force', and a comment by British military intelligence on the article supported this claim.[32]

If the capture of the orders did not affect Gort's decision to send 5th Division north, is it possible to identify any other critical factor in the late afternoon of 25 May? By now the German attack on the Belgians, which had started on the 24th, was giving serious concern. 4th Division, part of II Corps, was adjacent to the Belgians.

Their war diary recorded that late on the evening of the 24th the Belgians were driven back from the Lys. It was, of course, as a result of this vacant space on the left of the BEF that Burford's patrol was sent out on the 25th. Also on the 25th a motor contact officer sent out to reconnoitre the road running parallel with the Lys east of Menin reported: 'The Belgians here seem to have given up all idea of fighting and although within 2000 to 3000 yards of the front line were sitting about in cafes drinking beer and coffee.' 4th Division also noted reports that the Belgian army would be forced to withdraw farther north – that is, away from the BEF. At this point 4th Division's front was extended along the Lys to Comines in order to defend II Corps' flank. Brooke's information that there was growing German penetration through the Belgian front was mentioned earlier in the chapter. It may have come from 4th Division or from liaison officers with the Belgian army. He received it at 0200 on the 25 May and, as has been seen, visited Gort early that morning and obtained limited reinforcements.[33]

GHQ also had information from the BEF's mission to Belgian GHQ, headed by Major-General Needham. At 0700 on 25 May Gort had received a telegram from the mission stating: 'Position serious Belgian front between Menin and canal junction NW of Desselgem.'* By 0900 the mission was reporting a heavy attack on this front and significant German penetration, and during the day Gort received further reports from other sources along the same lines.[34]

Thus Gort was well aware of the potential hole on the BEF's left where the Belgians were meant to be, but from which they were being driven back. GHQ's reconnaissance regiment was 12th Lancers, an armoured car regiment under Lieutenant-Colonel Herbert Lumsden. Pownall referred to them as 'always most reliable'. At 0630 on the 25th they had been told to watch the left flank of II Corps north of the Lys and establish contact with Belgian forces in that area.[35]

12th Lancers' war diary was almost certainly written up afterwards, but the precise timings suggest that it was based on a contemporaneous record. It noted that Lumsden had actually been woken up by a staff officer, presumably from GHQ, at 0615, so Gort and Pownall obviously took the Belgian situation seriously. The Lancers quickly established that the enemy had crossed the Lys just east of Courtrai. By early afternoon the Germans were pushing westwards – hardly surprising in view of the lack of Belgian resistance noted by 4th Division's motor contact officer. The Lancers themselves were putting up some resistance, but there was not much a few armoured cars could do against a major German attack, nor was it their job to get

---

* Desselgem was east of Courtrai.

involved in battles. Major Horsbrugh-Porter, who was their liaison with the Belgian army, reported that he had visited three Corps HQs and one army HQ, which were obviously not in touch with the actual situation on the battlefront. They were 'busy making grandiose arrangements for a counterattack . . . Whereas in fact no very strenuous resistance was being offered to the German advance on this front.'[36]

Late in the afternoon of 25 May the Lancers sent two critical messages to GHQ. The first, probably the most vital, was received at 1703. The Germans were pushing forwards to the outskirts of Menin and advancing north through Moorsele, a village northeast of Menin: 'They are meeting with little resistance . . . our allies [the Belgians] are withdrawing . . . It appears that a gap is forming between our Allies and our troops.' Given that, when Archdale saw Gort and Pownall at 1730, they had clearly formed the opinion that the attack south might have to be called off, it seems most likely that they had already seen and digested this message. Coming on top of what they already knew about Belgian weakness, it possibly turned the scales.

The next message received, at 1725, might not have reached Gort and Pownall when they saw Archdale. However, if it arrived immediately afterwards, as seems likely, then it would have cleared up any remaining doubts: 'Am tending to get involved in infantry battle between Menin and Roulers [Roeselare] in which Belgians are taking no part.' This showed that the Germans had pushed a considerable distance north and confirmed the lack of Belgian resistance.[37]

A number of almost ineluctable facts shaped Gort's decision. Above all, these facts were the German attack on the Belgians, the clear evidence of its success, and the fact that by the afternoon of 25 May there was no Belgian resistance to speak of on a front extending ten miles north of Menin, the Belgian junction with the BEF. That front was itself just twenty-five miles from Dunkirk.

Ever since the series of meetings at Ypres on 21 May there had been doubt as to whether the Belgians either would, or could, pull back in a westerly direction towards the Ypres–Comines line if further German attacks were launched. Now the answer was clear: they were retreating northeast, away from the BEF, and there was a pressing danger that the BEF would be rolled up from behind if it did not construct a defence line running north from Comines. The attack south, a romantic project at best, would be of little avail if German troops were attacking from the east with no organised resistance being offered.

It, therefore, seems most likely that, when Gort made his historic decision to call off the attack south and send 5th Division to the Ypres–Comines front, he did it because of the information he was receiving about the Belgian collapse. He could not at that point have been aware of the captured German orders. But anyone observing the progress of Army Group B for the last fortnight could have inferred that it was not likely to rest when it had smashed up the Belgians, and that its next target was likely to be the BEF. It was not necessary to capture the orders in order to have a fair idea of what the Germans might do. The 12th Lancers' and other reports confirmed that they were doing it. Adam's phone call or calls may also have influenced Gort, but we can only be more certain about this if some primary source evidence about the time they were made comes to light.

In a sense, for Gort to describe his decision as based on a 'hunch' fits in with this conclusion. It is somewhat disingenuous, though, both as a description and as a piece of reportage by Pownall. Gort was not relying on some mystic impulse, but on what 12th Lancers and Brooke were telling him about the Belgians. And Pownall's remarks to Archdale suggest that he had shared to some extent in Gort's deliberations and cannot have been entirely surprised by them.[38]

Accepting that Gort made his decision first and only saw Brooke later also helps to make sense of another puzzling source. This is Franklyn's memoir of his time as commander of 5th Division during the 1940 campaign. Franklyn was sent for by Gort at about 1600 on 25 May. His memoir is inaccurate in detail in a number of instances, and there seems little doubt that he wrote it largely from memory, twenty-two years after the event. Therefore the time of the summons may or may not be correct, but certainly by the time Franklyn arrived Gort would have made up his mind about the change of plan. It is known that his final decision was made soon after the interview with Archdale, and he must have seen Franklyn after that.

Like other Second World War generals, for example Brooke, Franklyn in later years enjoyed having a dig at some of his erstwhile colleagues. He described how, after his arrival at GHQ, Gort wasted his time for an hour: 'He discussed this, that and the other; he even got a young tank officer to relate how he had engaged a German tank in single combat.' Then Pownall 'intervened to remind Gort that I was waiting for orders. Pownall surely might have done that earlier. Gort did then tell me that I was to hold the Ypres–Comines line with my division.' Apparently neither Gort nor Pownall mentioned that 5th Division, up to then assigned to III Corps for the attack south, was now to be under Brooke and II Corps: 'I was, therefore, surprised to find Brooke waiting outside to give me orders.'[39]

On the face of it, this bears out the critics of Gort, who have focused on his absorption in minutiae to the detriment of strategy. But in fact close attention to the timings puts Gort's apparent time-wasting in perspective. If, as set out above, Franklyn met Gort soon after 1800, and spent an hour or something like it with him, this was because Brooke only arrived at 1900, then had to attend a conference, and military protocol gave Brooke the task of issuing orders to Franklyn. Even leaving protocol aside, as such an emergency might seem to demand, it was probably sensible to let Franklyn and Brooke decide their plan together. They were experienced generals, who knew each other since 5th Division had earlier been part of II Corps. Finally there is no reason to suppose that Pownall seriously wasted time by not intervening in Gort's chitchat earlier than he did. There was no point in intervening until Brooke arrived and Pownall told him the new plan. This was no doubt the 'conference' to which Brooke referred.

Franklyn's other accusation, no doubt also made from memory, is similarly baseless. He stated that, while Gort was time-wasting, 'my division was streaming away southwards: one hour's progress entailed another hour to retrace their steps'. In fact, only some of the officers belonging to 13 Brigade units had gone south. The great bulk of the division was resting. The most precise timing as to when 5th Division units knew of the change of plan comes from 2nd Wiltshires, in 13 Brigade. As late as 1830 they received orders for a move south to the vicinity of Douai. No doubt this emanated from brigade HQ and would have been issued while Gort was still talking with Franklyn. Possibly Pownall could at 1800 have sent a holding order to 5th Division units that they should prepare for a move, not south but to an unspecified location. But such an order did not take long to get through, since the Wiltshires received a message to that effect, which also cancelled the move south, at 1933. The precise timing suggests that their war diary in which the messages were recorded was contemporaneous or at least based on contemporaneous notes. The order fits in with what else is known. No doubt as soon as Brooke and Franklyn had met they realised the urgency of the situation and arranged to have such messages sent out. Equally important, no battalion could actually move until motor transport was available, and that was under the control of GHQ. Thus the message at 1830 ordering a move south was not accompanied by any actual movement.[40]

Gort can, therefore, be absolved from most of Franklyn's criticisms. Of course his conversation with Franklyn was typical of the man and illustrates his fascination with military minutiae. One cannot imagine Brooke relaxing by talking for an hour about that sort of thing. But surely we can be sympathetic to Gort. He had just taken a critical decision after a period of anguished thought and his period of relaxation was both human and understandable. In the same circumstances even Brooke might have relaxed. Only he would have talked about birds.*

---

* Brooke's great hobby was birdwatching.

While Gort was deciding and then relaxing, the Germans were fighting and advancing. But their move westwards towards the Ypres–Comines Canal, although more or less definite by the time Gort made his decision, was not initially so preordained as the Sixth Army orders of the 24th, or the later British accounts of their capture, implied.

As noted earlier, Bock on the morning of 24 May had planned to attack the Lille salient at its outermost end, and had thought that the panzers would continue the task of cutting the salient off from the sea. So Reichenau's instructions to IV Corps in the captured orders, which were to 'continue the attack, the objective the heights of Wytschaete', may have been Sixth Army's own idea. Bock's later enthusiastic support, however, suggests that he probably had a hand in formulating the basic concept. IV Corps' attack on the Belgians had taken 2,700 prisoners on the 24th; IX Corps, farther north, a further 1,500. This number of prisoners suggests that there was not much real resistance and may have encouraged the Germans in the idea that the direction of attack could shift from northwards to westwards without running undue risks from a counterattack. And with Bock aware later on the 24th that the panzers were halted for the time being, he may have already grasped that any attempt to cut off the salient would now be the responsibility of Army Group B.[41]

It is important to realise, however, that the orders actually set out several objectives for Sixth Army units and that the army was not finally committed to all of them. IV Corps' attack on the canal was one. It would be shielded by XI Corps, who would attack towards Ypres. The wording of the latter order – 'The 11th Corps is to protect the right flank of the Army by attacks . . . in the direction of Ypres' – indicates clearly that the attack towards Ypres was subsidiary. And there was another attack equal in importance to IV Corps', that of XXVII Corps, with 'concentrated forces', on the French to the east of Lille. Finally there was the main attack on the Belgians, referred to in the first paragraph of the orders, which was to be made by Eighteenth Army.[42]

Thus Sixth Army actually had two main objectives and one subsidiary one. This is typical of German practice, in which during a battle objectives were relatively loosely prescribed and might be adjusted according to circumstances. They were also ambitious. After two weeks of steady marching and intermittent fighting, there was one overriding objective – to continue the advance.

Knowing that once the Germans turned west they had an undefended space between them and the canal, it seems obvious that it was their intention from the start to attack in that direction and cut across the salient that contained the Allied forces. But given the knowledge they had on 24 May, when the orders were issued, their ideas cannot have been so cut and dried. The fact that the Belgians were retreating north or northeastwards – away from the British – only became clear the next day. On the 24th, the planned westwards attack of IV Corps, which would not be likely to start until the 26th, might just as well have met Belgian opposition as an empty space. Therefore, if events on 25 May had come out rather differently, the Germans might have adjusted their intentions for IV Corps' attack. If the Belgians had put up tough opposition, the Germans might have had to find another way of cutting off the salient.

It is a tribute to Bock's ability to rethink quickly that, in the changed circumstances of 25 May, IV Corps' attack came to assume a central place in his plans. As we know, the Belgians were rapidly falling back. According to German sources, by midday on the 25th Sixth Army had taken Courtrai and reported weak resistance, with the Belgians retreating towards Roulers. Meanwhile Bock noted in his diary that the attack by the left wing of Sixth Army – this was the attack to the east of Lille – had 'got nowhere', although nevertheless the army wanted to repeat it. He refused and restricted Sixth Army's *Schwerpunkt* to the advance by IV Corps. Eighteenth Army, as before, was to carry on the main effort against the Belgians.[43]

Bock's intentions were furthered by the commander of IV Corps, Viktor von Schwedler. In a subsequent account of the battle by IV Corps' staff, they reported him as pushing Sixth Army on the 25th to give IV Corps its head in its westward drive. German discussion at senior command level was remarkably frank, and exact hierarchies were not important (except where Hitler was involved). Therefore the intervention of Schwedler was likely to be significant. At 1345 XI Corps was ordered to turn north and continue the attack on the Belgians, thus removing the flanking protection it was to have given IV Corps in the original plan. But no doubt also by that time the Germans, like the British, had discerned that west of IV Corps the Belgians had melted away. IV Corps' account continued:

> The Commanding General was faced with a very difficult decision. He had a better overview at that point of the position of his Corps than the army did. He saw success beckoning: could he, in spite of the overall [illegible] situation, risk suggesting to the army that the attack be continued? Could he lead his 4 divisions into a situation where the position on the flanks was uncertain, trusting only to the fighting strength [illegible] of his divisions and his opinion of what the enemy were doing – an opinion that had become reinforced over the last 15 days? The Commanding General made his decision and applied to the army for permission to continue the attack,

deploying the 14th Division to secure the flank to the north. The decision was the same one the Chief of Staff (*Chef des Generalstabes*) had reached independently, and there was no one on the Staff who didn't welcome it warmly.[44]

According to this, 'at 16.50 the army granted permission' – that is, for the move westwards as set out in the original orders of 24 May to go ahead. Whether it was Bock's or Schwedler's views that carried the most weight is unclear. But the main point is clear. German plans were not set in stone, and, although the original orders had set in motion the idea that IV Corps should drive westwards towards the canal, it required the favourable outcome of the battle on the 25th and the direction of the Belgian retreat to harden this into reality.

4. Into Position

W HEN BROOKE AND FRANKLYN finally met at around 1900 on 25 May, they 'sat down on the grass with the map between us . . . It was a lovely summer evening, quiet and without any sign or sound of war. It was hard to believe that only comparatively a few miles away a large German force was advancing steadily with only a weak brigade to bar their progress.' 5th Division was to move up to the Ypres–Comines Canal and take this brigade – 143rd – under command. But this still gave Franklyn only three brigades, the normal strength of a division, because in April a brigade had been detached from 5th Division for service in Norway. It had been a two-brigade division ever since.[1]

5th Division was concentrated around Seclin, a few miles south of Lille. As the crow flies this is fifteen miles south of Comines and twenty or so to the southern edge of Ypres, the point to which 5th Division's line was to extend. Allowing an extra four or five miles for travel by road, significant distances were involved. But the battalions would not have to march. They would be lifted by the RASC's troop-carrying companies.

The troop-carrying companies, described in Chapter 1, barely get a mention in most accounts of the BEF's campaign in 1940. Yet they were a vital component of the army's mobility. Most of them were under the direct command of GHQ, that is, not attached to divisions or corps. This ensured their most economical use, but meant that during the retreat they had to drive long distances from one assignment to another. And, of course, it was not always easy to find a strange unit in an unfamiliar location. Nevertheless in spite of vicissitudes the ready availability of transport meant that the defenders of the Ypres–Comines line could be transported twenty miles or more overnight and arrive at their destination reasonably fresh, rather than undergoing a lengthy night march.

Because there is so little about these troop-carrying companies in the literature, and because only three of their war diaries survive, all too little is known about them. They were not staffed by regular soldiers. Possibly their officers were older than the norm, perhaps called up out of retirement. They seem to have done a difficult job with remarkable dedication. They were often late but, in the war diaries seen, they rarely if ever failed to turn up at all. Their job may not have involved fighting, but it was not easy: for example, having to drive the twenty passenger trucks, without powered steering and with crash gearboxes, along the notoriously bad roads of northern France and Belgium; and having to drive at night with little light or by day with the constant hazard of air attack.

The one troop-carrying company that was involved in Ypres–Comines and for which a war diary survives was No. 4 Company, commanded by Major A. Proven. On 21 May two of the three sections had driven ninety-five miles. On the 23rd one section made a journey of more than a hundred miles, and that night the whole company moved elements of Macforce, one of Gort's scratch forces, from Orchies to Estaires, another seventy-eight-mile round trip. After maintenance and rest on 24 May, the company was sent on the 25th to move 143 Brigade. 143 Brigade was Brooke's first major reinforcement for the Ypres–Comines line, which he had obtained from Gort after he had been to see him on the morning of 25 May. The other brigades of 48th Division, 143 Brigade's original home, had already gone elsewhere – one to Dunkirk and one to defend the Canal Line on the BEF's southwestern front. 143 Brigade was in reserve in the vicinity of Aubers, a few miles west of Lille. It took considerable time to locate and pick up the battalions, and one of them – 1/7th Royal Warwickshires (1/7th Warwicks) – did not start moving until midnight – more than eleven hours after No. 4 Company had received its orders. The latter's war diary offered a partial explanation, reporting 'considerable delay in embussing owing to enemy bombing and machine-gunning'. By the morning of 26 May, however, 143 Brigade were getting into position on the Ypres–Comines Canal. Subsequently No. 4 Company carried elements of 3rd and 4th Divisions to north of Ypres before its own personnel were evacuated.[2]

5th Division's move to the canal was encompassed in a similar manner. As with 143 Brigade, there were difficulties due to the troop-carrying sections not finding their battalions. The last to go, 6th Seaforth Highlanders (Seaforths), started only just before dawn on 26 May, arriving at 1100. They were bombed twice and suffered some casualties, but this seems to have been the only example of air attack *en route*, for by now the Luftwaffe was increasingly occupied over Dunkirk.[3] As the lorries jolted through the night, they were frequently held up by traffic jams. The Wiltshires and the Cameronians both experienced them at Warneton, one of the bridging points on the Lys. Only a few hours earlier Gilmore, the Cameronians' commander, had been reconnoitring the mooted attack southwards. Now he was travelling in the opposite direction. North of Warneton, Gilmore remembered another block: 'This time it was a large convoy of French ambulances going south; we were going north.' When Gilmore looked he found the ambulances were empty or had unwounded men in them:

> As my task was operational and urgent . . . I told them to stop. Not a bit of it. At last I deliberately stood in front of one ambulance with my back to it, and my orderly ready with his rifle to shoot the driver if he knocked me down. The driver came up as far as he dared, his vehicle actually touching my coat. But he came no further.[4]

The 1st Oxfordshire & Buckinghamshire Light Infantry (Ox and Bucks) in 143 Brigade wrote a lengthy post-battle account, subsequently published in their regimental history. During their move they recorded:

> A traffic jam of vast proportions . . . on the main Warneton–Ypres road. Endless streams of mechanical transport were moving south towards Warneton. French horsed columns were trying to move up from the south and turn westwards to Messines. At the same time, other convoys of mechanical transport were coming in from the east, some heading for Messines and some for Warneton.[5]

The mechanical transport heading south perhaps included the ambulances confronted by Gilmore. The volume of traffic and the various directions in which it was heading illustrate the chaotic and disorganised state of the Allied forces. Not surprisingly artillery units with their heavy vehicles also experienced delays, and a number of units noted enemy air activity. No significant attacks were recorded, however. For example, 18th Field Regiment, attached to 48th Division and moving in daylight on 25 May in support of 143 Brigade, had a 'first taste of low-flying air attack' but suffered no casualties. Most moves took place at night, and the Luftwaffe does not seem to have carried out much in the way of night attacks.[6]

Most of the heavy and medium artillery was already in position. It was under the command of the Medium Artillery of I Corps (henceforth MA I Corps), which was to play an important part in the battle to come. The medium artillery of each corps was a separate command, the CO of I Corps' being Brigadier 'Ambrose' Pratt. When the BEF retired to the frontier position on 23 May, MA I Corps went to the general area of Ploegsteert Wood, the 'Plugstreet' of the First World War. According to 63rd

Medium Regiment's war diary, citing an MA I Corps' operation order, the medium artillery had withdrawn 'to form a reserve of artillery on wheels with [the] intention that it should remain in its present position ready to be put into action at any point at short notice, and if necessary to supply detachments of personnel and Guns to formations in need of them'. Presumably this idea had originated with GHQ.[7]

Wherever it originated, it was a sensible disposition, which was of great significance in the battle ahead. There was no real risk involved in withdrawing I Corps' Medium Artillery from the BEF's eastern front, because the front was much shorter now the Allies had retired to the French frontier. The British sector would still be covered by II Corps' medium artillery. Since some units notionally controlled by GHQ were reassigned to MA I Corps, a number of regiments were available to it by 25 May: 1st, 5th, 63rd and 65th Medium, along with four heavy batteries (3rd, 5th, 16th and 28th).[8]

The actual process by which MA I Corps came under Brooke's command has been related in Brooke's postwar memoirs. As so often with memoirs, the account raises as many questions as it appears to answer. Brooke wrote that, either on 26 or 27 May:

> Ambrose Pratt, commanding the Heavy Artillery of I Corps, came to me and asked me whether I should like the support of a Corps Artillery. I thought at first that he was joking, and asked him whether the I Corps had no use for his services. He informed me that apparently not, since he was receiving no orders from them . . . that his Corps artillery was just west of Ploegsteert Wood and had plenty of ammunition.

The reference to 'no orders' was a dig by Brooke at Michael Barker of I Corps, the least successful corps commander in the BEF.[9]

In fact Brooke's diary recorded the date as 25 May, and further light is cast on the episode by MA I Corps war diary – that is, the diary of Pratt's own HQ formation. According to this, at 1600 on the 25th Pratt had gone to I Corps' command post in Lille and had received orders there to deploy his regiments to cover the canal. The detail in the diary suggests that it was based on contemporaneous notes so it seems likely that MA I Corps' timings were accurate. If so Pratt's visit occurred before Gort made his decision to direct 5th Division north and defend the canal. Possibly Brooke had seen Pratt earlier and realised the importance of his artillery to the defence of the canal about which Brooke was already worried. Later Brooke wrote a summary of II Corps' operations, in which he stated that he 'picked up I Corps Heavy Artillery while at GHQ'. Perhaps Brooke gained permission to use the medium artillery at his early morning visit to GHQ on the 25th, having met Pratt before that.[10]

When the medium artillery had moved to the Ploegsteert area on 23 May, the locations of the regiments extended up to and included Kemmel a little to the northwest. With the change of command some of the regiments moved again, and most of the new gun positions were located on the western slopes of the Messines Ridge, of First World War fame. Observers on the ridge had a good view of the country to the east up to and over the canal. But regimental areas 'were extremely limited owing to the number of guns coming into action behind the ridge', and so the guns were sometimes close together. When daylight broke on the 26th, 5th Medium Regiment's war diary recorded that '1 Battery of 1 Med Regt was on right of 20/21 Battery [of 5th Medium], and there were twelve 6-inch howitzers in a row with little or no cover.' The quotation evokes those First World War photographs of big guns lined up before an offensive. And these howitzers would be the same type as is often seen in such photographs, although they would now have had pneumatic tyres, not the iron wheels usual in the First World War.[11]

Lack of maps was a major potential problem for the artillery, since it made accurate shooting impossible. 1st Medium, who had no maps at all, had already found it difficult to locate its position. In the end, there seem to have been just about enough. 5th Medium was able to lend one to 1st Medium, while on the night of 25 May Pratt sent a driver to collect some from Lille – presumably from corps HQ. His intention, in part, was to help out 5th Division's artillery, that is, the field gun regiments, which he knew would be on their way. At 0430 the next morning he met Brigadier Barry, 5th Division's CRA (Commander Royal Artillery) at a crossroads and gave him ten rolls of maps. Barry himself had had to make an overnight journey of around forty miles from the HQ he had established in Villers-en-Tertre, southeast of Douai, for the projected southern attack. His regiments had also travelled overnight, and they were reported as being in action by noon on the 26th.[12]

Franklyn had had a major accession of strength. Pratt's medium and heavy artillery were well supplied with ammunition and well led. Most importantly, the artillery was by reputation, and probably in reality, the best trained and most effective part of the British army.[13]

Leaving his artillery for the time being to sort out their own dispositions, Franklyn was engaged on the evening of 25 May in working out how to deploy his limited force of infantry. The frontage of his intended line started in the south at the junction of the Ypres–Comines Canal with the Lys, which divided the Belgian Comines to the north and the French town of the same name to the south. The British line then ran northwards, mainly along the canal. But at the northern end, where the canal bent to the west, the line continued almost due north along a railway to the outskirts of Ypres. It was about 11,000 yards,* or just over six miles, long.[14]

As it happens, one of Belgium's linguistic divides runs at right angles through the canal, roughly halfway between Comines and Ypres – in fact between the villages of Houthem and Hollebeke. It separates the small, French-speaking enclave of Comines in the south from Flanders. Franklyn was probably not much concerned with this geopolitical fact on 25 May. But he was familiar with the canal, having 'unhappy memories' of it from First World War days.[15]

Only the memoir exists to recreate his thought processes, and as has been seen it is not always reliable. But Franklyn was quite willing to be self-critical, so the memoir does not seem to have been a retrospective exercise in self-justification. Given the distances to be covered, he decided to put his three brigades in line, rather than keeping one in reserve. But he wrote in the memoir: 'Later I regretted not having a reserve brigade.' Franklyn's plan called for 143 Brigade, which for a brief period occupied the whole line, to shuffle to the right. It would then hold the southern 4,500 yards of the canal. The central section, of about 3,000 yards, was to be held by the 5th Division's own 13 Brigade. To the north was the virtually open flank of Ypres. Franklyn noted that 50th Division 'would come up on my left eventually', although it is not clear that any promise about this had been made by Gort on 25 May. Presumably Brooke told Franklyn that he, Brooke, would look after Ypres, but Franklyn knew that for the time being it was lightly held. He, therefore, assigned 17 Brigade on the left a frontage of only 2,000 yards. This would enable the brigade to put two battalions on the front and have one in reserve to cope with the open flank. However, 17 Brigade's front was a lot longer than Franklyn thought. 17 Brigade's war diary estimated it at 3,500 yards, and it was certainly at least 3,000 yards. Whether Franklyn simply misremembered or whether the original estimates of distance, perhaps made hurriedly on an inferior map, were askew, is not known. A more accurate assessment might not have made any difference to the deployments. All the frontages were long enough, the relatively short one in the centre being justified because one of 13 Brigade's battalions, 2nd Wiltshires, was held back in a reserve position on the forward slopes of the Messines Ridge.[16]

---

* From now on frontages will usually be given in yards, in line with British army practice; for distances in metres, reduce by about 10 per cent.

The line was sparsely manned. Most of the battalions in 5th Division at the start of the battle had already suffered casualties, in some cases quite heavy. 143 Brigade had been involved in the fighting on the Escaut. Their 8th Warwicks had suffered particularly heavily, the war diary recording six officers killed, one missing believed killed, six missing and four wounded. More than half their officers had been lost. On a pro-rata basis officer casualties were usually heavier than those of other ranks, but even so this suggests that the battalion was unlikely to have been at much more than half strength. This is borne out by the regimental history, which estimated the rifle companies at about fifty men each. The 1/7th Warwicks, by comparison, seems to have got off fairly lightly before 26 May. Like many regular formations the 3rd Battalion of 143 Brigade, 1st Ox and Bucks, had its eccentricities. It eschewed even the abbreviated version of its lengthy official name and called itself the 43rd Light Infantry, or 43rd for short. It was a title harking back to 1751, when it was one of the old line regiments. And as such, it liked to be known as a regiment and not as a battalion. Here, prosaically, it will remain the Ox and Bucks and be referred to as a battalion. It had clearly been engaged in fairly continuous action on the Escaut, but the war diary did not report heavy casualties.[17]

In 17 Brigade, the 6th Seaforths had been involved in fighting on the Scarpe and during the retreat from it on 23 May. Losses were heavy, including two entire platoons of one company and a 'considerable number' of other casualties. Further casualties were suffered in the air attack *en route* to the canal. Total losses up to the 26th were not stated in the war diary, but one hundred is probably a low estimate. The 2nd Northants suffered even more heavily on the Scarpe. They had 352 casualties, including both the CO and the second-in-command. In other words, they were at little more than half strength at Ypres–Comines, and it seems likely that the casualties were highest among the fighting troops. Like the Ox and Bucks the Northants preferred to call themselves by their old name, the 58th.[18]

In 13 Brigade, W. S. Giblett, then a sergeant in the 2nd Wiltshires, recorded that on the withdrawal from the Scarpe his company was ambushed and more than half ended as prisoners. On 25 May, the battalion war diary listed officer casualties to date: four missing believed killed, three others missing and two wounded. They reported two rifle companies at fifty men each and another at eighty. It seems reasonable to conclude that it was at no more than two-thirds of maximum strength. The Inniskillings' war diary recorded some action on the Scarpe, although as casualties were not stated they were probably not heavy. However the battalion had started the campaign almost 25 per cent under strength. Only the Cameronians in 13 Brigade and the Royal Scots in 17 Brigade seem to have started the battle without a significant deficiency in numbers, and even the latter recorded a 'steady stream' of casualties on 22 and 23 May from shelling and bombing.[19]

So most of the battalions were significantly under strength. Even at full strength, however, they would be taxed by defending around a mile of line each. The headquarters company would usually be some way back and, of course, contained personnel who fought only in dire emergency, such as cooks and clerks, as well as fighting groups such as the mortars and the Bren carriers. Most probably one rifle company would be in reserve. So two or three rifle companies would constitute the first line of defence, and they also needed some men in their HQs: signalmen and runners, for example. Only a proportion of each battalion, therefore, was actually in the front line.

The Ypres–Comines Canal, the destination of these units as they drove through the night of 25/26 May, is usually described in British sources as 'abandoned'. In fact, although it was almost completed, it was never used as a canal due to unstable soil and difficulties in construction at certain points. In some places it was almost dry; in others there was some water.* The area had been heavily contested in the First World War, especially around Ypres itself, where the Allied front line crossed the canal. Farther south, the canal was behind the German front line for much of the war and in 1914–15 one of the German units stationed in the area was Infanterie-Regiment (IR – equivalent to a British brigade) 16, the List Regiment. It was a Bavarian unit and in it served a *Gefreiter* (junior corporal) – the young Adolf Hitler. Hitler spent months in Messines and Comines and, as a regimental runner, he would have known the whole area well. Right at the end of the war the List Regiment returned to the area as the Germans retreated, and in October 1918 Hitler's war ended at Werwik, just two miles east of Comines, where he was gassed.[20]

The canal was on Gort's mental horizon before the German offensive got under way. In April he wrote a memo to Billotte about the possibility of improving the Franco-British line by advancing some distance into Belgium. This would presumably have been a move prior to and independent of any German attack, since in such a case the Dyle Plan was already agreed. The proposal would reduce the distance of the awkward step along the Lys, which ran at a right angle to the generally northwest to southeast direction of the frontier line. Probably more important, and the focus of Gort's memo, it would allow the French and British

---

* There is a clear, though brief, description in Dan Gamber's website, which is primarily designed for those cycling around Belgium. There are also some relevant postings on the Ypres Battlefield forum website.

to occupy the high ground 'on the general line Messines–Wytschaete–Kemmel', that is Messines Ridge and Kemmel Hill to its west. The canal was seen only as a forward line.[21]

With the Belgians' insistence on preserving their neutrality, nothing was done about Gort's idea. But the fact that the canal had already been noted as having some defensive value may account for its identification by GHQ during the retreat as a possible fallback position. Now, however, it was the canal itself rather than the high ground behind it that was deemed the main line of defence. There were good reasons for this. By 24–25 May the German forces to the south and west of the BEF – German Army Group A – were a matter of ten miles or so from Armentières. Armentières to Comines was less than ten miles. This gap of less than twenty miles was the funnel through which British forces would have to retreat, and across its neck was the river Lys, with only a few crossing points. The four divisions on the frontier line around Lille were even more constrained. If, when retreating north, they first had to go to Armentières before crossing the Lys, they would be travelling fifteen miles or more in the wrong direction. They needed all the Lys crossings available between Comines and Armentières. Since the first one after Comines was at Warneton, it was important to defend east of this if possible. Messines Ridge, however, lay farther west. Taking it as the main line of defence would have severely restricted the opportunities for crossing the Lys. In addition the canal had some potential as an anti-tank barrier, referred to by both Brooke and Franklyn. In view of the havoc wreaked by German tanks in the west, this was an understandable concern.

The canal also had a major disadvantage. It was not actually a good defensive position for infantry. Gilmore of the Cameronians, in the centre, described it as a 'poisonous position to hold. To the east, the German side, the ground rose fairly steeply with modern houses crowning the summit, and reaching halfway down the slope. On our side it was flat for some way and only rose where the canal was out of effective small arms fire.' 13 Brigade's war diary summed up the situation on this sector: 'The Ypres–Comines Canal, which was dry, was found to be of no value as an obstacle either against tanks or infantry, and the railway embankment running along the front seriously diminished the field of fire.' The railway was on the far side of the canal to the British but running close to it, mainly on a low embankment. On the northern sector, where the canal curved westwards, 17 Brigade had the railway as their main line of defence. On the right of this sector where it runs through a cutting they regarded it as a 'fair tank obstacle', although not on the left where it again runs on a low embankment. On the southern stretch of the line, held by

143 Brigade, there is less comment about the deficiencies of the position, although the Ox and Bucks regimental history drily observed of the canal: 'It was not a formidable obstacle.'[22]

For better or worse the canal and, in the northern sector, the railway, comprised the line chosen. And on 26 May, while units from the three brigades were hastening to get into position, Anthony Eden, the secretary of state for war, telegraphed Gort. The British government had become aware of the probable weakness of the planned French attack from the south on Army Group A. It held no prospect of 'junction with your armies in the north'.* 'In such conditions only course open to you may be to fight your way back to west where all beaches and ports east of Gravelines will be used for embarkation.' The political decision for evacuation had effectively been taken. But by his own decision of 25 May, Gort had made it far more likely that it would be successful.[23]

Blanchard, still Gort's titular commander, had by now also recognised the impossibility of the attack from the north, which Gort had pulled out of the day before. Independently of Eden, he issued orders calling for the Allies to retire into a bridgehead around Dunkirk, with the Lys as its southern boundary. Since the Lys would also be the interim staging post for the British withdrawal, for the time being they had the same aim as the French. It would soon become evident, however, that there was a fundamental disagreement as to what should happen next.[24]

At around the same time, Brooke was reconnoitring the line. Early on 26 May, his memoir recounts, he had arrived at Zillebeke at the northern end and had driven along the east side of the canal to Houthem. He was assessing the canal's defensive value and also, in the absence of reliable information, trying to find out how many Belgian and French troops were in the Ypres sector. (The answer was not many; those that were belonged to the postal service of a French division.) Brooke's car crossed the canal back to the west side at Houthem, where he 'noticed a couple of our men near the bridge running along in a crouching attitude'. Soon after crossing the bridge there was a heavy explosion behind him, followed by four more. Initially he attributed these to bombs but could see no planes. Then there were a series of other explosions and, hearing 'that well-known whistle of an approaching shell', Brooke realised that the German artillerymen had started work. The first explosion, however, he now attributed to British engineers blowing the bridge over the canal: 'If this is the case, which I have never been able to confirm, we had narrowly escaped arriving just too late to cross the bridge.'[25]

---

* Eden was right: not because the French attack was likely to be too weak but because it had been called off.

Brooke's supposition was quite possible since there were British engineers in the vicinity. The 5th Division engineer companies all seem to have been otherwise engaged, but Brooke's bridge, and others along the canal, may have been blown by the incredibly hard-working 2nd Lieutenant D. A. Smith, an engineer who was attached to 12th Lancers.[26]

Smith led a small detachment of sappers – nine including himself, the only officer – from 101st Field Company Royal Engineers. He wrote a wonderful account of their adventures, in turns dramatic and humorous. It is revealing about the dynamics of some parts of the British army: highly trained soldiers such as engineers, usually working in relatively small groups of company size or below. The detachment had been travelling and working – mainly, on the retreat, blowing bridges – for a fortnight since the German attack began. Smith interrupted his narrative of their exploits with an account of their first real rest on 24 May, at Fleurbaix, where 12th Lancers had their HQ in a wine merchant's house nearby:

> The detachment took over a carpenter's shop for a garage and a billet. While the drivers were attending to vehicles Lance/Sergeant Johnson went into the yard at the back and by alternate coaxing and cursing managed to get some of the carpenter's fowls into a shed. The encounter in the shed was short but very sharp and the final issue was never in doubt. Sapper Roach prepared the potatoes and Driver Clout provided leeks for a second 'veg'. Lance/Sergeant Johnson was unanimously elected cook and while the meal was cooking each member of the detachment had their hair cut by Lance/Corporal Hourigan who in turn had his cut by Sapper Roach. By the time the haircutting was finished Lance/Sergeant Johnson announced the lunch and everyone agreed that it was magnificent. It was greatly assisted by the wine merchant's champagne and topped off with his brandy. The war was then forgotten for 12 hours.[27]

The 25th was also a day of rest for most of the detachment, but on 26 May it returned to work. Neither the 12th Lancers' account nor Smith's are clear as to whether he was blowing bridges in the Houthem area during the 26th, although the Lancers refer to bridges on the canal and railway south of Ypres being prepared for demolition. The inference is that Smith was involved. Henri Bourgeois' book on the battle, which used Belgian as well as other sources, offered another possibility. He referred to the Belgian Sergeant Verstraete as blowing up canal bridges at Houthem. Brooke obviously thought he saw British troops so exactly who was responsible must remain a mystery.[28]

The 26th was also a busy day for 143 Brigade. It was the unit assigned to Brooke in the early afternoon of 25 May, although as the battalions were late in starting they arrived only a little before most 5th Division units. For a brief period the brigade held the whole line of the canal, but it soon shifted south to occupy the southern 4,500 yards of the line, from Comines to Houthem. The Ox and Bucks held the section nearest the Lys and the 8th Warwicks the middle part of the sector, with the 1/7th Warwicks on their left in and around Houthem itself. Some of the latter must have had a lot of marching to do that day – first from their debussing point to the north end of the canal, then almost immediately a move several miles south.

In the central sector, which was taken over by 13 Brigade, the 2nd Cameronians were on the right next to the 1/7th Warwicks; the 2nd Inniskillings extended the line farther north. The Wiltshires were in reserve. Next to the Inniskillings was 17 Brigade's right-hand battalion, the Royal Scots, defending the more favourable line formed by the railway cutting. In the north the Seaforths of 17 Brigade, having had a late start, only debussed at 1100, so must have got into position rather later than the others. The 2nd Northamptonshires (Northamptons), in reserve, occupied the canal as it skirted Ypres, running almost westwards.[29]

There were already a few troops occupying the general line Ypres–Comines apart from the ubiquitous 12th Lancers. The first arrivals were the 4th Gordon Highlanders (Gordons), the machine-gun battalion transferred by Gort to Brooke, along with 143 Brigade on the 25th in the first tranche of reinforcements. The 1/9th Manchester Regiment, another machine-gun battalion, was already with 5th Division. They only got their orders at 2200 on 25 May but had arrived at Wulveringhem, a few miles from the canal, by 0330 the next day. By the morning of the 26th the Gordons had been split up: one company under the command of 13 Brigade; and two under 143 Brigade. The Manchesters similarly were shared between 13 and 17 Brigades. Finally, the 13th/18th Royal Hussars, a 'cavalry' – that is, light tank – regiment had been placed at the northern end of the canal. Apparently they made contact with the French 2nd Division Légère Mécanique (DLM) but it 'did not appear willing to co-operate, claiming to have been badly knocked about in earlier fighting'.[30]

Gilmore of the Cameronians later recorded his memories of getting into line. He saw some – British – light tanks in front of their new position, 'but they were clearing off'. These may have been the Hussars or the armoured cars of the 12th Lancers, who, their reconnaissance and temporary holding job done, were off to Ypres to prop up its defences. He also saw Franklyn, who was on the front line himself at this point, and who called out to Gilmore by his nickname: 'Hurry up

Pop, they [the Germans] are just behind me.' When the Cameronians had settled in, Gilmore walked their line from Houthem northwards; when he reached the left of his front, the bridge over the canal was being prepared by engineers for demolition. The timing seems to fit in with Brooke's conjecture that the bridge at Houthem had been blown just after he crossed it. Very probably it was the same engineers, possibly Lieutenant Smith's detachment, who were working their way north.[31]

In a poignant vignette, Gilmore then described seeing near the bridge, 'a small prosperous farm and an elderly couple' who:

> ... had just come to the gate of the garden to look at us. They smiled and waved their hands. At that moment the bridge was blown, and simultaneously some German artillery opened fire. That couple went straight away as they stood. They did not even turn back into the house. I went in later; there was a rocking chair by the kitchen fire, the mending on the table, and a half emptied bottle of red wine, some in a cup with a broken handle, and a slice of bread that had been put down in the act of eating, to see what was going on outside.[32]

This picture of interrupted domestic peace was repeated elsewhere. The German advance had been so rapid that the inhabitants of the towns, villages and farms of the area had been taken by surprise. When 8th Warwicks went up into the line they noted that 'the inhabitants had no idea of the nearness of hostilities, and were following the normal routine of Sunday'. As with the Cameronians and other units farther north, the Warwicks and their companion battalions in the southern sector started constructing makeshift defensive positions. Corporal Hawkins of 1/7th Warwicks remembered his unit coming down a track alongside a 1914–18 war cemetery:

> Beyond the cemetery wall was this old wrecked canal, the embankment being about level with the cemetery wall. On this corner we started digging in, preparing a position which overlooked both the canal and countryside on other side of same ... As we dug our trenches through the roots of trees and bushes, we came across many macabre or rusting artefacts of the 'War to End all Wars'. There were bullets, cartridge clips, Lewis gun ammunition pans, shell fragments, personal equipment, barbed wire, parts of weapons and even the odd bone![33]

Apart from the preliminary shelling noted by Brooke and Gilmore, there was relatively little action on 26 May. In the north, the Seaforths recorded the arrival of some German motorcycle troops, then 'considerable numbers' on bicycles, as well as intermittent shelling, which continued during the night; but the brief RSF account implied only limited enemy activity. The Inniskillings recorded effective British artillery fire directed at Germans getting into position. The Cameronians on their right experienced some action, however. Gilmore recalled 'one or two determined attempts by the Boche' to cross the canal on that day, although these were not successful. And the Cameronians were suffering casualties, with men being killed by sniper fire from the houses on the rising ground opposite. 1/7th and 8th Warwicks both reported light fire during the night, but the southern sector seems to have been least affected at that point. Nevertheless Corporal Hawkins of 1/7th Warwicks probably echoed the feelings of many: 'We all knew that another battle lay ahead, and indeed recognised the importance of it.'[34]

As the experiences recounted above suggest, the British were only just in time. Indeed Franklyn said in his memoir that the Germans were 'advancing steadily' the evening before, but this had not been the case. Sixth Army's IV Corps was still mopping up the remains of Belgian resistance and getting into position for their advance westwards. ID 31 took Menin only at 1900 hours on 25 May, while IR 54 of ID 18 crossed the river at Courtrai during the day. It had presumably been in reserve as the rest of the division was fighting in the battle. Bock saw it and observed that 'the regiment was in a fabulous mood'.[35]

As discussed in the previous chapter, the canal had finally been set as the *Schwerpunkt* of Sixth Army's attack during 25 May, and IV Corps had been scheduled to carry out the attack, as it had been in the original plan of the 24th. But in fact there was still debate about this in Sixth Army until the 26th. Reichenau, its commander, clearly wanted to continue attacking the Belgians, whereas Bock wanted them to be the preserve of Eighteenth Army on Army Group B's right wing. Sixth Army's diary suggested that there was continuing tension with Bock, who insisted that the canal and then west to Kemmel remain its main objective. In the end, there seems to have been some compromise, because Sixth Army was allowed to attack the Belgians on the line Thielt–Roulers–Dixmude. Perhaps the obvious collapse of the Belgian forces led Bock to feel that attacking them with all available troops would not dangerously overextend the army.

Some light on Reichenau's role is cast by an entry in Bock's diary a few days later. On 29 May, after the Belgian surrender, he noted that units of Sixth Army had 'veered north into the sectors of the 18th Army', which was by now advancing west along the coast. He went on to comment that Reichenau was with the Belgian king in Bruges, instead of where he should have been – with his army: 'He is and remains a "big kid". Between 24 and 26 May Reichenau had wanted to go on attacking on as many fronts as possible, while Bock was more aware of the need for concentration of effort. In addition Bock was focused on the desirability of cutting off as large a portion of the salient as possible by a drive westwards, once the panzers had been halted by Hitler.[36]

Interestingly, this focus by Bock led to him countermanding what must have seemed at the time a relatively minor change in the direction of the attack, which was potentially quite critical. On the afternoon of 26 May, when they were already advancing towards the canal, IV Corps suggested that the midline of the attack should be Ypres itself. In other words, the axis of attack would swing about four miles north of where it actually was between Houthem and Hollebeke. Aerial photographs had shown that the British were occupying the line of the canal, so opposition could be expected. At the same time, the advance westwards was subject to 'extremely unpleasant flanking fire from the south'. This would have come from the British forces occupying the south bank of the Lys, along the other side of which the Germans were advancing. Moving the *Schwerpunkt* slightly to the north would move the German advance farther from the flanking fire and might at the same time bypass the British defences.[37]

Fortuitously for the British, Bock arrived at that point at corps HQ. Learning of the corps' successful advance so far he ordered it 'to keep going straight ahead, the most direct route to the Kemmel. This will cut off the enemy's retreat towards the north.' Bock knew that when the panzers started attacking again, as they did that evening, their most direct route would also be to Kemmel and, therefore, aiming for this seemed the best way of closing the pincers around the salient. Thus his order not to change the direction of attack was logical. But in fact it was fortunate for the Allies, because at that stage Ypres was still weakly defended by British troops and the area north of it virtually unoccupied. Bock's single-mindedness, invaluable as it was in keeping Reichenau focused, may have robbed the Germans of a considerable prize.[38]

ID 31 had been on the left of IV Corps' attack on the Belgians, but was to occupy the centre of the German line attacking the canal. Judging by the number of prisoners noted in Chapter 3, the attack on the Belgians was not a hard battle. German war diaries, however, tended to make the most of enemy opposition, and ID 31's report on the final stages of the battle on the morning of 26 May referred to 'constant fire' from enemy artillery on the roads around Menin and 'continual fighting' with enemy rearguards. Some of the artillery fire may have been from British and French artillery south of the Lys. On the 25th the division had also experienced a significant British air attack on its pontoon bridge at Marke, just west of Courtrai, causing at least twenty casualties. Therefore, even if Belgian opposition was not very formidable, the division had gone through a testing period. At 1100 it learned of the unblown bridges at Houthem, one of which Brooke was crossing around that time. It was ordered to take these 'at all costs ... a.s.a.p.' As we know these bridges were blown shortly afterwards, but in the meantime the division's IR 82 was ordered forwards to try to seize them. IV Corps later noted that the division 'came across entrenched British forces who put up a stubborn defence' and 'the fight for Houthem goes first one way, and then the other'. The 1/7th Warwicks, who held Houthem village, did not report significant fighting on the 26th, so this must refer to the attacks on the Cameronians just north of Houthem, which were repelled.[39]

ID 61 on the German left was echeloned back from ID 31. It was on the north bank of the Lys, making its way westwards 'through wet cornfields'.[40] Around Menin ID 61 was fired on, it thought from the forts at Lille, although it seems more likely that the attack was from British II Corps artillery south of the Lys. As the division approached the canal the danger became more immediate. The platoon of Feldwebel Muller-Nedebock, belonging to the division's IR 162, was suddenly caught by machine-gun fire when it was roughly opposite the boundary between 1/7th and 8th Warwicks. From his perspective: 'The enemy had perfect positions and an excellent vantage point on the other side of the canal.' This is interesting, because as has been seen the British thought the canal in many places anything but an adequate defensive position. ID 61 had not been in action before, and the inexperience of Muller-Nedebock's platoon commander 'caused agitation which seemed very much like panic'. Muller-Nedebock took command. As he was in the machine-gun company they were able to return the British fire. Discussing the situation at nightfall with the forward infantry, they decided to ask for gunfire on the British positions, starting at dawn.[41]

The other division attacking the canal, ID 18 in the north, was some way behind the others. With a disjointed attack line and the realisation that British resistance was likely to be significant, IV Corps decided that 'the enemy can only be defeated by a concerted Corps formation attack'. The local decision taken by Muller-Nedebock and his infantry colleagues was now subsumed within the larger plan for a major attack on 27 May. By then IV Corps was aware of the wider perspective, its history noting: 'The British are fighting to allow the retreat of their columns heading north in a continual stream.' The corps had been told that the panzers were attacking again, also with Kemmel as their target: 'Competition for the hill now begins ...

This should affect our divisions. They are told this at once and it adds to their fighting spirit.'[42]

While Franklyn and Schwedler, the IV Corps commander, were making their dispositions prior to battle on the canal, momentous decisions were being taken by the British government. During the afternoon of 26 May Eden again contacted Gort. His suggestion of the morning that Gort 'may' have to fight his way back to the coast was changed, effectively, to a 'must': 'In these circumstances no course open to you but to fall back upon the coast . . . You are now authorised to operate towards coast forthwith in conjunction with French and Belgian armies.' The latter phrase was just a face-saver for the British government, since if the French and Belgian armies would not co-operate Gort could hardly wait for them to come round to the British point of view. In the evening, at 1857, without further consultation with the Allies, the Admiralty signalled that the naval operation for full-scale evacuation, codenamed 'Operation Dynamo', should commence.[43]

In theory there was still a possibility that evacuation was a staging post to allow the troops to return to France south of the German forces, but in practice the British government realised that they might have to continue the fight alone. Whether or not they would was the subject of another battle – a battle of words within Churchill's own War Cabinet. It was over what seemed a technicality, but was in reality a critical decision – whether or not Britain should associate itself with a planned French attempt to ask Mussolini to act as an intermediary in peace talks. (Italy was not yet in the war). The idea was supported by Lord Halifax, the foreign secretary, and over the next three days the Cabinet was to thrash out the options. There seems little doubt that, had Italy accepted such a role, it would have been psychologically difficult to keep the British people focused on a continuation of the war.[44]

5. Crisis in the South

MORNING TO MID-AFTERNOON, 27 MAY

THE 27TH STARTED BADLY for 5th Division. At the southern end of the southern sector of the front, where the Ypres–Comines Canal ran through the Belgian Comines before joining the Lys, Lieutenant-Colonel Whitfeld of the Ox & Bucks was inspecting his forward positions at 0200. Passing a farmhouse a little north of Comines, his party heard a rustle. They went on but soon had to retrace their steps to find their direction. Lance-Corporal Bailey, one of the party, cautiously approached the gate to the hedged-in garden of the farmhouse, and Whitfeld, believing that his own men might be in the vicinity, called out to him not to shoot. Whitfeld was correct, as the garden contained an Ox & Bucks section. Unfortunately, in the state of nerves that prevailed, it was they who opened fire, wounding Whitfeld in the left arm. He was escorted away and Major Charles Colvill assumed command.[1]

There were plenty of other more serious setbacks for the British battalions in the day ahead. For the first part of the day the most critical situation was in the southern sector, occupied by the Ox & Bucks and the other battalions of 143 Brigade.

The German division opposite 143 Brigade was ID 61, an East Prussian division that had been formed in August 1939. Up to now it had had only limited combat experience. Since 22 May it had been in army reserve, before being assigned to IV Corps for the attack on the canal. ID 31 in the centre was formed in Braunschweig in 1936 and was nicknamed 'Lowen' (Lion) Division. At the northern end was ID 18. This had been formed surreptitiously in 1934 in Liegnitz, in Silesia, before Hitler denounced the limitations that Versailles had placed on German troop numbers. Hermann Hoth, later to become one of Germany's most successful generals, was its GOC 1935–8 and von Manstein 1938–9, so it had a distinguished lineage of commanders. Both of these divisions had significant experience, having been engaged on several occasions since 10 May, including against British forces on the Escaut.[2]

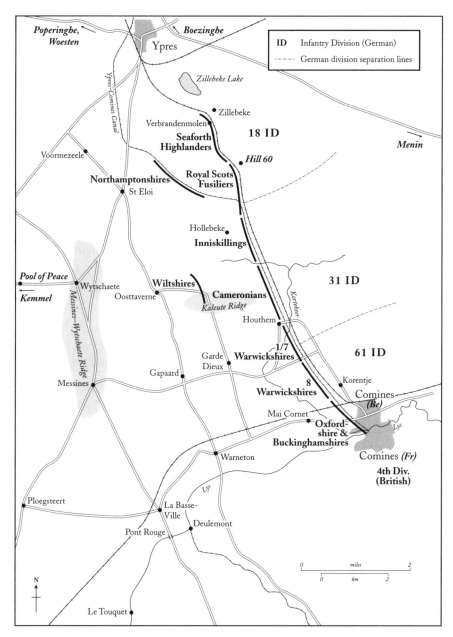

MAP 3: Ypres–Comines, morning 27 May

Some of the tactics these divisions were to use in the battle ahead are well known. The German army had always stressed the doctrine of the *Schwerpunkt* – 'the concentration of overwhelming superiority at the selected point', to quote a 1941 British analysis. The *Schwerpunkt*, however, is an operational principle applicable at any level from a campaign to a platoon advance, and provides only the general context for infantry tactics. The key German tactics in the Ypres–Comines battle are summarised in this and other British analyses. After noting the German emphasis on flexibility and close co-operation between all arms, the 1941 British analysis stated: 'The Germans still firmly believe in their well-known theories as regards infiltration.' It continued:

> An attack by infantry acting without the support of tanks usually starts before dawn. First comes the advance of small parties, armed with machine carbines and grenades, which infiltrate by approaches previously reconnoitred and penetrate as far as possible behind the enemy's forward positions. Later the artillery opens fire and the infiltrating elements try to penetrate further, to cut line communications and to disorganise the defence in general. [But] if the infiltration fails to achieve its object, the German principle is to launch an attack in force after the artillery has increased the volume of its fire. The attacking force then advance in mass formation making little use of the ground.[3]

It would not be surprising if these had been the German tactics at Ypres–Comines, because the pamphlet was clearly written mainly from the experience gained during the retreat. The points made above can be traced back in War Office notes on the German army issued in August 1940.[4]

It is, however, interesting that before the German attack in May the 'well-known theories as regards infiltration' were *not* stressed at all in the same series, which seems to have begun in March 1940. The first edition included a substantial section on the experiences of British officers who had visited German units as late as August 1939. They noted some aspects which, like those above, would become familiar to British troops in May 1940: the German emphasis on speed of movement; the rapid shifting of machine guns from point to point; and the use of the light artillery attached to infantry regiments at close range. But there was no real discussion of infiltration, nor was it discussed in subsequent notes before May 1940. Instead space was allotted to a discussion of armoured and artillery tactics in Poland. No doubt the Germans in 1939 were not going to reveal some essential aspects of their tactics to foreign observers. Given the importance of infiltration in the later battles in the

First World War, however, it is curious that pre-May 1940 notes on German infantry tactics did not say something about it. As it was, the extent of infiltration seems to have been a surprise. It, therefore, achieved exactly what it was intended to, which was to destabilise units by giving them the impression that they were surrounded.[5]

The main sources for this and most battles are the unit war diaries. War diaries were, in theory, written up every day and contained a record of the main events of the day. In practice they are very varied. In many cases the appendices containing orders and other messages are missing, so supporting evidence is lacking. At least for the busy and chaotic period leading up to Dunkirk, it is evident that many diaries were written up after the units had returned home, although these might be based on contemporaneous notes and messages. To add to the difficulties of interpretation, it is not always clear which diaries are contemporaneous and which not. Sometimes diaries are dated in June, which makes it clear that they were written after the event. Sometimes this is indicated by obvious anachronisms, such as incorrect dating of events, or references to events that occurred subsequently. But with some diaries there remains uncertainty about when they were written.

In the 'fog of war' contemporaneity does not necessarily mean accuracy. War diaries may well get the location of adjacent units wrong, and they may even be uncertain about the location of troops within their own units. The British infantry still relied largely on telephone communication. That meant cables, which would be quickly cut, by infiltrating enemy troops or by artillery fire. As a result HQs, whether of battalions, brigades or divisions, often lost touch with their subordinate formations.

Conversely, those diaries that were written up later might incorporate information from a number of officers in these subordinate formations. Therefore they might be more complete, although obviously such information is subject to the dangers of hindsight and the distortions of memory. That also applies, but even more so, to the detailed regimental and other unit histories, which appeared soon after the war. Such sources are valuable but also need to be treated carefully. Numerous memoirs have subsequently appeared, sometimes published but often in manuscript form or tucked away in obscure publications. Memory distortion becomes an increasing problem, but such accounts do widen the range of sources and can be useful.

War diaries have another characteristic that poses a hazard to the historian. It is clear that they were influenced by a natural pride in the writer's own unit, leading to difficulty in admitting that it was at fault or that men and officers within it may have behaved in a less than exemplary fashion. This was probably exacerbated by that fact that diaries were usually written by junior or middle-ranking officers, who were no doubt reluctant to write anything too critical when it might be read by their own CO. Therefore war diaries tended to minimise the shortcomings of their own unit, but correspondingly dwell on those of other units. As will be seen, these might be real but were sometimes imagined.

In spite of the dangers of taking too literally the criticisms made by war diaries of other units, however, this propensity to criticise can be useful to the historian because it draws attention to problems that otherwise might never have seen the light of day. Some vivid examples will be revealed in this chapter, which takes the story roughly up to 1700 on 27 May in the southern sector, and subsequent ones.

The main German attack on 143 Brigade started in the early morning of 27 May. The 1/7th Warwicks were at the northern end of this sector, around Houthem and adjoining the Cameronians of 13 Brigade, who were on their left. According to the 1/7th Warwicks' war diary, heavy shelling started at about 0700 on their forward posts. By 0900 the German attack had developed, and both the forward and the support companies on the left were being engaged by machine guns. Then infantry attacks began in earnest. The 8th Warwicks to their right and the Ox & Bucks at the far southern end had similar experiences.

The latter's account is supplemented by a letter from Captain G. D. (Tony) Jephson, commanding the carrier platoon. He recounted how enemy machine guns were firing, almost certainly from the other side of the canal on fixed lines. However, just before dawn a young officer of the . . . (here Jephson leaves a blank): 'rushed up to regimental headquarters and announced that the area of the road and railway down to the canal was "ringed with submachine-gunners" '. The regimental chronicle later revealed that the officer came from the 4th Gordons, the machine-gun battalion on the southern sector. As Jephson thought, this was a false alarm. Then at about 0700 or 0800, Jephson relates – he was writing from memory on 30 May, having been wounded and evacuated to a hospital in England – enemy shelling started. It was on and around the HQ location, about half a mile back from the canal. So the German artillery was shelling in depth.[6]

The contemporaneous British records from the southern sector are limited. The 1/7th Warwicks' war diary was quite full, however, and although it may have been written up later it contained enough detail in the form of map references and suchlike to suggest that it was based on contemporaneous notes. In addition substantial amounts were written quite soon after the event, by officers such as Jephson, in a lengthy 'chronicle' put together by the Ox & Bucks, which substituted for their missing war diary. The detailed reconstruction by Henri Bourgeois, a Comines' local historian, which used German and Belgian testimony as well as written sources, supplements other records.

For all the battalions in 143 Brigade, once the German infantry attacks started it was only a matter of time before not just the forward outposts but most of the forward companies were overwhelmed. One reason for this was that 143 Brigade faced the heaviest German assault. The German separation lines placed the left flank of the 1/7th Warwicks, in Houthem, within ID 31's attack frontage. As a result four battalions of ID 61 and one of ID 31 attacked the three of 143 Brigade, one of which was the weakened 8th Warwicks.[7]

The left flank of 1/7th Warwicks around Houthem was involved in a particularly bitter battle with ID 31, and by around midday on the 27 May both A and B Companies on the left had been overrun. Nevertheless a counterattack at that point by 2nd Lieutenant B. A. Stapleton with some cooks, batmen and pioneers occupied a farm behind A Company's position for some time. Stapleton won the Military Cross, but perhaps equally important was an action that went unrewarded. Private A. G. Wynne, manning a Bren gun, continued to occupy a house in Houthem until around midday on the 28th, preventing the Germans re-establishing the bridge over the canal, which had been blown by Allied troops on 26 May. Eventually he was killed, and his bravery was unknown to his own side until after the war.

Stapleton's force later fell back, as did C Company on the right, who had not been so seriously attacked. A new line facing east was formed along a road near battalion HQ about a mile back from the canal. It was extended to the south by D Company, which had been in brigade reserve but evidently came back under battalion control.[8]

Although 1/7th Warwicks had taken a severe pasting, they still retained two rifle companies and HQ company. They were strengthened by a party of 5th Division engineers belonging to 245th (Welsh) Field Company. The company had been assigned on 26 May to 143 Brigade, delivering tools on that day but not doing much else. On the 27th Major Garwood, the CO, had made up parties to dig for each battalion. But then alarming reports began to come through about a withdrawal among the Cameronians, to the left of 1/7th Warwicks. Brigadier Muirhead, 143 Brigade's CO, sent Garwood's ninety men to reinforce 1/7th Warwicks as infantry. Garwood reported to Colonel Mole of 1/7th Warwicks in the early afternoon, the engineers' diary recording that Mole's HQ was: 'in a farm built around an old Blockhouse. R.A.P. [Regimental Aid Post] full of wounded and more coming in all the time.' The men of 245th Company joined 1/7th Warwicks' line.[9]

The 8th Warwicks' experience was similar to that of their sister battalion. The CO, Major Kendal, was in touch with the flank companies by phone for a time. His last message from B Company on the right was the signaller reporting: 'There's merry hell going on up here, Sir, and Captain Burge . . .', at which point the line died. Cunliffe's postwar history, informed by the memories of captured survivors, has the forward companies resisting until around midday. Captain Lewthwaite in C Company's HQ held out all morning in a cottage about 200 yards back from the canal, until he and all his men were wounded as the Germans mortared the cottage and followed that with stick bombs. Burge of B Company and many of his men were likewise wounded before surrendering. One platoon of A Company and various stragglers got back from the front line.[10]

Kendal managed to form some sort of line about a mile back, continuing 1/7th Warwicks' line south. It consisted, however, of little more than two isolated positions. The remains of the reserve company, D, under Lieutenant Gibbs, strengthened by the platoon from A Company and two carriers, constituted one called Gibbsforce. Gibbsforce was based in a farm and, in Gibbs' words: 'took up excellent defensive fire positions from the buildings. Some posts were in the barns and others were outside watching my flanks. From the roof of the farm [we could see] the bank of the canal, which appeared to be entirely occupied by large numbers of Boche troops.' Kendal collected stragglers, and these were placed under Captain Waugh on the right of the battalion position, as Waughforce.[11] According to Waugh:

> . . . the enemy attacked repeatedly, supported by heavy mortar fire and shelling. The accuracy of his mortar fire was remarkable. His effort was directed towards 'finding the soft spot' and when his attacks were held up he did not press them but a new attack would be seen to develop on the right or left. It seems probable that a strong attack pressed home with determination would have overwhelmed the scanty forces holding the line, but the enemy was held at about 400 yards and suffered heavy casualties.[12]

Meanwhile the Ox & Bucks were experiencing similar problems. After a time HQ lost touch both with the rifle companies and with HQ 143 Brigade, no doubt because the cables were cut by artillery fire. German troops were infiltrating up the Kortekeer stream, which had overgrown banks, from Comines. In addition, before the lines were cut Captain Godman from B Company reported German troops crossing the canal unopposed to his left, on the 8th Warwicks' front. As a result battalion HQ 'formed a flank' – that is, occupied a defensive position along the Warneton–Comines railway facing north, at right angles to their main front to the east. Jephson was in command of this flank guard, which consisted both of the carriers with their Brens and a scratch force of 'cooks, signallers, the immaculate Corporal Creed and all the odds and sods'. Also included were stragglers from the forward companies.[13] Jephson continues with the story:

> After about half an hour the leading Boche appeared, storm troopers dressed in black, later ordinary field-grey. They emerged on the ridge beyond the wood and the re-entrant [the Kortekeer stream] and dead on the Warwicks' (late) front. Charles got the mortars onto them, and I got my chaps into action. Range about eight hundred to one thousand two hundred yards. They obviously expected no resistance, and in spite of the range we were hitting them. The troops were steady but apprehensive, and needed all the reassurance we could give them.[14]

Sometime in the early afternoon Jephson was hit and wounded in the hand and arm. He recorded that he 'fell into the Leech's hands' – the Leech being Captain S. McCallum, Royal Army Medical Corps (RAMC), the battalion medical officer. McCallum 'was magnificent, with shells and mortar bombs actually hitting, but not destroying, his regimental aid post. He was quite unshaken.' Fortunately by around 1400 there was a lull, and the Ox & Bucks could take stock. D Company, the southernmost company, was more or less intact. Although the Germans had been infiltrating up the Kortekeer, they had not launched a major attack across the canal in Comines itself. One reason for this may have been the fact that the southern bank of the Lys both west and east of Comines was occupied by British troops of 4th Division. German troops attacking close to the Lys were, therefore, exposed to fire from their left flank, a fact mentioned by the ID 61 history.[15]

At 1430 Major Colvill, the Ox & Bucks' acting GOC, took the decision to pull the remains of HQ Company and D Company back to Warneton. Whereas the Warwicks could retreat up to higher ground, where both battalions formed their new defensive line, the Ox & Bucks occupied a strip of almost flat country stretching for about a mile north of the Lys with few natural defensive positions. At that stage Major E. C. Richards, the commander of the reserve company, C, appeared with some of his men. According to Jephson they had moved during the night: 'The Baron [Richards' nickname] did not indicate his new headquarters and was, therefore, out of touch with the Regiment.' In fact C Company had been quite near battalion HQ. After a scuffle with infiltrating German troops they had pulled back. The combined forces, including stragglers from A and B, the centre and left companies, which had been overwhelmed like most of the forward companies of the Warwicks' battalions, formed a defensive position. They were, however, about a mile farther back than the remains of the Warwicks. So by mid-afternoon on 27 May the three battalions formed a disjointed new line.[16]

The outline of what happened in the morning to the battalions of 143 Brigade seems clear. There was a combination of frontal attacks on the forward companies and infiltration. The forward companies were largely overrun but had put up enough resistance to take some of the sting out of the frontal assaults. The infiltration had been only partially successful. The 1/7th Warwicks actually recorded taking numerous German prisoners. It seems likely that these were troops who had infiltrated between the 1/7th Warwicks' widely spaced frontal positions but who had then lost their nerve when isolated. Meanwhile, as has been seen, the Ox & Bucks successfully fought a flank action against infiltrating troops throughout the morning.[17]

That was not quite how it appeared to all of those on the ground, however. The 97th (King's Yeomanry) Field Regiment was positioned in and around Warneton. Its diary described the German breakthrough and the fact that British troops were pushed back out of Comines. Then in a low-key but dramatic entry it recorded that around midday: 'One gun was placed on the main road in Warneton, and preparations for local defence were made. The infantry were told they would be fired on if they came back any further, so they stood firm.'

It seems clear that the gun on the road was to deter British troops from retiring any farther. Lieutenant-Colonel Lushington, commander of the 97th Field, wrote a history of the regiment after the war, which adds more detail about the events of the day. According to him: 'Our territorial infantry, who were neither well-trained nor well-led, gave way and by four o'clock [in the afternoon] small parties of Germans were seen advancing on the far side of Warneton.' Lushington was clearly referring to the Warwicks. The 97th Field's account is backed up by the Ox & Bucks' chronicle. According to Jephson, some time in the morning the 8th Warwicks were seen retiring, and the Ox & Bucks then formed their defensive flank. Apparently the 4th Gordons' machine guns had also disappeared.[18]

Neither testimony, however, is quite as robust as it might appear. No doubt Jephson saw British troops retreating, but whether he could be sure, at a considerable distance, that they were 8th Warwicks seems less certain. Some might have been Ox & Bucks soldiers, since we know that survivors from the battalion's forward companies were later gathered together at Warneton. Also the account of Kendal, the CO of 8th Warwicks, mentions him collecting 'stragglers – not all ours – with drawn revolver' to make up Waughforce on his right. His right abutted the Ox & Bucks, so it seems likely that some of those stragglers were theirs.[19]

97th Field's gun on the road certainly lends a dramatic touch to the proceedings, and no doubt some Warwicks did retreat to Warneton. But Lushington's own testimony should be taken with a pinch of salt. Although the 97th Field was itself a territorial regiment, Lushington seems to have been imbued with the view that, at least in the infantry, the regular battalions were the top dogs. A striking instance of this will be given later in this book. His assumption that it was the territorial battalions – that is the Warwicks – which gave way, and his strictures on their commanders, may have been generated as much by prejudice as by evidence.

There is another set of witness statements as to what occurred when the German troops were advancing in the southern sector. On the morning of 27 May three companies of Royal Engineers were preparing a defensive line. They were from 4th Division, and their concern when they started work that morning was not the Ypres–Comines Canal, but the canalised Lys running at right angles to it. As part of Brooke's plan for the withdrawal of II Corps, 3rd and 4th Divisions would swing back on the night of the 27th/28th and move up behind the Ypres–Comines line towards the Dunkirk perimeter. It was for these units and the rest of II Corps that the bridges over the Lys were needed so badly. The manoeuvre would mean abandoning the line of the Lys east of Comines, where currently the British held the southern bank, but defending the northern bank between Comines and Armentières on 28 May, so that 5th Division itself could make its escape. The sappers had been tasked with constructing defences on that bank.[20]

The engineers, like so many of the troops of the BEF, had been almost ceaselessly at work during the retreat. On 23 May, for example, 7th Field Company had been 'digging and wiring infantry positions in front of Halluin, continued through the night'. On the 24th it had again been preparing infantry positions and wiring, as well as demolishing a brick wall and destroying some barges. The same sort of work had been done on 25 May, although on the 26th – a Sunday – there had been a rest day. Then overnight the companies moved, and for some there had been as little as three hours sleep. Coincidentally Captain (later Major) Charles (Bill) Hedley, subsequently my stepfather, was an officer with 225th Field Company, who were on the left, that is nearest Comines. Hedley was not with the company on 27 May, however, or at any rate he left during the morning. He had been sent up to HQ 4th Division Royal Engineers, which had established itself near Bray Dunes, soon to be one of the evacuation sites. Presumably they were making preparation for the evacuation.[21]

225th Field Company was virtually on the front line in Comines, and was aware as early as 0900 that the infantry on the Ypres–Comines Canal had been pushed back. The unit acted quickly and swung 90 degrees so that they faced the canal, about half a mile short of it, and formed their own defensive line. By 1000 7th Field Company, next in line around Warneton, became aware of the situation: 'Infantry withdrew through Warneton in some disorder and stated that the enemy were following.' It also pivoted and started establishing defensive positions facing towards the canal, behind those of 225th Field Company. This formed the basis of a new line with 59th Field Company on the left of 7th Field Company, and 225th Field Company moving back to the left of 59th Field Company.[22]

The remains of the Ox & Bucks, according to their chronicle, linked up with the sappers who were 'digging furiously'. Meanwhile Major Brunker from 5th Division HQ had been sent to organise a 'Brunker force' of stragglers to guard the bridge at Warneton. But because there already was an organised defence there, Brunker returned to HQ.[23]

Because of this information from the engineers, it is possible to say a bit more about the vexed question of who gave way where. Certainly elements of the 8th Warwicks did make an unauthorised retreat. Their CO, Major Kendal, said so in his later account, which mentioned a platoon under a company sergeant-major which 'came back' in the early part of the battle. Perhaps it was this party that was seen withdrawing through Warneton by 7th Field Company. Kendal later put the same platoon between the groups in his reserve line, Gibbsforce and Waughforce, but at some stage they retreated again. He related that, back in England, 143 Brigade's brigadier decided not to 'wash dirty linen' over the affair. In other words there was no formal enquiry into it.

Other comments suggest that nerves were showing among the 8th Warwicks as the Germans came forwards. Cunliffe in his history stated: 'Assisted by the admirable firmness of Corporal B. Wareham (who won the Military Medal), Lieutenant Gibbs made it clear to his men that there was to be no withdrawal.' There is an inference here that it needed considerable powers of persuasion to hold Gibbsforce in position. And as already seen Kendal found it necessary to draw his revolver to assemble Waughforce from stragglers. Of course, nerves are very understandable. Some of these men would have seen most of their comrades either killed or wounded; all would have been shelled and aware of the close proximity of the advancing Germans.

Nevertheless the 8th Warwicks also had troops who were willing to hold the line to the end. Apart from the officers mentioned and Corporal Wareham, there were the numerous individuals who remained in the forward positions. Burge and Lewthwaite were both awarded the MC. Corporal Bennett, in Burge's company, took command of a platoon when 2nd Lieutenant Pratt – also awarded the MC – was wounded. Bennett received the Military Medal. In the reserve line Sergeant Fendley manned the battalion's one remaining 3-inch mortar, and a number of runners were mentioned in the regimental history.[24]

Furthermore, the 8th Warwicks' rifle companies were probably no more than 50–60 strong to start with, while inter-battalion boundaries were notoriously weak spots. In those circumstances, and especially if the companies had already been weakened by artillery fire, the Germans were very likely to find undefended places to cross the canal between the Warwicks and the Ox & Bucks. The latter's version omitted the fact that their left forward companies, A and B, were also overwhelmed, thus allowing more Germans to cross north of the Armentières–Comines railway and attack Jephson's flank guard. According to Henri Bourgeois, presumably using Belgian oral testimony, south of the railway the British withdrew from the Ferme Blanche on the outskirts of Comines. The unit responsible must have been D Company of the Ox & Bucks, and this could have left the way open for the German infiltration up the Kortekeer. The fact that 225th Field Company of Royal Engineers knew quite early on that troops on the canal were being pushed back is very suggestive. 225th Field Company was stationed on the Lys towards Comines and could not have been aware of anything happening to the Warwicks farther north. They were only in a position to observe what was happening to the Ox & Bucks.[25]

There was, therefore, no justification for the Ox & Bucks to put all the blame for the retreat in the southern sector on the 8th Warwicks. The fact is that all the battalions' forward positions ultimately crumbled under the weight of attack. At the same time, the Germans were infiltrating and, once the British forward positions had gone, they could push up new groups of infiltrators to make more ground.

As is evident, infiltration had achieved exactly what the Germans intended. The Ox & Bucks were confused, jumping to the conclusion that the Warwicks had retreated behind them, when they had not. This judgement may also have been influenced by the Ox & Bucks' already poor opinion of the 8th Warwicks. They noted an alleged retirement of the 8th Warwicks – no other source mentioned it – on the evening of 26 May. And on 20 May they recorded that, according to the 8th Warwicks, German infantry were across the Escaut. A reconnaissance by Jephson, however, found no Germans. The Ox & Bucks' confidence in the 8th Warwicks was no doubt shaken, whether justifiably or not is not known.[26]

Bad communication was a contributory factor. If the Ox & Bucks' own reserve company, C, had stayed in touch with HQ overnight on the 26th/27th, there might have been more chance of organising a counterattack against the German breakthrough. Radios would have helped, but even without them Richards, the company's CO, could surely have let battalion HQ know his position. A final factor in the failure to stop the Germans getting between the Warwicks and the Ox & Bucks was the disappearance of the Gordons' machine-gunners. Although the young officer whom Jephson excoriated for the false alarm was presumably also responsible for their disappearance, it indicates a problem caused by the British policy of putting the Vickers heavy machine guns in separate battalions. During an action these were often split up into companies or platoons that might be complete strangers to the units with which they were working. In contrast German infantry battalions directly controlled their heavy machine guns. However hopeless the machine-gun officer was, it would have been difficult for him to scarper if he had been in the Ox & Bucks, rather than just attached to them.

In fairness to the Gordons, however, this seems to have been exceptional. Another machine-gun section of the battalion continued to give the 8th Warwicks assistance until silenced by enemy fire. And on 28 May the 1/7th Warwicks recorded 'wonderful support from a Platoon of MGs from the Gordons, which [had] its guns right up in the front line with our Brens'.[27]

From the German perspective, until mid-afternoon progress in the south was highly successful, although costly. ID 61 at the southern end seems to have launched its attack on 143 Brigade with four battalions forward, out of a total of nine. On its left, opposite the Ox & Bucks, there were two battalions of IR 176. On the right, Muller-Nedebock's account, in Bourgeois, implied that IR 162 also had two battalions forward. IR 151 remained in reserve. ID 61 would have had the entire divisional field artillery in support, whereas 143 Brigade seems to have had only one field regiment, the 97th, although some of the field guns on the Messines Ridge may also have been supporting them. The British may, however, have had more medium artillery in support.[28]

ID 31 in the centre also seems to have attacked with four battalions. The division's war diary was partially burnt in a fire in 1942, but enough survived to make an adequate reconstruction. The next day it certainly had four battalions in the fight, so this also seems likely on 27 May, when it was launching its attack. The left battalion of its left regiment, IR 82, probably attacked Houthem village, which was held by the 1/7th Warwicks. The rest of the division was engaged against 13 Brigade, and this is discussed in the next chapter. ID 31's report had limited details, but clearly British resistance was fierce. This is known not through the incomplete narrative description but through hard figures: twenty-two officers of IR 82 were dead or wounded by midday. It seems likely that they include senior NCOs (*feldwebel*), as otherwise they would amount to around one-third of the commissioned infantry officer complement, an almost impossibly high figure given that one battalion was in reserve. Also they must include those lost in the fighting with the Cameronians of 13 Brigade. Even so they are high. IR 82's slow progress meant that around 1430 the regiment stopped its attack for a time, presumably to regroup.[29]

To the south of ID 31, Muller-Nedebock of ID 61 recollected that, as a result of German artillery fire on the British front lines, these were largely destroyed when his regiment, IR 162, crossed the canal. Nevertheless the Warwicks were still resisting – from his description, he was probably more or less on the boundary between their two battalions. When his platoon crossed they were attacked from the right, and he was wounded. Furthermore his troops were still under fire from their own artillery. He sent up rockets to stop this.* 'I then led my soldiers to an assault on some farms beyond the canal which were not very closely defended.' Presumably by this time the Warwicks' forward companies were crumbling under the combined weight of German artillery fire and infantry assault. Muller-Nedebock then retired to the first-aid post, where his wound was dressed, but he refused to stay – fortunately for him, as the first-aid post was struck soon afterwards by a British shell. By then the platoon was 800 yards or so from the canal and, since he was armed only with a pistol, Muller-Nedebock used a British machine gun to fire from the Bonte-Descamps' farm. Finally, another battalion coming up, his positions were moved south and he ordered his men to dig in.

The scratch line formed by 1/7th Warwicks and 8th Warwicks was about a mile back from the canal, and so the British artillery was able to paste the area in front of this, where the Germans were located. Muller-Nedebock observed: 'During the course of the afternoon we were subject to intense artillery bombardment.'[30]

On the left wing of the German attack, by contrast, IR 176 'gained particularly good ground . . . in the direction of Warneton'. This was, of course, where the Ox & Bucks had fallen back to the line the engineers were digging. As noted earlier, however, the German troops remained exposed to fire from the flank, which may have hampered their advance south of the railway.[31]

---

* The Germans made extensive use of rocket signals, and British war diaries often mention this German practice.

By mid-afternoon 97th Field in Warneton, in the direct line of IR 176's attack, was almost on the front line. Lieutenant-Colonel Lushington recalled: 'By four o'clock small parties of Germans were seen advancing on the far side of Warneton. David Warner rang up to say that there was no one between the oncoming Germans and his guns except a small but gallant party of sappers who could be seen digging in in front of Warneton.' Lushington 'rang up the Division and told them the situation. The C. R. A. [Commander Royal Artillery], Brigadier Barry, replied that they had no reserves and that the line must be held at all costs even if it was by the guns alone.' Some more messages were exchanged. Then: 'a quarter of an hour passed with no further news except from David who said that most of his O. P. [observation post] parties had been driven back to positions close alongside the guns which were now firing at ranges of 900 yards and under.'[32]

6. The Wider Battle

THE CENTRAL SECTOR OF the Ypres–Comines line, occupied by 13 Brigade, stretched for about 3,000 yards from just north of Houthem to just north of the village of Hollebeke. Houthem itself was occupied by the 1/7th Warwicks of 143 Brigade. The 2nd Cameronians (Scottish Rifles) were next in line to the 1/7th Warwicks, their line stretching for 2,000 yards or so.

The Cameronians were a Lowland Scots regiment, a distinction to which they attached great importance. Their origins lay with the Protestant Covenanters of the seventeenth century and Gilmore, their commander, spent some time in his memoir lamenting the tendency of people to confuse them with the Cameron Highlanders.

North of them defending Hollebeke were the Inniskillings, another regiment whose origins lay in the religious conflicts of the seventeenth century. From Enniskillen in Northern Ireland, they also had Protestant origins, but this time Ulster Protestantism. The 2nd Wiltshires, a traditional county regiment, were in reserve about a mile back on the low ridge that forms an advance guard for the larger Messines–Wytschaete Ridge of First World War fame.[1]

Although the attacks on the central sector were heavy, the front companies withstood them for longer than did the battalions to their south. The latter, however, had a longer front and were attacked both by ID 61 and the left wing of ID 31; 13 Brigade faced the remaining three battalions of ID 31, which were deployed in the attack – still a superior force but by less of a margin. Nevertheless quite early on, the Cameronians were in difficulties, their front giving way in various places on several occasions during the morning. According to the 1/7th Warwicks: 'the Cameronians on our left started to withdraw ... in disorder, and wild rumours about large enemy breaks were rampant. The CO [of the Warwicks] sent out the Intelligence Officer to the Cameronians and the latter intercepted the Colonel about 1 mile away and turned him round.'[2]

The Cameronians, of course, painted a rather different picture. According to Gilmore's own memoir, based on notes written soon after the events although published much later, the continuous enemy attacks had led to infiltrations, which had to be met with counterattacks. It seems most likely that, when the Warwicks' intelligence officer met Gilmore, the latter was trying to organise one of these counterattacks. Although Gilmore was perhaps not the most dynamic of commanders, he showed no lack of personal courage and it was unlikely that he himself was retreating.[3] In spite of localised difficulties, the Cameronians and Inniskillings hung on in or near their forward positions until mid-afternoon.

Meanwhile the British troops to their north had retired, beset by the usual confusion caused by German infiltration. There is least documentation for the fighting in the northern sector of the British front line, since the battalion war diaries were all fairly terse. 17 Brigade's war diary was quite full, however. It contained some detailed timings, presumably based on contemporaneous notes, but the diary itself must have been written up later. This is known because it mentioned an officer by name and then on the same line added that he was killed – which he was, but the next day. Apart from the war diaries, there are two reasonably detailed regimental histories.[4]

The dispositions of 17 Brigade were simple. Since the Ypres–Comines Canal bent back westwards just north of Hollebeke, the brigade line continued northwards along the railway for about 3,000 yards to just south of Zillebeke. It was held by the 6th Seaforths in the north and the 2nd RSF in the south. The 2nd Northamptons, who had suffered most in the fighting around Arras, held a reserve line along the canal. One of their companies was sent forwards to fill a gap between the Seaforths and 150 Brigade in Ypres, but the Northamptons could not gain touch with the latter so there was still an open flank.[5]

The gap may have contributed to the problems that the Seaforths were shortly to have, as may the length of their line, which they estimated at 2,000 yards. And yet another problem was that for most of their front the railway runs along an embankment that is so low that it is virtually indistinguishable from the surrounding countryside and which cannot have been of much use as a defence line.

Enemy artillery started up at 0400 on 27 May and infantry attacks followed, much earlier than farther south. At 0645 Captain Goldie of the Brigade Anti-Tank Company 'visited Brigade HQ to report that 6 Seaforth had retired from their left FDL [forward defence locality] on the railway, leaving one of his Anti-Tank guns unguarded'. It seems likely that Goldie knew that more was at stake than one of his guns, and realised that he needed to inform brigade of what was happening. The brigade war diary continued the story:

> Brigade I.O. [Intelligence Officer] immediately left for HQ 6 Seaforth to make enquiries and to take Brigadier's order that the line was to be re-established at once. On arrival at Seaforth HQ he discovered that the left company ('C') was retreating under enemy pressure and that approx 2 companies enemy had taken the line of railway from Halt extending 300 yards Southeast. Plans were made for 'B' Company (reserve) to retake line. Artillery support arranged. This counterattack never got back to the line of the railway owing to heavy enemy mortar fire.[6]

Apparently the commander of C Company had not reported his withdrawal to battalion HQ, and there is other evidence that the Seaforths at times retreated in a disorganised fashion. One of 18th Field [Artillery] Regiment's officers, Major Barff, was in an observation post (OP) well forward in Verbrandenmoelen, a small village just south of Zillebeke. As has been shown earlier, regular formations sometimes held a rather jaundiced view of territorials and 18th Field carried on this tradition, their war diary recording that 'the T.A. Battalion' near where Barff was stationed 'had no stomach for the fight and were fading to the rear'. They carefully refrained from naming the battalion, but the Seaforths were the only territorials in 17 Brigade. Barff won the MC by rallying six anti-tank gunners – presumably some of Goldie's men. His small force then 'held the village for another 90 minutes until a storm of fire burst on them and drove the gunners out'. By 1300 the brigade diary reported the Seaforths to be 'almost back on the line of the canal'.[7]

While the perception by units of general retirements by neighbouring battalions could sometimes be an illusion, in the case of the Seaforths there is too much evidence that a general withdrawal, at times fairly disorganised, took place. There were extenuating circumstances – the length of their line; and the open left flank being two. Also enemy artillery and mortar fire was undoubtedly heavy, so that, for example, all the officers of A Company became casualties. This example shows that effective leadership at a local level could and did occur. Sergeant F. Stewart took over command of the company, winning the Distinguished Conduct Medal (DCM).[8]

The Royal Scots also demonstrated how effective leadership and determination could enable a strong defence. They were only pulled back because of the perception that they were isolated in a salient. The left flank of the RSF's defences was Hill 60, one of the First World War landmarks which loomed so large in the battle. Actually an artificial mound created out of spoil from the nearby railway cutting, it had been occupied by the Germans in 1914, subsequently seeing much fighting and changing hands several times before 1918. In 1940, as fighting broke out around Hill 60 once more, the Royal Scots' good defensive position caused the Germans problems. The ability to command ground locally from the hill, a contrast to most battalions' front line on the canal, helped the Scotsmen, although Hill 60 itself was vulnerable to mortar fire.[9]

The RSF held on until about 1300. Then Lieutenant-Colonel Tod, their CO who had shared Gilmore's adventurous journey back to France, thought that the Inniskillings were retreating. With the Seaforths on 17 Brigade's left already back to the canal, its brigadier, Montague (Monty) Stopford, decided to bring back the RSF. The battalion had considerable problems in retiring, particularly from Hill 60, which lay to the east of the railway. At that point the railway runs through a deep cutting, which must have been difficult to cross. 2nd Lieutenant Cholmondeley and his 'Fighting Patrol' covered the withdrawal, Cholmondeley being killed leading the patrol into action against a German machine-gun position.[10]

The canal where it was bent back then became 17 Brigade's new front line. The Northamptons already stationed there became the brigade left wing and the Royal Scots the right, while the remains of the Seaforths went into reserve behind the canal. The RSF's problems in retiring continued. Most of their 'A' Echelon transport – transport used for ammunition supply and other immediate needs – was forward of the canal. But the bridges on this had been blown on 26 May, thereby trapping the transport; the regimental history tartly observed that this 'had been pointed out to the Brigadier before the bridges were blown'. Nonetheless the battalion withdrew successfully, although with heavy casualties, and occupied its new position on the canal to the right of the Northamptons. By late afternoon on 27 May, like all the other units of 5th Division, 17 Brigade held a tenuous line well back from the original.[11]

13 Brigade, however, was still forward: Lieutenant-Colonel Tod had been wrong in thinking that the Inniskillings had retired. As so often, it is likely that a localised withdrawal had been interpreted as meaning that a full-scale retreat was taking place. Ironically the Inniskillings had simultaneously thought that the RSF was retreating. The confusion illustrates the problems caused by inadequate radio provision. As will be seen later, other battalions and brigades had radio trucks, and so presumably the units in question also had them, although they might have been destroyed or damaged in previous actions. More likely, as will be seen when the artillery are discussed, the sets just did not function reliably. Whatever the reasons for its absence, radio contact would have made life easier for the British.

Around 1500 13 Brigade finally withdrew the Inniskillings. Some of them came back too far and, after leaving behind numerous men who got lost, were brought forward again. They then established a new line in the late afternoon to the left of, and in touch with, the Wiltshires. The latter remained more or less where they were, and there seems to have been no significant further change until around 1800.[12]

Meanwhile the Cameronians on 13 Brigade's right were also retiring, in accordance with brigade orders. During the withdrawal Gilmore was co-ordinating his new line of defence with Lieutenant-Colonel Eric Moore, the Wiltshires CO. Mindful of the potential shortage of rations, he had given orders for men to forage for food and in particular – a delightful detail – to collect eggs and hard-boil them. The withdrawal started satisfactorily, but quickly became confused because Germans had infiltrated onto the ridge that was the Cameronians' intended new position. As a result of the confusion many men overshot the ridge on the way back and, as with the Inniskillings, arrived back on the Warneton–St Eloi road. But unlike the Inniskillings, who had retraced their steps relatively easily, the Cameronians faced a different prospect. They had to go back 1,000 yards or so without cover to retake ground on which the enemy had a footing. At that point Gilmore arrived. How the Cameronians got back to the ridge will be told in the next chapter.[13]

In contrast to 143 Brigade, one of whose two companies of 4th Gordons had proved to be a dud, 13 Brigade seem to have benefited from some stalwart machine-gunners. They were B Company of the 1/9th Manchesters and A Company of the Gordons. Captain S. I. Derry of the 60th Field Regiment had his troop of 18-pounders stationed forward on the Inniskillings front in an anti-tank role, sharing his position with eight Vickers of the Manchesters. Two pairs of these were located in houses, two pairs in gun pits. He noted at one point that the machine guns were firing 'at short intervals' and appearing to draw the enemy artillery fire. One of the gun pits received a direct hit. At that point Derry met an Inniskillings officer who informed him that they were withdrawing and ordered Derry to withdraw also, as the infantry were going back and no German tanks had appeared: 'I informed the Manchester subaltern what I was going to do, but he replied that he was staying as he had over 2,000 rounds and six guns still in action.' Whether his action was foolhardy or not, it exhibits an extraordinary degree of sangfroid.[14]

Farther south, Gilmore recorded that in the thick of the battle 'some Scottish machine-gunners reported. I don't know where they came from, or where they were supposed to go, but I gave them a task.' They were probably the platoon of the Gordons that 13 Brigade's war diary stated were moved to the right of the Cameronians as flank protection when touch was lost with the 1/7th Warwicks.

According to the Cameronians' diary they 'proved of great value throughout the action'. The brevity of the machine-gun battalions' own war diaries unfortunately means that there are only odd references such as these to their role.[15]

Although the situation in the north was serious, it might have been worse if the Germans had carried out fully the original orders captured by Sergeant Burford. As discussed in Chapter 3, Sixth Army on 25 May had decided to change the original intention of sending XI Corps towards Ypres in order to screen IV Corps in its attack on the canal. Instead XI Corps was to go north to attack the Belgians while IV Corps both attacked the canal and screened Ypres. The decision seems to have arisen from haggling between the various levels of German command mentioned in Chapter 4: Bock wanted to focus on the attack westwards; Reichenau sought the glory of defeating the Belgians; and Schwedler, the corps commander, wanted the opportunity for his corps to attack but perhaps was also attracted by the idea that it should do the job itself and not be beholden to anyone else. The upshot was that the attack was to go ahead as planned, ID 14 would act as flank guard, and ID 18 would have to screen Ypres as well as attacking the northern sector of the canal. The effect of this decision will shortly become clear.

From the German perspective, ID 31's fight against the 1/7th Warwicks in Houthem was reviewed in the previous chapter. As noted there IR 82, the regiment on the division's left facing the 1/7th Warwicks and the Cameronians, suffered heavy losses. On the division's right, where its IR 17 was attacking the Inniskillings, the attack was stopped from 1400 and 1730, as it had been for IR 82. Hollebeke was only taken when the attack was restarted.[16]

Farther north, analysis of the German part of the battle is difficult because ID 18's diary is fuller than usual of hyperbole about the division's accomplishments, but relatively short of facts. Undoubtedly the division had a difficult task, since it had much farther to go than the others as it wheeled round from the Courtrai area towards Ypres. After completing this manoeuvre it attacked before dawn and fought 'through difficult wooded terrain southeastwards of Ypres by dint of sustained bitter combat against small groups of enemy and tanks. The railway line between Zillebeke and Kleine Zillebeke was reached. English and French troops had settled in here for determined resistance in bunkers from the world war.' The division's attack started so much earlier than those farther south because it considered the attack on the railway essentially a preliminary operation to get ready for the main attack ordered by the corps at 0900.[17]

The last section of the quote above must refer to the RSF's stand on Hill 60, which lies between the two Zillebekes and where there were (and still are) some old First World War bunkers. The 'French troops' may have been a reference to units of the 2nd DLM, an armoured division. 17 Brigade recorded a liaison officer from the DLM arriving at 1810 on 26 May to explain that it was in position around Zillebeke. When Stopford went back with him, however, he found that the French HQ had disappeared and that the tanks were withdrawing to Ypres. Perhaps a few units stayed and attacked the Germans the next morning, and hence the reference to 'tanks'. But these might equally have been British Bren carriers, which the Germans usually referred to as 'tanks'. The RSF did not mention any French troops on Hill 60 itself, so ID 18's diary must be confused here.[18]

At some later stage one of the two regiments in the attack – IR 30 – 'struggling hard, was ordered temporarily for defence'. After that the attack was carried on by the other regiment – IR 54. The diary then confirmed what is known from British sources: the Germans captured the wooded area south of Verbrandenmoelen and reached the canal. One battalion managed to reach the 'bridge at Voormezeele', probably meaning the bridge over the main road from St Eloi to Ypres.[19]

IR 30 may have been reassigned in part because its reserve battalion had already been ordered up to protect IR 51, the regiment screening Ypres. This suggests that the British troops in and north of Ypres were perceived as a considerable threat. The fighting in that sector is discussed in Chapter 10, but it can be noted at this point that 'because of multiple enemy incursions from the north' IR 51 had been ordered not to attack over the river – probably meaning the Yser Canal north of Ypres – but to 'secure the north flank in a wide arc'. This suggests that it was tasked with holding the ground to the north of Ypres and east of the Yser Canal. The discovery that Ypres itself was 'strongly occupied' then led IR 51 to be given the further task of sealing off Ypres 'from the east' – presumably meaning that it had to defend the rest of the division from possible British attacks from Ypres. Thus IR 51 was more than fully occupied with its multiple roles around Ypres, which spread it over a wide area. One can infer also that fear of counterattacks discouraged the Germans from getting too close to Ypres on the south side. This decision constrained the width of their attack frontage and made it more logical to go on with IR 54 only.[20]

It is clear, therefore, that ID 18 was never able to give 17 Brigade its undiluted attention. Given the rapid demolition of the Seaforths' position this was a very good thing for the British.

While the British battalions had taken heavy punishment from German artillery fire, the British were returning it in equal measure. The medium artillery had moved into position on the evening of 25 May. Two regiments, 63rd and 65th, supported 143 Brigade in the south. 1st Medium Regiment supported 13 Brigade in the centre and 5th Medium Regiment and 1st Heavy Regiment the northern sector up to and including Ypres. Both 1st and 5th Medium Regiments were behind Messines Ridge, and the other medium regiments were probably there too. The BEF had about four times as many 6-inch howitzers as 4.5-inch guns in its medium armoury, so this is the likely composition of the medium weapons supporting 5th Division. The remains of 1st Heavy Regiment's war diary mentioned that its four four-gun batteries had a mixture of 6-inch guns and 8-inch howitzers, all of First World War vintage. The heavy howitzers were massive affairs, throwing 200-pound shells.[21]

With the guns placed in position overnight, on 26 May I Corps medium artillery war diary noted: 'All Regts. M.A. I Corps reported in action by 0600 and firing by 0615.' 5th Medium Regiment recorded: 'All guns except 2 of B troop were brought into action during hours of darkness with 40 R.P.G. [rounds per gun] on the ground.'* At that stage, and throughout the 26th, guns would have been firing mainly 'harassing fire' on crossroads, copses, farm buildings and other locations where there might be enemy troop or vehicle concentrations.

OPs were also established to observe enemy movement and direct fire onto it, rather than just firing onto targets established by map references. 5th Medium Regiment's OPs, for example, were on Messines Ridge, forward of the batteries. 5th Heavy Battery's was in Wytschaete church. Although the artillery had radios, 63rd Medium Regiment's detailed war diary – probably contemporaneous from the precision of its timings – reported atmospheric interference, and the unit seems not to have persevered with the use of radio. In general, judging by the war diaries, telephone communication was used as with the infantry. Unlike the infantry, however, links were broken less often – the medium artillery was well back from the battlefield and less fire was concentrated on it – and they could usually be restored. MA I Corps recorded that its Signal Section 'did excellent work in keeping through by line to all Regts. in spite of bombing on the main road'.[22]

Until the late afternoon, the 27th itself was another day of normal service for the medium and heavy artillery. As they were well back they did not need to move in spite of the enemy advances. The records, such as they are, indicate that fire was often directed on observed targets, whether a few rounds 'GF' (gunfire) or

---

* A medium artillery regiment had two batteries of eight guns each.

heavier bombardments. This is to be expected because the Germans had no time for elaborate camouflage as they advanced, and would have been easily observed by eye. Some of the bigger guns were still concentrating on targets well back from the enemy's front line: 5th Heavy Battery, for example, 'harassed villages and woods and roads behind the canal'.[23]

Whereas the medium regiments were several miles behind the front line, some of the field regiments were much closer, and for them 27 May was emphatically not normal. Captain Derry of 60th Field commanded the guns that were probably closest to the action. His experiences say a lot about the determination with which some units, and the men in those units, could fight.

Derry was encountered earlier pulling his guns out of their anti-tank position on 27 May. Presumably there was a perceived lack of the specialist anti-tank 2-pounders and so field guns were drafted into the role. The anti-tank role, which meant being in or near the front line, may have gone to 60th Field because it was a territorial unit with old First World War 18-pounders. They were probably judged more expendable than the 18/25-pounders many units had – similar guns, which had been 'retubed' to take the 25-pound shell. The elaborate precautions taken against tanks reflect the experience of the Blitzkrieg and the subsequent German attacks from the southwest on the BEF. In the event the Germans had precisely no tanks on the Ypres–Comines front, and Derry's unit actually carried out a variety of other tasks.

Derry's troop of four guns – C Troop – was in position in 13 Brigade's sector by early morning on 26 May.* He recorded that 'the infantry officers seemed extremely pleased to see me and seemed rather surprised to find the "Gunners" were so near to the front line . . .' There is no record of his troop carrying out harassing fire, presumably because they did not want to give away their positions, which would have been vulnerable to enemy artillery.

Derry's first active contribution came at about 2000 on the 26th, when Major Shaw of the Inniskillings thought that he saw some enemy infantry enter a farmstead about 2,000 yards away. Derry looked through his binoculars and, 'after a few minutes I saw small detachments of men make a dash across some open country from a wood to the farmstead'. Shaw and Derry agreed on a map reference for the farm, which the latter 'sent through on the W/T [radio] set' – so here the radio is being used. His battery picked up the message and sent it to 5th Division's HQ. About twenty minutes later Derry and Shaw saw 'a "crump" of gunfire fall minus

---

* There were three troops per field battery, and two batteries per regiment – twenty-four guns in all.

the farmstead, this was followed up with a "plus", and the third salvo scored a direct hit on the farmstead itself – we were both delighted and the Major asked me to stay for supper'. But Derry excused himself as he had to visit his guns. Later on 26 May, as it was getting dark, Derry found that Shaw had pulled back his forward positions to get a better field of fire. As Derry was moving his two forward guns back in conformity, Shaw told him that a German patrol had entered a small factory just 400 yards in front of them. When the guns came along the road:

> I gave the order to drop into action and fire twenty rounds H.E. [high explosive] at the factory, I ordered the drivers to keep their engines running and the Nos 1 to keep their trailers hooked up. Everybody seemed to work faster than I have ever seen them before – we were all in a state of tense excitement. Major Shaw stood with me between the guns and smiled with satisfaction as each round hit the objective. The whole thing was over in about five or six minutes, and we hooked up and made our way back to the cover of some woods.

On 27 May, when battle broke out in earnest, Derry initially found himself more concerned with tending British wounded than with the enemy. Walking wounded and stretcher-bearers were coming back and, seeing Derry's vehicles around his HQ in a farm, were congregating there. One man had lost two fingers and was 'bleeding violently'. Derry's memory went back 'to a lecture given by Captain Harris in the gunpark at Lille' and, assisted by Bombardier Barnard, Derry applied a tourniquet to the injured man and stopped the bleeding. Barnard then set off on what turned out to be a heroic marathon. He motorcycled to Wytschaete along a road that was being heavily shelled in order to get hold of an ambulance. There were none left but he managed to persuade an officer to lend him a 15-cwt truck. Barnard arrived back at HQ, and eventually had to make four journeys to clear the thirty or more wounded.

Subsequently Derry set off in a truck to visit his forward guns. It is not clear if they were firing, although Derry recorded that a gun of A Troop, which had ended up near his position, fired shrapnel at the enemy, whose infantry were about 1,000 yards away. Derry left his truck in woods to avoid drawing fire and went forwards on foot. It was at this point that, as recounted earlier, Shaw ordered him to pull out and the Manchesters' subaltern decided to stay. Derry returned to his truck and ordered Barnard, who had also returned there, to go off on his motorcycle and tell the other two guns to pull out as well. After Barnard departed, Derry was told that the truck had been shelled and Barnard had been hit in the stomach. But in Derry's words: 'Barnard had not mentioned this, but had gone off on my order.'[24]

Derry then left again to pick up his forward guns. The sergeants in charge of the two forward guns managed to pull them out, although the one from A Troop had to be left behind. One of Derry's other guns had already departed, but he picked up the final one.

When Derry returned to his truck he found that Barnard was already there: 'I questioned him regarding his wound, and he replied that it was nothing. I actually saw the wound later that evening, the piece of shell after penetrating his leather DR [dispatch rider's] suit had made a gash in [his] stomach about two inches long and about a inch wide.'

The radio link had been lost hours earlier, indicating its relative unreliability, but later contact was regained and Derry received orders. C Troop and other remnants of 60th Field ended up at La Basse-Ville, a little place just west of Warneton. It seems likely that they were sent there as a backstop in the vulnerable southern sector.[25]

Another gun of 60th Field, under the command of Sergeant Welburn, was farther down the line on the Cameronians' front. The gun was near their battalion HQ, and at some stage Welburn and his crew 'volunteered to manhandle it forward and deal with some snipers in a house, and some mortars located nearby. This the gun detachment did in no uncertain manner and with great skill and daring.' Welburn used up all his ammunition before withdrawing, later being awarded the Military Medal.[26]

'Devotion to duty' is an old-fashioned phrase, but it seems about the only one that can be applied to Barnard, Welburn, Derry and the 60th Field gun crews.

Also near the front line were the guns of 97th Field, which had been helping to stem the German advance – and the British retreat – at Warneton. 97th Field's war diary recorded that it began harassing fire from 1600 on 26 May. On the 27th, as the Germans crept ever nearer: 'The Regiment was firing incessantly, both on observed targets and on targets dictated by the Infantry.'

91st Field Regiment, in contrast, was up on the Messines Ridge. Regimental HQ was in the vicinity of Wytschaete, although the batteries may have been farther north. On 27 May they similarly 'fired continually on D.F. [defensive fire] and C.P. [counter-preparation] tasks'. Even up on the ridge the troops well aware of the German advance in the central sector and, to the gunners: 'at one time it looked as though both flanks were going'. This may have been the point in the afternoon when both the Seaforths on the far left and the Cameronians on the centre-right came back too far. The 91st Field was to undergo further adventures that evening as the battle continued.[27]

Another field regiment on the ridge was 9th Field Regiment in the Spanbroekmolen area, about a mile from Wytschaete. The area was named after a windmill that the Germans destroyed in 1914. Subsequently it was the site of one of the huge mines that the British blew up in June 1917 at the start of the Battle of Messines Ridge. The mine crater, which had filled with water, was purchased in the 1920s by Lord Wakefield and named, hopefully but as it turned out fruitlessly, the 'Pool of Peace'. One of 9th Field's batteries, 20/76, fired during the night and into the morning of 27 May on defensive fire tasks. As the Germans advanced in the centre and left of the British front, there was 'continuous observed shooting by both batteries during the afternoon and evening'. 20/76's targets included a motor transport column east of the canal as well as mortars and machine-gun posts established by the advancing Germans.[28]

It is a tribute to the speed with which the mechanised British artillery could move that 5th Division's Commander Royal Artillery (CRA) war diary recorded that all regiments were 'in action' – that is ready to fire – by noon on 26 May, and some such as the 97th Field and the 9th Field's 20/76 battery were ready much earlier. These guns had moved twenty miles or more on the night of the 25th/26th and then had to get into position. Most field regiments did not, in fact, fire much on 26 May, but if the Germans had attacked earlier than they did the artillery would have been ready.[29]

The 5th Division field regiments had been joined by others such as 18th Field, attached to 143 Brigade. On 27 May its batteries were close together near Hollandscheschurr Farm, another First World War landmark about 1,000 yards northeast of Wytschaete: 'Ammunition was none too plentiful, but our "Q" [Quartermaster] staff had orders "Ammunition, ammunition, ammunition; think of nothing else; steal it, loot it, send it up as you get it", and we knew they would produce all they could.' But no other references at this stage to shortage of ammunition were found in the war diaries or memoirs, although there the odd one or two may have been missed. Although some secondary sources suggested that the BEF was running short by this time, there is little sign of it in the records.[30]

During the day, 18th Field's diary recorded the retreat of the Seaforths and the resistance of Major Barff. Perhaps it was at this point, although no time is given, that 18th Field's commander, Lieutenant-Colonel G. N. Martin, issued a 'Special Order of the Day'.

1. The present position held by 5 Division is vital to the security of the British Expeditionary Force. It must be held at all costs until further orders.

2. The Royal Regiment of Artillery must be prepared to take their full share in the defence of the line, not only at their own job but as rallying points for the infantry.

3. The guns of 18th Field Regiment will NOT be moved without orders. The Colonel knows that he can count on all ranks whom he has known so well in peace and war to serve them to the end, and if necessary to take part in the infantry fight with small arms.

By doing this they will not only ensure the getaway of others but of themselves.

TO BE COMMUNICATED TO ALL RANKS.[31]

Martin's order may seem melodramatic. But there is plenty of evidence that, in the artillery at least, the *esprit de corps* which it implies was not just a fiction in the mind of a few officers. There have already been examples of this, and there are more in subsequent chapters.

No German artillery war diaries were consulted for this book. The German artillery effort has, therefore, had to be reconstructed mainly from British accounts of its impact and the general principles governing German artillery deployment. Clearly there was no lack of artillery support for the German attack, as the British front-line infantry units all referred to heavy shelling and indicated that this extended well back from early on in the battle.

Assuming the full complement of artillery, each German division would have had twenty 75-mm field guns, forty 105-mm field guns and fourteen 150-mm guns.* The first were very light infantry support weapons, which could be manhandled if necessary, and they fired a 13-pound shell. The second fired shells of 33 pounds. The 150-mm guns were the standard medium weapon, which threw a shell weighing around 96 pounds. This was bigger than the British 4.5- and older 60-pounder medium guns (both of which actually fired shells of 56 pounds) but similar to the 6-inch howitzers with which most British medium regiments were equipped.[32]

On the distribution of the field guns given above, the shell weight of a German division with sixty field guns approximately equalled that thrown by an equivalent number of British field guns, split one quarter 18-pounders and three quarters

---

* Technically most of these weapons were howitzers.

25-pounders – roughly the proportion in the BEF as a whole.* With three divisions, the Germans would have deployed a maximum of 180 field guns. The British had the equivalent of about eight field regiments, including two deployed to support 50th Division around Ypres, which should be counted because some of ID 18's artillery was also deployed against Ypres. At full strength the British would have had 192 guns, although in reality there were probably less. Thus there was approximate equality in field artillery.

The Germans could also make some use of their anti-tank guns. There are references to Bren carriers being disabled by anti-tank gunfire, while according to ID 18 its anti-tank units did 'excellent service in keeping the bunkers under fire' in their attack on Hill 60. By contrast there was little for British anti-tank guns – firing small armour-piercing projectiles – to usefully engage.[33]

On the same basis of computation, the Germans would have had forty-two medium weapons. But they also deployed separate medium and heavy artillery units under army control and on the 26th IV Corps was allocated one of these – I assume a standard artillery battalion of twelve medium guns. At some stage on the 27th IV Corps was also allocated three 'heavy units', presumably also meaning artillery. One can guess that this was late on after the news of likely Belgian ceasefire and, if so, the guns would probably not have been available until the next day. At the initial deployment, therefore, the Germans had a likely maximum of fifty-four medium guns, rising to a possible ninety. The British started with four medium regiments and one heavy – a maximum of eighty guns. One further medium regiment was deployed late on the 27th, which brings this up to ninety-six. So for the 27th, at least, the British medium/heavies probably had a significant superiority in shell weight.[34]

On at least one occasion on 27 May some British medium units were employed on counter-battery work, while there is very little mention in British artillery diaries of them being shelled in return. Given the undoubted impact of British artillery on German advances – more will be said of this later – it would be expected that counter-battery work, usually carried out by medium guns, would have been a German priority if they had had enough weapons. This again suggests a British superiority.[35]

It is probably sensible to conclude that both sides could fire about the same weight of shell in total, possibly with some British superiority on 27 May.

In contrast to the battle on the ground, where there are plenty of British sources but they tend to contradict each other, there are relatively few sources for the higher

---

* The British at Ypres–Comines also had one battery of 4.5-inch field howitzers, throwing a heavier shell than the other field guns.

command during the battle. We are no longer concerned with GHQ. By this time there was not much Gort and Pownall could do. They had virtually no reserves left, as Brooke discovered when he visited them on 27 May, and their main concern was the details of the evacuation. Nonetheless it was a surprise to Brooke when he revisited Premesques later on the 27th to find that they had disappeared 'without saying where they were going'. In fact Pownall had set off early to try to establish GHQ at Cassel, but German shells were already landing there. Eventually he established it for one night at Houtkerque on the way to the coast before moving to La Panne, east of Dunkirk, on 28 May. Wireless messages were sent from Houtkerque to corps HQs, but Brooke presumably missed his.[36]

Whatever the truth in this case, GHQ has been accused elsewhere of not doing their job properly at this stage. According to Bryant, writing about 26 May, Brooke was 'co-ordinating the movements both of his own Corps and of the 1st Corps on his right and in retreat behind him, without orders from above and on his own sole responsibility'. This seems greatly exaggerated. Brooke's own diary referred to a GHQ conference on the 26th, which discussed plans for the evacuation, suggesting that the general lines had been mutually agreed first. According to Pownall: 'we spent the whole day [of the 26th] one way and another, laying on the arrangements not only for the withdrawal by bounds but also for the other end' – that is, the evacuation. Brooke may have had to bear some extra responsibilities, because Michael Barker of I Corps was not a very effective commander. But Brooke's diary discussed below suggests that, at least on 27 May, he was primarily concerned with his own corps.[37]

Apart from Bryant's account, Brooke's associated memoir and his diary, the other main source for higher command decisions during the battle is Franklyn's memoir, with a few letters he wrote after the war. The memoir is hit and miss over timings, but it is not self-glorifying and probably gives a reasonable insight into Franklyn's thoughts and feelings. The corps and division war diaries have nothing of real value.

Franklyn set up his HQ at Ploegsteert Chateau. Ploegsteert had good road links with all areas of the front and was far enough back to be out of range of most German artillery. According to Franklyn his HQ was 'not really a chateau but nothing more than a small villa. There were steps in front leading down to a pleasant garden, now rather neglected.' He took one of the small front sitting rooms for his own use. 'I prefer to be alone when wrestling with knotty problems and it seemed likely that there would be plenty of these in the near future. Besides, I have a habit of pacing up and down in moments of stress.'[38]

For much of 27 May until the late afternoon, however, his memoir adds nothing to what is known from elsewhere and is unreliable over timings. Brooke's diary, on the other hand, is likely to be a fairly reliable account of his movements, although it lacks timings except at the beginning. Brooke started at 0800 with a conference with Montgomery of 3rd Division and General Dudley Johnson of 4th Division to settle the details of their withdrawal from the frontier line, which was scheduled to take place on the night of the 27th/28th. He called in at Wambrechies, the HQ of Harold Alexander of 1st Division, which was in I Corps: 'to ensure that they stop sending traffic on 3rd Division road'. This sort of intervention may be the reason for Bryant's statement that Brooke was co-ordinating I and II Corps' movements. At this point Brooke's memoir adds some detail to the bare diary entry. 'From there across the Lys to Ploegsteert Wood to see 5th Division.'

Franklyn at this point was out visiting his brigadiers – clearly he did not run the battle entirely from his HQ but preferred to see the situation on the ground. Brooke had a talk with Grover, Franklyn's GSO1 (general staff officer 1, that is chief of the divisional staff) and then went to see Martel of 50th Division at Ypres. One of his brigades was in position there but had not gained touch with 5th Division on its right. Brooke went south to GHQ, pausing again at Ploegsteert to stress the importance of 5th Division establishing contact with 50th Division. At that point he learned that the situation at Comines was giving concern. GHQ had no reinforcements, so Brooke went back to his own HQ to tell Johnson to detach a brigade of 4th Division and send it up to Franklyn. But its move would take some time and Brooke wanted to give Franklyn help more quickly. He continued: 'As I had heard that the 1st Division had already started withdrawing three battalions from the line and that these battalions were somewhere west of Ploegsteert Wood, I decided to endeavour to secure their assistance.'

Brooke went to I Corps HQ, since 1st Division was in that corps, and 'after some hunting' found the HQ in an old Lille fortress. He obtained Barker's agreement to the transfer and went again to Alexander at Wambrechies, who issued the relevant orders to the battalions – 3rd Grenadier Guards, 2nd North Staffordshire and the Sherwood Foresters. He then went to GHQ again and secured seven infantry tanks: 'which were dispatched at once to 5th Division front'.[39]

Brooke's next few journeys that day were less significant to the battle itself. They included his third visit to GHQ, when he discovered that the personnel had disappeared. When he did return to 5th Division HQ again, it was late in the evening. Of the reinforcements he had organised, both the brigade – No. 10 – of 4th Division and the three battalions of 1st Division were to play an important part.

In spite of Brooke's belief that the tanks were instantly dispatched to the front, they were not because they were somewhere else entirely. GHQ was clearly out of touch with the situation. At that point the remnants of the infantry tanks were taking part in fighting on the La Bassée front, in the southwest on the Canal Line, which dealt the *coup de grâce* to most of them. Brooke may have got confused with the light tanks of the 13th/18th Hussars, which had been placed under his command earlier and were to take part, as the next chapter will reveal, in a vital counterattack.[40]

Brooke's role, and importance, are obvious. He started by making sure that Montgomery and Johnson knew what they to do over the next day and night. His ceaseless movements from then on were devoted to ensuring that, as far as possible, Franklyn and Martel's divisions formed a joined-up front line and, even more importantly, that Franklyn had all the forces that Brooke could possibly muster for him to deploy against the German attack. Here Brooke's knowledge of the German orders of 24 May may have played a part, in that he knew the attack would be in three-divisional strength, and that Franklyn would likely need more than his initial one division to withstand it. He also was aware that the Germans were *not* planning any significant action on II Corps's original front, so he could move troops from there if necessary. In the course of doing all this, Brooke certainly seems to have kept a watchful eye on what Michael Barker of I Corps was doing, but it seems too much to say that he was responsible for co-ordinating the retreat of both I and II Corps.

Less is known about Franklyn's activities, although he was clearly attempting to keep a grip on what his brigadiers were doing. Major Brunker's visit to Warneton to organise 'Brunker force' – which was not in the end needed – shows that Franklyn and 5th Division HQ were taking some sort of action to deal with the situation in the southern sector. Soon after, however, Franklyn was forced by the steadily deteriorating position there to take a much more important decision.[41]

No German material appears to cast new light on any of their command decisions beyond divisional level for this period of the battle. The significant German decisions were to come later, when the Belgians surrendered. In the British War Cabinet the momentous question of whether Britain should join the planned French approach to Mussolini to act as mediator was still being discussed on 27 May. While Halifax, the foreign secretary, still supported this, three War Cabinet members – Churchill himself and Clement Attlee and Arthur Greenwood for Labour – opposed it. Neville Chamberlain, once the appeaser, was inclined to join them, as was Archibald Sinclair, the Liberal leader who, although not a member of the War Cabinet, had been invited to join the discussions.[42]

7. Counterattack in the South

A T ABOUT 1630 ON 27 May, according to the war diary of the 3rd Grenadier Guards: 'Information was received from a Gunner Battery Commander and also from 5 Div that the line held by 5 Div on the Ypres–Comines Canal north of Comines had broken.' The battery commander belonged to 97th Field, and the German breakthrough was on the front occupied by 143 Brigade. The diary entry marks the beginning of a dramatic period in which the British fought back against the German advance. It culminated when, two-and-a-half hours later, the Guards were ordered to launch a counterattack to restore the position.[1]

By mid-afternoon 143 Brigade's southernmost battalion – the 1st Ox and Bucks – had been pushed back from Comines almost to Warneton and were digging in with some Royal Engineers. Not far behind them the OPs of 97th Field were driven back level with its guns, which were firing at ranges of half a mile or less. But soon after this the situation was to change. Before the Guards' counterattack got underway, the engineers from 4th Division – and other troops – had also launched a counterattack against the Germans, pushing westwards. Their participation illustrates 5th Division's precarious situation, since it was almost unprecedented for such specialised troops to act as infantry in an attack. As usual, there is conflicting evidence about the two successive attacks.

According to Franklyn: '. . . it was reported to me that an officer of the Black Watch, commanding two companies of his battalion, was thirsting to make a counterattack'. Franklyn gave the go-ahead. The 6th Black Watch, the battalion in question, was in 4th Division, which had been stationed on the frontier line some distance to the east of Comines. The division had initially moved the Black Watch to guard the south bank of the Lys from Menin to Comines. Although there were various alarms, there was in fact no German penetration in that sector. There would have been little advantage to the Germans in opening up a new front, when success in the attack on the canal would cut off the British forces south of the Lys. And with

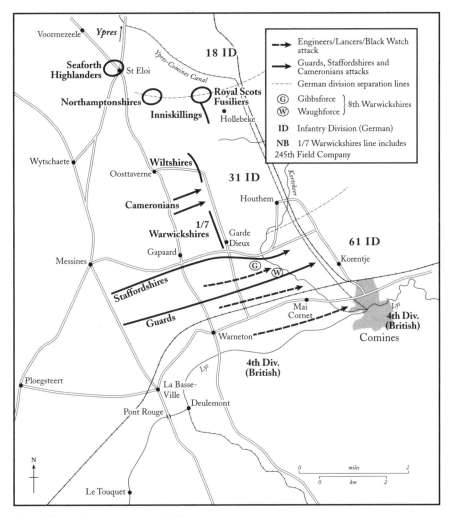

Map 4: *Ypres–Comines, evening 27 May*

attacks on the Belgians, French and British impending or under way, Sixth Army had its hands full anyway.[2]

In fact, only part of the Black Watch's A Company was involved in the first counterattack. The other participants were the 4th Division engineers, who had started the day digging defences on the Lys, and the 13th/18th Hussars with their light tanks. The Hussars had been in Ypres but had been relieved when 50th Division moved in on the morning of 27 May. However the Black Watch's commander,

Lieutenant-Colonel M. A. Carthew-Yorstoun, was in charge of the attack, and it can be assumed that he suggested the attack, as Franklyn's statement inferred.[3]

It is not known how many men the attack involved. The war diary of 97th Field referred to '300 R.E.s'. The diary is otherwise inaccurate about the attack, but the number is plausible. An R.E. company contained more than 200 men, and there were three companies – 7th, 59th and 225th. If allowance is made for those held back in reserve or not in the attack for other reasons, a figure of 300 engineers could be about right. To these can be added a few troops from the Black Watch, but probably not many – 7th Field Company's war diary stated: 'One platoon of 6 B.W. alone was found on the Company left', although it is not the most reliable source. No source recorded the number of Hussars, but given the number of casualties they suffered it seems likely that there were quite a number. Three squadrons were involved, all the men from one being 'dismounted', the ex-horsed cavalry squadron's term for on foot. Therefore there might have been 400 men or more in the attack, or the strength with which a single infantry battalion might have attacked.[4]

Charles Miller's history of the Hussars puts its A Squadron on the right or southern end of the attack, south of the Warneton–Comines road. C Squadron, the dismounted one, was astride the railway, which ran parallel to it. B Squadron was on the left, that is, north of the railway. 7th Field Company were on the same axis as C Squadron; presumably the dismounted Hussars and the engineers joined forces. 7th Field Company's diary located the Black Watch and then 59th and 225th Field Companies in succession on its left, each echeloned 400 yards back. 225th Field Company's diary added that it was on a front of 500 yards. This seems plausible, and if all the formations except the small Black Watch contingent had roughly the same front, then the attack stretched from south of the road to about 1,500 yards north of the railway.[5]

There is other evidence about the attack frontage in the account of Major Kendal, of the 8th Warwicks. Kendal is hopelessly unreliable about times and even dates, locating the attack on 28 May. But his memory probably served better when recalling the surrounding detail of an event. Kendal stated that a counterattack by the Black Watch and '95 Field Company' (probably 59th) passed through or near Captain Waugh's position, and the latter had been in contact with them. 'Waughforce', as the Warwicks called this *ad hoc* group, seems to have been located about 800 yards north of the railway. So this statement also suggests that the Black Watch and 59th Field Company constituted the left centre of the attack frontage. 225th Field Company, still farther to the north, may have passed between Waughforce and

Gibbsforce, the 8th Warwicks' other group of defenders, which were separated by another 800 yards or so.[6]

The attack got under way at around 1900, starting from the Royal Engineers' positions just east of Warneton. As it went in, there was strong German resistance at Emile Ghesquiere's farm, which was close to Waughforce. Lieutenant Furness of the Hussars 'drove his tank into the yard and fired into the hay until it was well alight, the entire farm soon catching fire'. The Deltour Farm, another half mile towards the canal and on the same axis, was also retaken. Farther south 7th Field Company advanced along the railway, relieving two sections of the Ox and Bucks' C Company, which had hung on under Sergeant Roby at Mai Cornet, about 1,200 yards west of the canal. Roby was awarded the DCM for his gallantry. They pushed on beyond the river Kortekeer to attack Remi Masschelein's farm.[7]

Artillery support for the counterattack was provided by 97th Field and 63rd and 65th Medium Regiments. According to 97th Field's diary, during the entire day it was 'firing incessantly, both on observed targets and on targets dictated by the infantry'. 63rd Medium bombarded a target just behind Comines at 1940, then at 2012 the enemy were 'seen to run from 656524 after shelling and mount [a] large truck'. The map reference was to a road near Korentje, just north of Comines. 13th/18th Hussars noted that there was a creeping barrage during their advance and also counter-battery fire on the German guns.[8]

The attack reached the river Kortekeer and in some cases went beyond it, although at the time, in the half-light, the engineers thought they had reached the canal. 7th Field Company experienced heavy machine gun and small arms fire, but 'the enemy fire was ill-aimed and grew progressively worse as the Company closed and pushed him back'. Then – according to 7th Field Company's diary – at 2100 hours 59th Field Company arrived on the left 'in perfect order under heavy fire'. Pakenham-Walsh in his history of the Royal Engineers mentioned some heroic actions during the attack. 7th Field Company's advance was covered by the fire of the HQ Bren gun, manned by company Quartermaster-Sergeant Fryer, 'who continued to fire the gun, although his foot had been smashed in the action'. Major MacDonald, the CO of 59th Field Company, was killed while on a bicycle reorganising the company after a fight for a wood.[9]

A few elements of the attack almost reached the canal. B Squadron of the Hussars only stopped at a point where they faced some rising ground on the near side of the canal held by German machine-gunners and infantry. The right wing of the attack by A Company of the Hussars with a troop of tanks, operating south of the Warneton–Comines railway and road, drove the Germans back across the canal.

Charles Miller, their historian and CO at the time, noted that this advance reached 'a ditch two hundred yards from the bank' (of the canal). The detailed nature of Miller's account suggests that, although written after the war, it was put together after consulting officers who were there as well as drawing on his own experience.[10]

Collating the casualty figures from various sources suggests there were around sixty, concentrated in the sector just north of the railway where 7th and 59th Field Companies, and B Squadron of the Hussars, attacked. This was, of course, where ID 61 had advanced farthest, and most ground had to be reclaimed. In view of the substantial casualties and the fact that only a small part of the attack reached the canal, could it be called a success or was it a forlorn hope? Analysis of the next attack, in which the 2nd North Staffordshires participated with the 3rd Grenadier Guards, throws more light on the first.[11]

Together with 2nd Sherwood Foresters these regular battalions had marched up from I Corps' positions southeast of Lille, which were being thinned out preparatory to the whole corps moving north. They belonged to 1st Division, the crack formation led by Harold Alexander, later to be C-in-C in the North African and then the Italian theatres. Both the Guards and the North Staffordshires had marched on foot, presumably because there were other calls on the transport companies on the night of 26/27 May.

Having marched eighteen miles, they had lain up at Le Touquet – not the French seaside resort so popular in the interwar period but a tiny Belgian hamlet just across the Lys, north of Armentières. It was the location of one of the few bridges by which the BEF could cross that river. As the Staffordshires laconically put it in a later summary of their time in France, the night of the 26th/27th onwards 'proved to be one of the toughest 48 hours we had to deal with throughout the period under review'.[12]

Initially the two battalions were to occupy a position on the Lys, covering 1st Division's retirement.[13] According to the Guards, a message was received at about 1630 ordering them to go direct to Dunkirk, and this was followed by the information from 97th Field quoted at the beginning of the chapter. Then at 1700 the Staffordshires received a message to come under 5th Division. Brooke had no doubt become aware of the battalions on one of the visits he made to Alexander's HQ that morning, and subsequently, as outlined in the previous chapter, he obtained their loan from Barker of I Corps. The Guards received their message via Captain George Thorne, a liaison officer with 1st Division. Thorne had travelled by motorcycle and saw Major Allan Adair, the Guards CO:

[Adair] was his usual, cheerful, optimistic self, lying in a ditch with his feet up. He told me he was delighted to see the son of his 1917 Commanding Officer doing his bit, and of course the battalion would set off at once to plug the gap. The Battalion Second in Command, Osbert Smith, took a different line, and said it was a pity I had not fallen off my bike miles away.

The battalions set off to march the three miles or so to Franklyn's HQ at Ploegsteert.[14] Franklyn had been anticipating their arrival and pondering how to use them. He knew that there were problems on all his sectors and that his left – the northern sector – was almost as vulnerable as his right. He wrote: 'of one thing I was determined, and that was not to use these fresh battalions passively to plug gaps. I must use them for counterattack. I remember pacing up and down my small room. I essentially came to the conclusion that it was vital to hold fast on my right and secure the hinge with Comines.' As it happened, while Franklyn was taking the decision, the Black Watch CO volunteered his services. But Franklyn did not think the Black Watch-led counterattack could be very strong. He referred to it being joined by 'a few engineers', whereas, as has been seen, there may have been as many as 300, plus tanks. So Franklyn resolved to follow it up with another one, involving both the Guards and the North Staffs. As he admitted, the operation on which the battalions were about to embark was highly unorthodox:

> The textbooks of the time laid it down that a counterattack on a strength greater than one company must never be launched without most careful reconnaissance, yet I was proposing a counterattack by two battalions over ground which they had never seen. Moreover, they would be starting the operation in the half-light and it would end in the dark.[15]

Adair and Lieutenant-Colonel Butterworth, the Staffordshires' CO, arrived at Franklyn's HQ between 1900 and 1930.[16] Franklyn 'sat them down on each side of me on the steps of Ploegsteert Chateau and I remember feeling that I just had to impress these two with the importance and feasibility of the task which I was going to ask them to perform'. He found Butterworth 'somewhat dour' but felt 'he was a determined person who could be relied upon'. Adair 'was entirely different, gay and light-hearted'. 'I wondered if he would succeed in tackling such a difficult problem. Now I know that his gaiety was due to complete confidence in himself and his Grenadiers.'[17]

Although the action was hazardous, Franklyn was not unconfident. He remembered a British counterattack, without preparation, which had been launched towards the end of the retreat following the German offensive of March 1918: 'The result had been a sweeping success.' Now as then Franklyn thought that the last thing the Germans would be expecting was a strong counterattack. But, he concluded, 'one is never sure'. After Adair and Butterworth left, 'I went and had a strong whisky and soda: I needed it.'[18]

The battalions now had to march another three miles or so to their start line on the La Basse-Ville to Messines road. So after their march the night before they had marched about six miles to get to this position. It was a total of twenty-five miles or so, and the Staffordshires, at least, had had no meal. And these were not fresh battalions. Both had been involved in heavy fighting on the river Escaut on 21 May, the Guards suffering 186 casualties or around a quarter of their strength. They still had to advance three miles across country to reach the canal, although advanced parties of the enemy were much nearer.[19]

At some point Adair called on Lushington, presumably to discuss artillery support during the advance. Lushington, who it seems did not know Adair's name, wrote:

> He was a little man, very neat and well-dressed, and his manner suggested that he had just dropped in for a cup of tea and a friendly chat . . .
>
> Twenty minutes later the whole battalion in line of battle moved past my headquarters. The setting sun was shining on their bayonets, their bren carriers were on either flank; in all my life I have never seen a finer and more inspiring sight. They walked through the guns and the men on them cheered them and made jokes as they passed.[20]

While the engineers' counterattack had one or two medium artillery regiments supporting it, during the second attack all four medium regiments and the one heavy were turned on the German positions.

Headquarters Medium Artillery (HQMA) war diary gave a summary of the 'Tasks in support of counterattack'. From 2000 to 2100 63rd Medium, 65th Medium and the 8-inch howitzers of 1st Heavy Regiment in the north were engaged in counter-battery work. Then until 2130 all the regiments except 63rd Medium were firing on villages, road junctions and copses – locations where German troops were likely to assemble or through which they might move. Some of these were north of the axis of the counterattack, presumably to prevent the Germans bringing up reinforcements. Other target areas were close to the flanks of the attack or on Korentje and adjacent locations just behind the German front. Apart from the 97th Field, the field regiments seem to have been fully engaged in the central and northern sectors – whose troops certainly needed their support.[21]

The attack was meant to start at 2000, but not surprisingly, given the distance they had to march to get to the start line, both the Staffordshires and the Guards were late. The Staffordshires timed their start precisely at 2012, the Grenadiers at 2030, which may be an approximation given that their diary was written later. The intended frontages were about 1,000 yards for each battalion. Because of the distance they had to travel across country, they lost touch with each other and seem never to have regained it.[22]

The Staffordshires advanced along the road running roughly west to east, which has the hamlets of Gapaard and Garde Dieux lying just to the north of it. When they reached the vicinity of Garde Dieux: 'Very heavy enemy Artillery and Mortar fire was put down, and the X-roads [near Garde Dieux] was heavily shelled.' It was now about 2115 and getting dark. 'However in spite of the darkness and the heavy fire, the Battalion pushed on.' Battalion HQ was established 100 yards east of the Garde Dieux crossroads. About 600 yards farther down the road, near the Kortekeer, was Gibbsforce, one of the 8th Warwicks' strong points. Gibbs and some of his men, with others from the 1/7th Warwicks, joined the Staffordshires. The river describes a curve, swinging away from the canal and then bending in towards it near Comines. At this point it was at its farthest from the canal, around 1,200 yards.

The Staffordshires crossed the Kortekeer and irrupted into the Bonte-Descamps' farm, only a few hundred yards from the canal, scattering the Germans in the yard. This was the farm from which Muller-Nedebock of IR 162 had fired a British machine gun earlier in the day. One German fled into the cellar, which sheltered civilians, and hid in the barrel for churning butter. The British went on towards the Noterdame Farm, even nearer the canal, apparently suffering heavily at this point from machine-gun fire. Bourgeois thought that they reached the canal in several places.[23]

Like the German advance earlier in the day, the Staffordshires had bypassed some obstacles and a second wave was mopping up. This included some engineers from 245th Field Company (not to be confused with 225th Field Company) who had been fighting with the 1/7th Warwicks. The engineers' CO, Major Garwood, led an attack on a house still occupied by Germans. Garwood, a character reminiscent of Uncle Matthew in Nancy Mitford's *The Pursuit of Love*, first had to neutralise two machine-gun posts. He 'stalked one of these and killed the team with his revolver and took charge of the post'. He then shot two more Germans with a rifle. Meanwhile 2nd Lieutenant John, who was with him, captured four enemy from an anti-tank gun team and attacked the house. Both his and Garwood's groups were, however, driven back. Garwood seems to have got detached and went forwards to get reinforcements – an action that somehow seems typical of the man, since most people's reaction would have been to go back. Presumably he overestimated the Staffordshires' strength and thought that significant numbers were ahead of him. He reached the canal, but found it 'still held by the enemy' and returned.[24]

From about 2330, wounded and lost men from the Staffordshires began returning down the road to battalion HQ. Clearly the attack had not taken a significant amount of ground. Soon after midnight, the shelling having died down, Butterworth went forwards and located the 8th Warwicks' sketchy line, with positions containing a mixture of men from the Warwicks' battalions, the Staffordshires and the 4th Gordons. Then he gained touch with the HQ of 1/7th Warwicks, a few hundred yards north of the Garde Dieux crossroads, and with them co-ordinated a defence line for the night.

Butterworth's role is easy to overlook. Even during the battalion's short period of rest, when they arrived at their position at Le Touquet, he had been busy marking out positions for other 1st Division battalions, which were on their way. After two nights and a day of what seems almost superhuman activity he had ensured that the position on his immediate flanks was secured. He was evidently not a flamboyant figure, and the brief history of the North Staffordshires has nothing of value on the battle. As a result the battalion's and Butterworth's roles have been somewhat neglected.[25]

Although active fighting died down, there was little comfort for the Staffordshires that night. The summary recorded: 'Frequent outbursts of shelling and MG fire rendered the task of holding positions and rescuing wounded extremely difficult and apart from all this there was still no food nor rest for anyone.' Casualties had been heavy, although it is not clear from the records which officers were killed or missing during the night and which the day after. Certainly one of the commanders of the leading companies was killed in the attack, and the other subsequently died of wounds.[26]

After passing the guns of 97th Field, the Guards initially advanced under less fire than the Staffordshires. Like the Staffordshires, the Guards advanced on a two-company front, with Captain Roderick Brinkman's No. 2 Company on the right next to the Warneton–Comines railway. On the left, they picked up elements of Waughforce of the 8th Warwicks, which included men from the 1/7th Warwicks who had been reinforcing the 8th Warwicks' denuded line.

Once the Guards crossed the Kortekeer, however, German fire increased. Brinkman was hit by a piece of mortar bomb in his right eye, and both his platoon commanders were killed. He was hit again by small arms fire in the right shoulder and left elbow. He then saw Lieutenant Dick Crompton-Roberts' company, No. 1, advancing to his right. According to Brinkman, the companies, in what was now complete darkness, had crossed over.

Continued heavy fire meant that more men became casualties. Brinkman told Crompton-Roberts that they must mount a bayonet charge: 'When I get back to my company I will blow a whistle, and we will get up and go for them.' In the course of doing this, Brinkman was slightly wounded again. By now there were just three standing including, amazingly, himself. He threw a grenade at a cottage on the canal used by the Germans, and they retreated back across the canal. Bourgeois thought this could have been the Woestyns' house, about 1,000 yards north of the railway, showing how easy it was to lose direction. Almost certainly this final attack was one Miller mentioned in the Hussars' history as continuing up the rising ground in front of the Hussars towards the canal. Brinkman then sent one of his two companions back to Adair to get more troops, but was hit again and fainted. He woke up the next morning to find himself a prisoner in the cottage on the canal, used by the Germans as a first-aid post.[27]

In spite of the heroic actions of Brinkman and Sergeant Ryder, who was with him throughout and was also wounded and captured, the Guards' attack had effectively run out of men as the leading platoons were cut down by enemy fire. Crompton-Roberts was killed and 2nd Lieutenant Aubrey Fletcher wounded and taken prisoner. Adair consolidated his front line along a field ditch just behind the Kortekeer.[28]

What did this series of counterattacks achieve? And can those achievements be credited to the first attack – that of the engineers and their companions in arms – or to that of the Guards/Staffordshires, or to both? One way of answering the question is to see what the German records stated, but before doing this it is necessary to try to reconcile conflicting accounts in the British sources. These shed a revealing light on how there could be entirely different perceptions of the same sequence of events.

The most egregious example is that of Major Gillespie, the CO of the engineers' 7th Field Company, who claimed in his letter to Major Joslen, the official history 'narrator', that no one in any of the engineer companies 'saw or heard of any further attack, or fighting during the night'. However he admitted that the engineers in the first counterattack did not reach the canal, and it seems clear that, although elements of this attack penetrated beyond the river Kortekeer, the engineer units at least then pulled back to it. Most of the fighting in the second counterattack, therefore, went on well forward of them. Some of the Hussars did remain forward, and as noted above they saw the Guards' attack going in ahead of them.[29]

Another example, which crops up in a number of sources, is the belief that the Guards, as they advanced to the attack, saw the Black Watch, silhouetted in the flames, attacking a burning farm ahead of them. How on earth anyone could tell it was the Black Watch is not explained, and the timing is wrong.[30] Because of the distance they had to travel, it would have been at least 2100 before the Guards could possibly have seen an attack going in some way in front of them, and by that time the participants in the original attack, including the Black Watch, had reached the Kortekeer. It seems far more likely that Adair's own explanation, which was that they saw Brinkman's men silhouetted in the flames, is the correct one.[31]

Different conceptions of what happened in the battle could be established in people's minds, because – even in such a relatively small area – a combination of darkness, and confusion between the Korketeer and the canal, could lead to disorientation. Finally there was probably a dash of believing what one wants to believe, either because it makes a good story (the Black Watch) or because of loyalty to one's own unit (Gillespie).

Although the confusion of the evening is mirrored in the German sources, much of the account above is validated. In Chapter 5, battalions II/176 and III/176 of ID 61 were left making good ground towards Warneton at the southern end of the Canal Line, while on the British side Lieutenant-Colonel Lushington of 97th Field was contemplating a last-ditch defence by his gunners. Then, in the words of ID 61's history: 'A British counter attack with tanks rolled over the scattered companies but was brought to a standstill at the Ypres canal.' This must have been the Royal Engineers' attack with the Royal Hussars' tanks, because after it the divisional history recorded several other British attacks. The first reference to these ran: 'Renewed attacks and counter attacks alternated, accompanied by heavy artillery activity.' The last few words suggest that this might refer to the Guards' and Staffordshires' initial advance during which the British medium artillery was unleashed.

There was then a 'further attack', which was repulsed, followed by the British 'in the night making a breakthrough among the III/176 when it came to bitter hand to hand fighting'. The first could refer to the Staffordshires' attack, the second to the Guards' final effort. The result, however, was clear. III/176 had lost heavily, with several officers killed. The whole of IR 176 was taken back behind the canal and replaced by IR 151. Muller-Nedebock recollected that IR 176 'withdrew in a panic losing many men in the bombardment'. He was by this time behind the canal getting treatment for his injury suffered during the earlier German advance, so he may have been close enough to have first-hand experience of the retreat.[32]

Earlier in the afternoon Muller-Nedebock, at that time farther north with IR 162, had been sheltering from another heavy British artillery bombardment. His account is not entirely clear, but it seems that his company was withdrawn because of its losses. However the relatively limited penetration of the Staffordshires' attack, which must have been on IR 162's front, is confirmed because when he returned with his platoon on 28 May he rejoined the German front lines almost at the spot where he had been the day before. He noted that during the night there had been a 'very confused situation. The Germans and the British had been so intertangled that most of the time there was no means of distinguishing the posts held by the enemy and those we controlled.'[33]

'Intertangled' just about summarises the whole story of the counterattacks: both the accounts of them in various sources, and the actual details of the attacks so far as they can be reconstructed. But in spite of the impossibility of getting a complete account, it is clear that the successive British attacks achieved practically everything Franklyn could have hoped for, although at a heavy cost. What threatened to be a German breakthrough was converted into a serious setback for ID 61, with its positions at the southern end of the line forced back to the canal and the division compelled to bring up its reserve regiment. Farther north on the front that had been occupied by the Warwicks' battalions, where progress by the Germans had been slower anyway, they were effectively brought to a halt and must have also suffered considerable losses.

There are some puzzles about the earlier German advance, which may be accounted for by ID 61's inexperience. After the breakthrough at the southern end, the Germans seem to have been slow to exploit it. Having overwhelmed the British forward positions by around midday, they had only advanced one-and-a-half miles from the canal by 1600. (They had got to within half a mile of 97th Field's guns at Warneton, which is about two miles from Comines.) Obviously this was partly due to the defence by the engineers, the flanking fire from the Ox and Bucks and 97th Field's artillery fire. But the Germans do not seem to have pushed many troops into the gap they had made in the south, judging by the comment about 'the scattered companies'. At the same time only slightly farther north they were hammering away at the Warwicks' reserve line without any discernible impact. Perhaps a more experienced divisional command might have read the battle better and fed reinforcements into the southern advance. After all one of the precepts of German tactics – illustrated very well by IV Corps' advance in the previous days – was not to worry too much about the flanks of an attack but to press forwards where opposition was weakest.

On the British side it seems unlikely that the Guards could have achieved what they did unless the engineers' attack had gone in first. On the central axis just to the north of the railway, the engineers and their fellow soldiers had already driven IR 176 back around a mile to the Kortekeer. The regiment was dealt a further blow by the Hussars' advance south of the road, while the latter's tanks clearly had a major impact on the Germans. These preliminary advances in the centre and south may account for the relative success of the Guards' attack compared with that of the Staffordshires. On the latter's front 225th Field Company had got up to the river Kortekeer, but at a point where it was much farther from the canal than farther south. So they had not cleared the way for the Staffordshires, as the companies farther south had for the Guards.

The Staffordshires also seem to have suffered more from artillery fire than the Guards, although it is not clear why there was a difference in the volume of fire on their respective fronts. The late start the attack made did not help. The British medium and heavy artillery were engaged on counter-battery work until 2100, which should have suppressed German artillery fire, and it may be no coincidence that the Staffordshires recorded very heavy enemy fire on the Garde Dieux crossroads at 2115 after the British medium artillery had switched to other targets. Apart from 225th Field Company, the engineers did not record significant artillery fire. Possibly the element of surprise in their attack helped here; perhaps also the Germans were uncertain about the location of their own troops.[34]

Clearly Franklyn suffered in making his decisions from the limited information he possessed. The engineers' attack was stronger than he thought. If he had known that, he might have revised his dispositions and simply aimed to relieve them. That would have reduced casualties, but German morale and strength would have remained higher for their renewed attack the next day.

5th Division had had to draw up a hasty plan and its staff, Franklyn and the artillery should be given credit for organising a well-supported attack at such short notice. But over-optimism about the timings probably reduced the impact of the artillery support. It was also unfortunate that the battalions were made to march first to Ploegsteert and then to the start line, a distance of about six miles. They could have saved about two miles of this if they had gone direct to the start line from Le Touquet, and surely Franklyn could have gone by car to meet them. However, it is easy to carp at the details of an action that must rank as an overall success – as well as an example of bravery and discipline on the part of the troops involved in both the first and second attacks.

8. Crisis in the North

B<small>Y LATE AFTERNOON</small> M<small>ILES</small> Dempsey of 13 Brigade had ordered a general retirement to the higher ground about a mile west of the canal, but the Cameronians in the south of his sector had come back too far. At 18.30 'Pop' Gilmore, their CO, ordered a counterattack to regain the Kaleute Ridge to the east of the Warneton–St Eloi road. As Gilmore told the story, there was no time to make a sophisticated plan. He simply strung out the 200 men or so he had available, some of them administrative personnel from HQ Company, in a line about 400 yards long, with two carriers on each flank. They started from the Warneton–St Eloi road south of Oosttaverne, with British artillery firing concentrations in front of them. Gilmore's own carrier patrolled up and down in front of the attack. There are a number of examples during the battle of German troops being intimidated by carriers, which they seem to have mistaken for light tanks. This was one such, and according to Gilmore two German machine-gun teams ran away as his carrier made towards them, even though it was unarmed.[1]

The Cameronians themselves had exhibited nerves on several occasions during the day, with neighbouring formations disapprovingly relating stories of Cameronian units coming back. But Gilmore seems to have inspired them to drive forwards successfully, even though the attack was over open ground with little cover. According to the regimental history heavy casualties were inflicted on the Germans, and hand-to-hand fighting took place on the ridge. Gilmore remembered his intelligence officer, Michael Turner: 'dashing forward, with a pistol in each hand to attack a house from which a machine gun was firing'. By about 1930 a line had been re-established on the ridge. The cost was heavy, though. Five officers were wounded, three killed – Turner among them – and apparently there were about 120 casualties among other ranks.[2]

Gilmore was one of the wounded. With a few other men, one of them his orderly Stephenson – like Gilmore a First World War veteran – he had ended up forward of the main Cameronians' line. He was prevented from going back by heavy German fire on the open ground behind him, so lying in a small field of crops he sniped at the Germans: 'I was kneeling up firing when a shell burst practically on top of me.' This wounded him in the leg, then he was hit shortly afterwards in the stomach. Gilmore was heavily built, leading Franklyn to comment unkindly: 'This portion of his anatomy was so considerable that vital damage was not done.' The leg wound was, in fact, the more serious, and Gilmore was bleeding heavily: 'I thought that the end had come at last, but strangely enough I did not worry overmuch. I felt detached and rather glad to think that all this worry and anxiety would trouble me no longer.' Stephenson dressed his leg wound and Gilmore tried to move, but could only shift himself a few inches with intense pain: 'It was then that I really gave up hope . . . I was sad, and I thought of my wife and all that home meant.'[3]

But then the 121st Psalm, 'the old metric psalm of the Scottish Covenanters' came into Gilmore's mind: 'I to the hills will lift mine eyes, from whence cometh mine aid.' He sang it quietly to himself and gained fresh hope. Knowing 'the methodical Boche of the last war', he expected that when darkness fell the Germans would keep shelling on the same targets. He watched the fall of the shells and planned a route back to the British line. With dusk, aided by Stephenson who, although the smallest man in the battalion, helped shift Gilmore's bulky frame, he began an agonising trip back to the British lines.[4]

Just to the north of the Cameronians were the 2nd Wiltshires. Their war diary was terse, but had a lot of timings. Therefore the sequence of events is known, but not much detail about them. All through the afternoon German troops had been getting closer, and in response the battalion had reinforced their forward companies with carriers. Enemy planes were overhead, although there are no reports of air attack. On two occasions companies fell back, but Eric Moore, the Wiltshires' CO, sent them forwards again. Then darkness fell, and it became clear that the Germans had packed up for the night. This was the signal for a reorganisation of 13 Brigade's front. The Cameronians, having gained part of the ridge east of the road at such cost a few hours before, were now pulled back, although the Wiltshires remained forward on their section of the ridge. It is possible that Dempsey thought the right of the Wiltshires' line extended farther than it did, since 13 Brigade diary placed it in map square 6154, which was (from the imprecise sources available) exactly where the Cameronians attacked. The remains of the Cameronians marched some distance north, to end up between the Wiltshires and the 2nd Inniskillings on the left of 13 Brigade's front. The Cameronians formed a new centre for the brigade, linking the other two battalions, but there was now a gap to the right of the Wiltshires.[5]

The Inniskillings had also retired too far and then returned, although in their case the return was achieved without opposition. They and the RSF of 17 Brigade still occupied the woods on the high ground west of the canal at its big bend just north of Hollebeke. The Inniskillings' denuded front-line posts were 100 yards apart, and the Germans were infiltrating between them 'firing Tommy guns as they went'. The forward companies from both battalions withdrew, each in their diaries accusing the other of being the first to go. The Inniskillings' HQ was not aware of its companies' withdrawal and was subsequently overrun, with Lieutenant-Colonel Lefroy, the CO, and his second-in-command being captured. By the morning the remaining Inniskillings were reunited near Oosttaverne.[6]

In spite of manifold problems, 13 Brigade preserved some sort of line and its battalions some sort of organisation. Equally important, ID 31 had received a real shock that evening as it was hit by counterattacks, of which the Cameronians' was the largest.

ID 31's report summarises what it thought happened. At 1700 Hollebeke had been taken, but Houthem still held out. Here there was continued resistance from Private Wynne, while the remainder of the 1/7th Warwicks were resisting about a mile back from the canal: 'So the south wing of the division is stuck again.' 'At 2200 the British attack the 17th and 82nd infantry regiments with tanks after preparatory shelling which is more than anything the troops have ever experienced. The regiments have lost contact with the battalions of the front line; the division has lost contact with the regiments.'[7]

The entry suggests a major setback. However, even allowing for the fact that German time was one hour ahead, the timing given is much later than the Cameronians' attack, which took place about 1830. Fighting on the ridge went on for some time, but even so there is a discrepancy. There are probably a variety of factors accounting for this, all of which affected ID 31's perception of the battle.[8]

Both the 1/7th Warwicks and the engineers of 245th Field Company, who were with them, launched some localised attacks on IR 82 – ID 31's left-hand regiment – as the Guards and Staffordshires went forwards against ID 61 to the south. The 1/7th Warwicks recorded: 'The Commanding Officer walked calmly along the line and with his encouragement a few local advances were made. The Adjutant retook one farm with his miscellaneous force and the Intelligence Officer another.' The map reference (624534) given shows that this occurred right behind Houthem and so must have been on IR 82's front. Since three Bren carriers from the Staffordshires had joined the Warwicks, the German troops affected might also have got the impression that tanks were involved.[9]

According to ID 31 its other forward regiment, IR 17, was also attacked. On the division's right, this would have faced the Inniskillings and the Wiltshires next to them. The Inniskillings were pulling back, but the Wiltshires may have contributed to the German perception of aggressive British action. At 2130 they reorganised their line on the ridge, the carrier section 'forming the backbone of the defence'. So the Germans there would have seen considerable activity and some forward movement as Moore sent back the companies that had retired, although the amount of actual fighting seems to have been limited.[10]

Nonetheless it seems likely that it was the Cameronians' attack that had the most impact on ID 31. It was accompanied by a heavy bombardment, while the Cameronians' carriers were no doubt taken by the Germans for tanks. The attack may have affected both IR 17 and IR 82, although probably hitting the latter hardest. But how can the discrepancy in timing be accounted for? ID 31's report must have been written up the next day, since it contained comments about events extending into the small hours of the morning. By that time the divisional staff would have become aware of the Wiltshires' movements and the Warwicks' counterattacks, both of which occurred late on. Given that the division's communications with both battalions and regiments were interrupted, presumably because the British bombardment had cut cables, it is not surprising that the staff became confused about the times of attacks, which were spread over a long period. This confusion would have been heightened by the attacks on ID 61, which also went on until late. And yet another factor was the British medium artillery's softening-up fire prior to and during the second southern counterattack, which was directed at ID 31 as well as ID 61. Thus whoever wrote the report probably conflated the various times to arrive at 2200.[11]

The Cameronians' attack may well have led the Germans to think that the counterattacks were more connected than they were and that the British had stronger forces than they actually possessed. Unfortunately a critical section of ID 31's diary has been burnt, but there is still quite a lot of information. It shows that the division was hard hit and needed to rest. IR 82 was so badly affected that it asked to be relieved. This was too complicated and the regiment had to stay in position, but there is a reference to 'restructuring, preparation and vital rest for the troops'. As a result the division's main attack on 28 May was postponed until 1400. 'The Corps was happy with that', since according to the diary ID 31 was now ahead of the other divisions. Presumably IV Corps wanted the other divisions to catch up with ID 31 before beginning a general attack. In the event ID 31 did go on attacking the next morning, but as will be seen most of these attacks were distinctly half-hearted.[12]

Although in the context of the battle as a whole the Cameronians' attack was no more important than the attacks farther south, for ID 31 it was probably decisive both in halting their attack on 27 May and in delaying their attack the next day. The Wiltshires' and Warwickshires' determination to hang on was also a significant factor.

In contrast with the centre, where the day ended not too badly for the British, the situation grew steadily worse for 17 Brigade in the north. The brigade's lead battalions were now stationed on the canal where it bent back and ran almost due west, the RSF occupying the right-hand sector and the Northamptons the left. The Seaforths were in reserve south of the canal, in the vicinity of St Eloi. Subsequent to the battalions' retirement Stopford, the brigadier, faced major problems. The RSF was seriously weakened by their losses in defending Hill 60, and the Inniskillings and Northamptons on either side of them lost contact. The RSF had some respite for a few night-time hours, because as usual there was little German activity apart from machine-gun fire. A brigade message to Tod, the RSF CO, stressing that he should hang on was met with the reply that the Royal Scots 'would do all that was required of them'. This was later parlayed by the War Office Public Relations Department into 'tell Brigade I'm not going a foot back' – a melodramatic statement that Tod may or may not have made. At 0300 Stopford, who cannot have had much rest that night, visited battalion HQ to convey the brigade message personally. Since the RSF were probably already surrounded, Stopford may well have passed through the enemy to reach them.[13]

The Northamptons were not involved in the battle until the afternoon of 27 May, but by 1800 the forward companies reported strong enemy attacks. They were forced back onto the ridge east of St Eloi, which overlooked the canal. Major Watts, the second-in-command, took up a party of officers from battalion HQ together with RSF stragglers to reinforce the ridge, while RSM [Regimental Sergeant-Major] Howard brought up ammunition 'across a heavily shelled area'. 'By now everyone was intensely weary, but there was little chance of rest for the officers, who had to visit the men continuously to ensure that they were on the alert.'[14]

Stopford visited the Northampton's HQ some time after midnight in order to pass on his message to stand firm, before going onto the RSF. According to the brigade war diary, the Northamptons' Major R. M. J. Wetherall, who was in command, 'appeared to have a good grasp of the situation and was unruffled. [The] brigadier discussed the arrangements to be made for sending out patrols across the Ypres–Comines Canal which was now the line of the FDLs.' The Northamptons' war diary put this rather differently. Stopford 'gave orders for B and D companies to try to re-occupy their positions on the canal'. Given that they were now some way back from the canal, this version is a more accurate description of what had to be done. The orders seem unrealistic, since the Northamptons had started the day well below strength and suffered further losses. They certainly proved impossible to fulfil. The battalion diary continued: 'B and D Companies attacked at first light but met with strong enemy opposition, and were unable to advance.' Under continuing heavy fire, the Northamptons waited on the ridge.[15]

If Stopford had received some comfort from Wetherall and Tod, he had not received much from the Seaforths' CO, Lieutenant-Colonel Reid, whom he visited first that night. The Seaforths had given way in the morning, when they had been stationed on the railway and had, it can be inferred, been put in reserve in the vicinity of St Eloi to enable some reorganisation. This did not seem to have done much good. The battalion was still being shelled, and at 2030 the brigade liaison officer reported: '6 Seaforth were retiring from their reserve line having been outflanked by enemy infantry and were coming under M.G. fire from the left.' The war diary stated: 'Brigade-Major and Brigade Information Officer went to discover what the situation was, and gave orders from the brigadier to all officers and NCOs whom they met that the original position was to be re-occupied forthwith.' When Stopford visited them later, both the CO and the adjutant 'appeared to be somewhat shaken'. Stopford contented himself with 'verbal orders regarding reorganising and holding the reserve position'.[16]

ID 18 was the German division facing 17 Brigade, but its diary is short of detail on this stage of the battle. It merely stated that a battalion of IR 54, by that time the only regiment actively engaged in the attack, managed to get a bridgehead west of Hollebeke 'by dint of sustained hard fighting'. Hollebeke itself was on ID 31's front, and the implication of this is that IR 54 crossed the canal where it runs almost due west and obtained a lodgement near St Eloi, where the Seaforths were stationed. There it made contact with the right wing of ID 31, 'whose bridgehead turned out to be much less deep'. ID 31 had said much the same about ID 18's depth of penetration, so clearly the British were not the only ones to be confused about the location of neighbouring units. In this case ID 18 was correct, since St Eloi is farther west than the ridge above Hollebeke, where ID 31 were still fighting the Inniskillings during the evening.[17]

Fortunately the artillery was still in position and able to pour fire on the advancing Germans. The Northamptons' history indicated the sort of impact this could have. The forward companies:

> got good support from the Gunners: for example, within ten minutes of the receipt from 'B' Company of the map-reference of an enemy mortar a 25-pounder battery just behind Battalion HQ had engaged the target and ten minutes later the company signalled 'Magnificent show! Men very pleased with R.A. Blown up men and mortar in wood.'[18]

However the enemy advance was itself posing problems for some of the field regiments. During the afternoon and early evening 20/76 battery, west of Wytschaete, twice had to move its OPs, which were east of Wytschaete, and it was in danger of being outflanked on its left. At 2015, as the tension increased, 20/76 battery recorded: 'Large number of enemy infantry attacking. Advancing across the open in lines. Engaged by the whole battery.' At 2045 the OP was moved again to the Warneton–St Eloi road and the battery again 'engaged advancing enemy infantry'. As with 97th Field at Warneton, the artillery acted as a rallying point – and a stiffening – for the infantry: 'Stragglers coming back into Wytschaete were pulled up and made to man the ditches by the roadside.' At 2200 the OP was withdrawn and, because the forward positions of British troops was not known, there was no firing during the night.[19]

The 91st Field Regiment, supporting the northern sector, was also close to the action. Its HQ was in the Wytschaete area and during the evening its diarist noted that the situation in the St Eloi area became more critical, implying that the batteries were near there. By 2000: 'Enemy infantry [were] reported within few hundred yards of D, E and A Troops' positions. Our own troops were holding line just in front of these positions.' Later, the diary recorded: 'C.O. orders Gun Control owing to proximity of enemy.' The Headquarters Royal Artillery (HQRA) 5th Division diary claimed: '91st Field Regiment and 1 Platoon of 9th Manchesters staged counter attack to save their guns, gaining 500 yards and holding off enemy until gap filled.' Since the regiment's own diary modestly did not mention this, it may be a garbled version of what happened. At 0330 on 28 May the regiment was ordered back to Kemmel, completing the move successfully with the exception of D Troop, who 'were caught by enemy infantry in process of winching their guns out of position', losing two guns as a result. The Germans started their attack on this sector at 0430, and this early start may have caught the British by surprise.[20]

Meanwhile all the medium artillery regiments bar one were supporting the counterattack farther south. 69th Medium, which only started firing at 2100 hours on 27 May, was not involved and instead its fifteen 4.5-inch guns were tasked with harassing fire on the Menin–Ypres road, but this would have been of little immediate value to the British troops facing attack in the area round St Eloi. At 1800, before the counterattack started, there is a puzzling entry in 5th Medium's diary, which stated: 'Regt fired on and practically destroyed St Eloi.' At that time St Eloi was still behind the British lines and indeed, technically, held by the Seaforths, although there was German penetration going on in the area. If the entry is accurate then the orders to fire must have been given without full knowledge of the situation, and 5th Medium may have been shelling British troops.[21]

As the crisis at the northern end of the line loomed, there was help at hand. Events ran roughly like this. Realising on 27 May that 5th Division was facing an extremely difficult situation, Brooke had told Johnson of 4th Division to detach a brigade and send it to Franklyn. Johnson chose 10 Brigade, under Evelyn Barker (not to be confused with Michael Barker, GOC of I Corps). However, the move took time, because 4th Division was still south of the Lys, 10 Brigade itself being in the Tourcoing area between Menin and Lille. As Barker remembered it in a postwar letter to Joslen, the Official History 'narrator': 'About lunch-time on the 27th May I received orders that the brigade was to move to Ploegsteert and come under command of 5 Div.' Barker went to Ploegsteert and met unit reconnaissance parties that had already arrived there. This speaks well for the British ability to move fast when necessary. He then went to 5th Division HQ nearby, where he was told that the situation had changed. Evidently Franklyn had been alerted to the growing difficulties in the centre and north, and the brigade was now directed to Wytschaete Ridge. Barker left his batman at a crossroads to redirect units already on the move, hurried back to Tourcoing to give fresh instructions, and then proceeded to Wytschaete, 'where I found HQ of 13 and 17 Brigade together in an *estaminet*, and found out the latest situation'.[22] According to 17 Brigade's war diary:

> [Barker] arrived at Brigade HQ to say that his brigade had been ordered up to help restore the situation. He proposed to push his carriers on to the Ypres-Warneton road at once to form a stop and then to move up battalions during the night with a view to carrying out a counterattack in the morning. After discussing plans with the Brigadier [Stopford] and Brigadier Dempsey he said that he would return later the same night to arrange details for

tomorrow's counterattack. He did not re-appear until the morning of 28 and the counterattack did not develop until the afternoon of that day.[23]

The diary entry is a trifle acerbic. Barker was probably unwise to make promises, but in fairness he and 10 Brigade were not having an easy time. Their initial orders had been changed and, since the battalions could not simply walk away from their positions in the front line, some units had to be left behind to maintain a defence. Furthermore transport was difficult – not surprisingly, as the transport companies must have been working under extreme pressure.[24]

10 Brigade's three battalions – the 2nd Bedfordshire & Hertfordshire (Beds & Herts), the 2nd DCLI and the 1/6th East Surrey – trickled into the Wytschaete area during the night or the next day. On arrival at Wytschaete the DCLI were the farthest forward on the 5th Division front, prolonging 13 Brigade's line north of Oosttaverne along the road to St Eloi. By 0600 on 28 May the left of the battalion, nearest St Eloi, was under attack and a party of Seaforths was withdrawing through them.[25]

Franklyn freely admitted that, in concentrating on the southern sector, he had to leave 13 and 17 Brigades to their own devices, even though the situation in the north was almost as bad as that in the south: '. . . I knew that no one could cope more effectively with such a difficult situation than Stopford. In any case, I could do nothing to help him and I had to leave it to him to work out his own salvation.' True to form Franklyn in his memoir then had a dig at Stopford, suggesting that it was a pity that he should have placed 'the one territorial battalion in the whole division' – that is, the Seaforths – on the exposed left flank.

Stopford's dilemma was that the Northamptons, which initially he put in reserve, were seriously under strength. Given the length of the line that his left battalion had to occupy – which Franklyn never seems to have appreciated – Stopford may have felt that he needed as many men as he could in the front line. And as has been seen two other territorial battalions, 1/7th Warwicks and 8th Warwicks of 143 Brigade, put up a good resistance.[26]

The basic problem was that 17 Brigade had far too few men to fill the gap between them and 50th Division in Ypres. Once they had been forced back on the canal where it bent westwards, the gap was even harder to fill, and presumably Stopford then took the Seaforths back into reserve rather than placing them on the new front line because they were too demoralised to be of much immediate use.

Knowledge of the gap may have influenced Stopford in his orders on the night of 27/28 May, when he chose to leave the battalions where they were – the RSF near the canal and the Northamptons on the ridge behind it. His dispositions can be questioned: Dempsey had drawn 13 Brigade's line back to the main Warneton–St Eloi road, and this withdrawal seems sensible. Stopford must have known about it as the two brigade's HQs were together. He could similarly have drawn back the remains of the RSF and the Northamptons, thus forming a coherent and shorter line linking with 13 Brigade and running up from Oosttaverne through St Eloi. Shortening his line would have given him spare troops to block German infiltration round his left flank. Whether Stopford made the best arrangements will be discussed in the next chapter.

Apart from the hope of linking up with 50th Division, one other factor clearly influenced Stopford. This was the possibility of speedy relief by 10 Brigade, stimulated by Barker's rash promise. Both the Northamptons' diary and the RSF's history recorded Stopford as saying on his late night visits to them that relief was at hand. Given the difficulties that everyone had had with transport in the previous few days, it was perhaps oversanguine to take Barker so literally.[27]

The gap with 50th Division exercised Franklyn from time to time, as Brooke was nagging him about it. Franklyn wrote later that he was 'constantly being urged to get in touch with 50th Division, but I still think it would have been more reasonable if that division, which was never engaged, had been asked to fill the gap themselves'. In fact 50th Division did have some fighting in and around Ypres, and Brooke was also urging them to close the gap. On 28 May he issued more definite orders to Martel, the division's GOC, to clear the situation up.[28]

The crisis on the evening of 27 May was also reflected in Franklyn's memoir. He had committed the Guards and Staffordshires to the counterattack in the south when Stopford reported his critical situation:

> Brooke was in my office. For the first and only time during the battle he expressed his anxiety and asked me what I was going to do about it. I replied with some heat that it was my responsibility and not his. He just smiled and left. Of course there was nothing I could do but leave the matter to Stopford.

Franklyn recorded that Brooke subsequently sent him 10 Brigade, but this allocation had, of course, been made much earlier, and Franklyn had already directed 10 Brigade to Wytschaete Ridge. Thus Franklyn's account of this meeting must be confused, because surely he would have told Brooke what he planned to do with 10 Brigade before venting his irritation. In fact, in an interview in connection with Bryant's book, Franklyn remembered two visits from Brooke on the 27th – one in the morning and one in the evening – at both of which Brooke had used the phrase: 'What are you going to do?' It was at the first that Franklyn had expressed his anxieties about his right, which led Brooke to allocate him 10 Brigade and to get hold of the battalions from 1st Division.[29]

Franklyn freely admitted his anxieties in his memoir, as Brooke did in his, although both appeared imperturbable to others. Brooke's responsibility was not just to 5th Division but also to II Corps and, as II Corps guarded the eastern flank, to the whole BEF. On the night of 27/28 May the remainder of the BEF south of the Lys was due to move north. 10 Brigade had already moved up, and on the 28th the rest of the 4th Division infantry also was deployed to support 5th Division. But 3rd Division, also in II Corps, had to make a longer move, to north of Ypres, where they would continue the line along the Yser Canal to Noordschote.[30]

Brooke in his memoir has left a graphic description of 3rd Division's move. By jettisoning much equipment it was able to travel in its own vehicles, supplemented by troop carriers. Brooke's HQ was in a farm near Ploegsteert on the road that 3rd Division was using:

> There was little possibility of sleep that night, as the 3rd Division were moving past and I repeatedly went out to see how they were progressing . . . with the congestion on the roads, road-blocks outside villages, and many other blocks caused by refugees and their carts, the division was frequently brought to a standstill. The whole movement seemed unbearably slow; the hours of darkness were slipping by; should daylight arrive with the road crammed with vehicles the casualties from bombing might well have been disastrous.
>
> Our own guns were firing from the vicinity of Mount Kemmel, whilst German artillery was answering back, and the division was literally trundling slowly along in the darkness down a pergola of artillery fire, and within some 4,000 yards of a battle-front which had been fluctuating all day somewhat to our disadvantage. It was an eerie sight which I shall never forget. Before dawn came, the last vehicles had disappeared northwards into the darkness . . .[31]

The next morning, 28 May, Brooke visited Montgomery: 'Found he had as usual accomplished almost the impossible and marched from Roubaix to north of Ypres, a flank march past front of attack, and was firmly established in the line with French DLM* to the north.'[32]

---

* Brooke wrongly called the DLM (Division Légère Mécanique) the Division Lourde Motorisée.

1st and 42nd Divisions of I Corps were also on the move from south and east of Lille on the night of 27/28 May. They crossed the Lys at Frelinghiem and Houplines to the west of 3rd Division and moved towards the Dunkirk perimeter. Meanwhile 2nd Division in the southwest had fought a courageous and sacrificial battle on the 27th, and the German panzer forces made only slow progress on that front. It was in this battle that one hundred men of the Royal Norfolks were massacred after surrendering to the SS Totenkopf Division. The scattered remnants of 2nd Division also then made their way north.[33]

While the British divisions were escaping, not far away the final act of a tragedy was being played out. Leopold III, the Belgian king, capitulated, a ceasefire being arranged from midnight on 27 May. Leopold's actions have been the subject of much debate, but this is not of concern here. The immediate point is that there was now nothing to distract the attention of the Germans on the northeastern front. They could concentrate on attacking the British line stretching northwards from Lys to the coast. And north of Noordschote that line was defended only sparsely or not at all. The Belgian capitulation was not unexpected given the information about the Belgian army that the British were receiving from the 25th onwards. Nonetheless although the British mission at Belgian HQ heard of the Belgian armistice request on the evening of 27 May, its message to GHQ was misplaced or did not arrive, and Gort did not hear of the request until 2300 that night. So the news must have been a shock.[34]

To the Germans, of course, it was a triumph. The British perspective on the campaign usually discounts the Belgian contribution, in line with the views of Gort, Pownall and Brooke. But the Germans saw an enemy that originally possessed a larger army than the BEF and had absorbed much of Army Group B's fighting capacity for more than two weeks. IV Corps' history noted about their attack on 5th Division:

> The day that had begun with such high hopes did not fulfil our expectations . . . All the same, morale stayed positive because one event overshadowed everything else: the capitulation of the Belgian army. At 2200 the news came over the radio, intercepted by the 31st Division. It was a great moment no one on the staff will ever forget.

Army Group B's war diary devoted a considerable amount of space to the surrender, compared to only a small amount on the canal battle.[35]

9. Hanging On

28 May

As dawn broke on 5th Division on the 28th, the northern part of its line consisted of little more than isolated remnants of the 2nd Northamptons and the 2nd RSF holding out in forward positions. In the centre, however, a coherent line had been re-formed on or near the Warneton–St Eloi road, although it was thinly manned. Behind these troops, reinforcements from 10 Brigade were getting into position. In the south, German ID 61 had received a major setback in the form of a series of successful counterattacks. From now on, however, the British troops there would have to fight things out without much further help.

12 Brigade was on the north bank of the Lys or holding the crossings. It could only give limited assistance to the existing line-holders who were north and west of Comines: its prime role was to defend the Lys, because, now that British troops had virtually completed their pull-out from south of that river, the Germans could occupy the vacated territory and pose a new threat to 5th Division.[1]

The night was an uncomfortable one in the south for the troops, whether British or German. It was raining, and the fighting of the evening had left both sides occupying scratch positions, often in ditches or open fields. Lance-Sergeant Charles Constantine was in the open, prepared for a German attack: 'Everyone lay there silently in almost continuous rain, for hours, waiting for the next orders to come. So passed the rest of what was a most miserable night.'[2]

Constantine's unit, the 3rd Grenadier Guards, had taken part in the second counterattack the previous evening and was now holding the front line, running upstream along the Kortekeer river from the Warneton–Comines railway. North of the Guards the line was held for a further 2,000 yards or so by a conglomeration of 2nd North Staffordshires, also participants in the second counterattack, and the original line-holders – the 8th Warwicks and the 1/7th Warwicks. The latter occupied the most northerly section, their line running for about 1,000 yards north of the Garde Dieux crossroads.

The Staffordshires recorded intermittent shelling and machine-gun fire during the night, and the 1/7th Warwicks' diary noted: 'Nobody had any sleep this night, but by this time we were all accustomed to working without any rest.' In spite – or because of – this the 1/7th Warwicks were up early and anticipated the Germans in taking the initiative. At 0500 2nd Lieutenant Davies patrolled to a farm occupied by the enemy and 'successfully engaged this strong point'. Half an hour later Captain Holdich searched the cellar of another farm that had been captured in the Warwicks' counterattacks the night before and discovered nine Germans who were taken prisoner. Then the Germans began their attack.[3]

The diaries of the 1/7th Warwicks and 245th Field Company, the engineer unit fighting with them, convey the flavour of the second day of a hard-fought and exhausting battle. Lieutenant Evans' section of 245th Field Company occupied the farm in which the prisoners were discovered. This was 'defended throughout the day and heavy casualties inflicted on the enemy on left flank with Bren fire . . . German A-T [anti-tank] Gun team shot and dispersed and A. T. Gun captured in evening and later destroyed.' The 1/7th Warwicks were given 'wonderful support from a platoon of M.G.s from the Gordons, which [had] its guns right up in the front line with our Brens'. Although 'ammunition supply was excellent', physical conditions were anything but – 'no food other than bully beef and biscuits arrived' – while at about midday it started to rain. There was also continual shelling and mortaring, although this was answered by British artillery, so 'shells were constantly whistling overhead'.

In spite of this, German pressure seems to have been steady but never threatened disaster: 'On several occasions the enemy tried to advance in open formation to the South of Battalion H. Q. [that is on the Warwicks' right] but were very effectively stopped by the Gordons' and our own fire.' The British artillery also contributed – 245th Field Company's diary recording: 'On the right enemy massed in the wood and was obviously planning an attack. Field and medium artillery plastered the wood and assembly points. A magnificent bombardment in which they expended tons of ammunition. Enemy attack proved abortive.' In turn the 1/7th Warwicks said of 245th Field Company's Major Garwood that '[his] courage was an example to all of us', while his men 'fought stubbornly with us during the whole battle'.[4]

Next in line to the south, the Staffordshires and the 8th Warwicks were intermingled. The Staffordshires mentioned two attacks during the day, in the morning and the evening, and the 8th Warwicks recorded some bouts of heavy shelling, including twenty minutes from a British 25-pounder battery on their own lines. But the German effort here seems to have been limited. It was the Guards

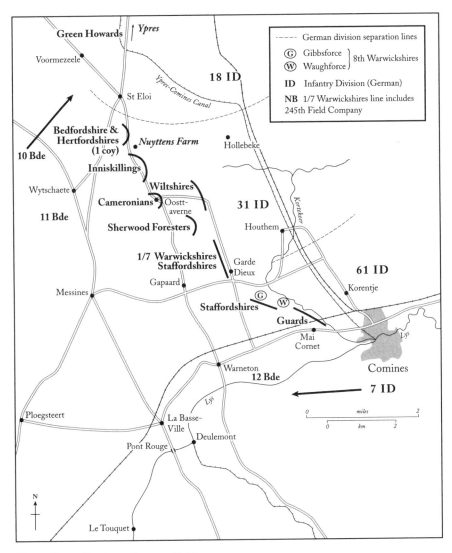

Map 5: *Ypres–Comines, afternoon 28 May*

farther south still who bore the brunt of German attacks in this sector. After the British counterattacks the original German regiment on the Guards' front, IR 176, had been replaced with IR 151. Thus the Guards faced a unit that was fresh, although it would have been exposed to the British artillery's harassing fire on 27 May. The Guards' forward companies occupied a ditch just to the west of the river Kortekeer.

The British had no tools but had deepened the ditch a little with their bayonets. As the regimental history described the action:

> In front of the ditch there was a downward slope ... which the Battalion kept covered by their machine guns pushed slightly ahead of the main infantry line. The German method of attack, which was repeated several times during the day, was to follow behind a heavy mortar barrage in groups of fifteen to twenty, spaced out in wide, arrow-head formation. The Grenadiers waited until they were close enough to see the detail of their equipment (the Germans, strangely enough, were all dressed in greatcoats) and then opened up with a stream of bullets which could scarcely miss their mark ... The enemy then withdrew out of sight, and in a few moments a belt of fire descended on the Bren posts; but this had been foreseen, and the gunners were back out of harm's way. The same performance was then repeated ... From behind, the 3-inch mortars, under Platoon Sergeant Major H. Wood, D.C.M., supported the forward companies with an accurate torrent of bombs.[5]

The history described the German tactics as 'futile'. But the Germans were also infiltrating round the flanks, and Captain Denis Dodd, from the 8th Warwicks but then commanding 143 Brigade's anti-tank company in theory – and in practice serving as a brigade liaison officer – had personal experience of this. He was carrying a message from the brigade to the Guards by motorcycle when, some way along the Warneton–Comines road, he was ambushed by two Germans hiding in a cemetery. Dodd was wounded and later picked up by German stretcher-bearers.[6] The road was just south of the railway, and it seems likely that the Germans had crept along here while the Black Watch and other units in the vicinity were preoccupied with the north bank of the Lys. Adair, the Guards' CO, takes up the story:

> At about 10 a.m. some enemy with Tommy guns, who had worked round the flank, started shooting at Battalion Headquarters, and from this moment we were in the thick of the fray. A direct hit from a shell on a carrier at the back of the farm set it on fire – ammunition in it was popping and banging in all directions – and shortly afterwards the barn behind us was ablaze. Luckily we had dug in some posts nearby, and from this the Second-in-Command, Major Smith, and Adjutant, Captain C. Earle, and others did some masterly shooting.[7]

The Guards were assisted by a platoon of 9th Manchesters with their Vickers machine guns, who had been sent up to battalion HQ: 'By the end of the day', according to Adair, 'they had fired over 35,000 rounds and thoroughly enjoyed themselves.'[8]

The Guards continued to hang on during the afternoon, although ammunition supply in the forward companies was becoming a problem. Two carriers were loaded up with ammunition cases and sent out from battalion HQ, but unfortunately most of the cases contained Verey lights. Apparently these had the merit, when fired, of confusing the Germans who mistook them for their own light signals, so mortaring ceased. Rations and that staple of the British army, tea, reached battalion HQ, but it was impossible to get them out to the forward companies, which had had no proper meal for thirty-six hours.[9]

Lance-Sergeant Constantine was with No. 4 Company, originally one of the reserve companies but now in the front line, and his reminiscence gives a vivid picture of the battle from the point of view of one small group at the sharp end of the fighting. He was sent just before dawn with his section to a small barn nearby. Evidently they were not defending the field ditch line, so presumably his position was at one end of the Guards' front. The enemy were behind a hedge in the adjacent field:

> The barn had been used as a storeroom and was empty except for a pile of potatoes against the far wall. I told the men to equal themselves around the walls and to knock out a brick or two for firing positions . . . We had just prepared ourselves when the enemy put in a big attack. I got myself in a good position, lying at an angle on the potatoes, and could see the firing had started from the far hedge of the field about two hundred yards to our front. We saw plenty of movement and returned the fire; much to our satisfaction we saw several enemy soldiers go down, not to move again. They had started to come forwards and some had managed to get into the long grass and small hollows in different parts of the field and were trying to surround us. Bullets were penetrating the brickwork of the old barn and one or two would ricochet amongst us. Now and again one would come through the wall and specks of white would appear where the bullets had gone through the potatoes.[10]

Constantine's Bren gunner was wounded in the eye and, in spite of efforts to help him, ran in agony out of the door. Then a German who had crawled close to the barn ran up to it with an 'automatic weapon' – probably a machine pistol – and Constantine shot him. Constantine feared that German mortars would soon get their range, but during the afternoon German fire slackened: 'At last we were able to light up a cigarette, something we had not managed to do these last few hours.' The German quiescence continued, and it started to rain heavily. Constantine could not stop looking at and thinking about the dead German close by and 'could not get these thoughts out of my mind. A tear came to my eye and I knew then that I must force myself to think of something different.'[11]

Although the fighting on the Guards' sector wound down in the afternoon, earlier on it had been quite heavy and losses had been actually greater than during the counterattack. On 27 May one officer was killed (Crompton-Roberts) and one wounded (Brinkman), and nine other ranks were killed. On the 28th no officers were killed although five were wounded, but fifteen other ranks were killed. This suggests that the counterattack incurred about forty casualties – most, no doubt, in the forward platoons of Crompton-Roberts' and Brinkman's companies. But on 28 May, even though the Guards were defending, they must have suffered fifty casualties or more.[12]

From the German perspective, the combination of the rain and the British defence was deeply debilitating. ID 61's history for 28 May described their situation:

In the wooded ground round the Kortekeer brook the companies were under heavy enemy fire. All efforts to get the attack under way again fizzled out. Probing enemy armoured cars and ever stronger machine gun fire kept the infantry under cover. From hedges and houses, from haystacks and roofs, the admirably camouflaged opponent, well organised for defence, maintained fire. Snipers behind trees with automatic weapons, swept the meadows with their fire, armoured cars standing well hidden behind hedges and adapted as armoured machine gun nests, reduced the effectiveness of the anti-tank units by swift and skilful changes of position. Lying on the flat slopes the companies were exposed to enemy fire and soon had to dig in. Unceasing rain hampered vision and made it even more difficult to attack the few enemy targets.

Enemy artillery fire systematically strafed the front line right up to the top of the regimental command post ... and soon the enemy armoured attack was under way. The situation of the previous day seemed to be repeated. A few tanks were wiped out, but on the other hand our own losses mounted: Oberleutnant Christofzik, Leutnant Mendritzki (both of IR 151) and numerous valued junior officers and men. Among the fallen was also the son of the divisional commander. The increasingly heavy rain had thoroughly soaked the clay soil. The men stood knee deep in water. Flanders mud clung

to the whole body and made weapons and equipment dirty. The tank straps
of the 08/15 automatic weapons were, for the greater part, unusable, our
own firepower was, therefore, much reduced.[13]

Some of this is almost a mirror image of the British accounts, although what was
to the British *ad hoc* resistance by different units who were not necessarily even in
touch becomes in ID 61's history a 'well-organised' defence. As usual with German
accounts of the battle there were references to tanks. By then there were no British
tanks taking part in the battle, and the 'tanks' must have been carriers, of which a
few were still operational. Given that the British forces in the southern sector on
28 May launched no significant counterattacks, carriers must have been mainly
used in static defensive positions. These were transmuted by the Germans into
well-hidden 'armoured cars'. The occasional forays by carriers, mainly to replenish
ammunition and food, became an 'armoured attack'.[14]

Although the British perceived the German shelling to be steady and at times
heavy, the Germans saw it differently. ID 61's history recorded: 'As a result of
shortage of ammunition, the intended heavy artillery fire did not materialise.' In
other words, whatever the British perceived, the Germans did not have the fire
support they thought that they needed. Sergeant Constantine remembered a virtual
cessation of German fire by the late afternoon, and the Staffordshires' war diary
also noted that 'fire quietened down', although it did not give any time.

On the British side 97th Field recorded that it 'was firing all day without
stopping', at times at the specific request of the Guards. According to Adair some
of the British fire was directed at the Guards rather than at the Germans, because
of the difficulty of establishing the exact position of the respective front lines. But
ID 61's history quoted above suggests that plenty of fire reached the Germans.[15]

The southernmost end of the sector was held by 12 Brigade, 4th Division's
rearguard. One company of 6th Black Watch, a 12 Brigade battalion, had participated
in the first counterattack on 27 May. The rest of the Black Watch crossed at Warneton
during the night and 'pushed forward on the North side of the canal [that is, the
canalised Lys] to contain the enemy as far to the East as possible'. Here they would
have faced the southernmost battalion of IR 151 somewhere to the west of Comines,
as well as guarding the bank of the Lys facing south. The other battalions of 12
Brigade – 2nd Royal Fusiliers and 1st South Lancashires – also crossed on the night
of 27/28 May and held the Lys from Warneton westwards. The carrier platoons of
these two battalions remained south of the Lys to cover the withdrawal of the final

British units – the final detachment of the South Lancashires crossing at around 1600 hours. It was probably the last organised British unit to go.[16]

Early on 28 May ID 61 launched an attack on the Black Watch, but it was successfully held with the help of the Royal Fusiliers. For whatever reason ID 61 seems to have concentrated its efforts on the main body of the Guards north of the Comines-Warneton railway – fruitlessly, as has been seen. ID 7 marching up south of the Lys posed even less of a threat. Apart from the obstacle of the canalised river itself – unlike the Ypres–Comines Canal, the Lys had plenty of water in it – ID 7 was constrained by the fact that it would be attacking at right angles to the existing attack by ID 61. Nevertheless there is a suggestion that some action was underway or planned, because at 1815 IV Corps was ordered by Sixth Army to stop ID 7 from going north of the river. The emphasis instead should be on ID 18's attack in the north, in order to cut off the British line of retreat.[17]

In the centre, on 13 Brigade's front, German action was even more limited than in the south, with little in the way of direct attack. On the right the Cameronians had been replaced by the Sherwood Foresters, one of the three battalions from 1st Division that had been allocated to Franklyn on 27 May. Unlike the Guards and the Staffordshires, which had immediately been swept up into the counterattack, the Sherwood Foresters had been resting overnight near Messines. Their move into the space vacated by the Cameronians was slowed by an air attack – one of the very few during the battle – which wounded the CO and killed the adjutant.

The battalion had taken up position by mid-morning, but the brigade right flank appears to have been undefended for quite a long period. It may be, as suggested in the last chapter, that Dempsey thought the Wiltshires' line extended farther to the right than it did. Whether or not this was the case the Wiltshires' CO, Eric Moore, and his men were unheralded heroes of the battle, since they stayed in the same position on both the 27th and 28th, and their only withdrawals were quickly rectified.[18]

In fact Dempsey's slowness in filling the gap did not really matter, because the northernmost part of 1/7th Warwicks' line, extended on the far left by 245th Field Company Royal Engineers, had a good field of fire over much of the territory to its left, that is, to the right of the Wiltshires. ID 31 had already reported its 'south wing', opposite the Warwicks/Engineers, stuck on 27 May. Yet again on the morning of the 28th the left wing of IR 82, the division's southernmost regiment, was held back by 'flanking fire from Houthem', while its report noted 'stout [British] resistance, fighting for every single house' in the village. Although Private Wynne

ABOVE: *Harold Franklyn (front, in profile) inspecting troops at Richmond, Yorkshire, in 1939.*

BELOW: *From left to right: Sir Winston Churchill, Lord Gort and Henry Pownall at Gort's billet at Avesnes, 5 November 1939.*

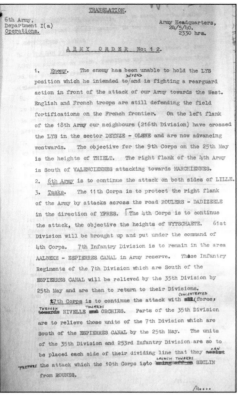

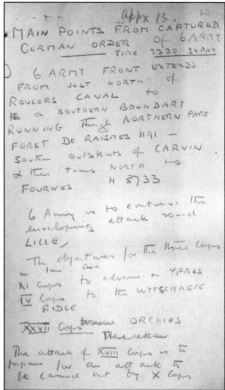

TRANSLATION.

6th Army,
Department I(a)
Operations.

Army Headquarters,
24/5/40.
2330 hrs.

A R M Y   O R D E R   No: 1 2.

1. Enemy. The enemy has been unable to hold the LYS
position which he intended to/and is fighting a rearguard
action in front of the attack of our Army towards the West.
English and French troops are still defending the field
fortifications on the French frontier.   On the left flank
of the 18th Army our neighbours (216th Division) have crossed
the LYS in the sector DEYNZE - OLSNE and are now advancing
westwards.   The objective for the 9th Corps on the 25th May
is the heights of THIELT.   The right flank of the 4th Army
is South of VALENCIENNES attacking towards MARCHIENNES.

2. 6th Army is to continue the attack on both sides of LILLE.

3. Tasks.   The 11th Corps is to protect the right flank
of the Army by attacks across the road ROULERS - DADIZEELE
in the direction of YPRES.   The 4th Corps is to continue
the attack, the objective the heights of WYTSCHAETE.   61st
Division will be brought up and put under the command of
4th Corps.   7th Infantry Division is to remain in the area
AALBEKE - ESPIERRES CANAL in Army reserve.   Those Infantry
Regiments of the 7th Division which are South of the
ESPIERRES CANAL will be relieved by the 35th Division by
25th May and are then to return to their Divisions.
27th Corps is to continue the attack with all forces
towards NIVELLE and ORCHIES.   Parts of the 35th Division
are to relieve those units of the 7th Division which are
South of the ESPIERRES CANAL by the 25th May.   The units
of the 35th Division and 253rd Infantry Division are so to
be placed each side of their dividing line that they can assist
prepare the attack which the 10th Corps is to launch towards SECLIN
from ROUNES.

/M.....

MAIN POINTS FROM CAPTURED
GERMAN ORDER OF 6 ARMY
TIME 2330 24 MAY

6 ARMY FRONT EXTENDS
FROM JUST NORTH of
ROULERS CANAL to
HE a SOUTHERN BOUNDARY
RUNNING Through NORTHERN PART
FORET DE RAISNES H91 —
South outskirts of CARVIN.
& then turns NORTH to
FOURNES   H 5733

6 Army is to continue the
enveloping attack round
LILLE,
The objectives for the three Corps
in line are
XI Corps to advance on YPRES
IV Corps to the WYTSCHAETE
RIDGE
XXVII Corps towards ORCHIES
Then either
The attack of XVIII Corps is to
prepare for an attack to
be carried out by X Corps

ABOVE LEFT: *First page of Whitefoord's full translation of the German orders of the 24th.*

ABOVE RIGHT: *First page of Lieutenant-Colonel Pat Whitefoord's summary of the German orders of 24 May.*

BELOW: *The Lys at Warneton. As can be seen, it was a much more formidable obstacle than the Ypres-Comines Canal (opposite).*

ABOVE: *The Ypres–Comines Canal at Comines. Although the banks have been tidied up, the photograph gives an idea of the state of the Canal for much of its length; from the descriptions given in war diaries, it was much the same in 1940.*

BELOW: *View from 245th Field Company's position on the far left of the 1/7th Warwickshire's line as on 28 May 1940, looking roughly north. With its extensive field of fire, the British position here held up the left flank of ID 31's attack.*

ABOVE: *Alan Brooke photographed while sitting for a portrait being painted by E. G. Eves on 30 April 1940, only ten days before the German attack.*

BELOW: *An extract from the diary of the 1/6th South Staffordshire Regiment, a pioneer battalion helping to defend Ypres, for 28 May. The diary is fairly typical, although rather fuller than most. It was evidently written up later.*

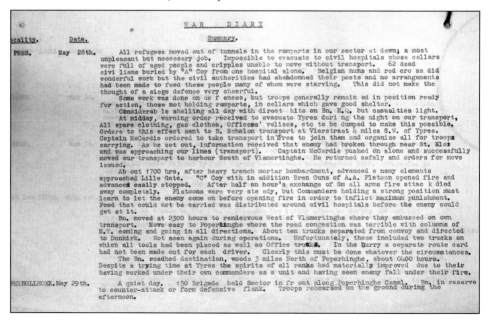

WAR DIARY

Locality.	Date.	Summary.

PRES. — May 28th.

All refugees moved out of tunnels in the ramparts in our sector at dawn; a most unpleasant but necessary job. Impossible to evacuate to civil hospitals whose cellars were full of aged people and cripples unable to move without transport. 62 dead civilians buried by "A" Coy from one hospital alone. Belgian nuns and red cross did wonderful work but the civil authorities had abandonned their posts and no arrangements had been made to feed these people many of whom were starving. This did not make the thought of a siege defence very cheerful.

Some work was done on defences, but troops generally remained in position ready for action, those not holding ramparts, in cellars which gave good shelter.

Considerable shelling all day with direct hits on Bn. H.Q. but casualties light.

At midday, warning order received to evacuate Ypres during the night on our transport. All spare clothing, gas clothes, Officers' velises, etc to be dumped to make this possible. Orders to this effect sent to B. Echelon transport at Vierstraat 4 miles S.W. of Ypres. Captain McCardie ordered to take transport in Ypres to join them and organize all for troops carrying. As he set out, information received that enemy had broken through near St. Eloi and was approaching our lines (transport). Captain McCardie pushed on alone and successfully moved our transport to harbour South of Vlamertinghe. He returned safely and orders for move issued.

About 1700 hrs, after heavy trench mortar bombardment, advanced enemy elements approached Lille Gate. "C" Coy with in addition Bren Guns of A.A. Platoon opened fire and advanced easily stopped. After half an hour's exchange of Small arms fire attack died away completely. Platoons were very steady, but Commanders holding a strong position must learn to let the enemy come on before opening fire in order to inflict maximum punishment. Food that could not be carried was distributed around civil hospitals before the enemy could get at it.

Bn. moved at 2300 hours to rendezvous West of Vlamertinghe where they embussed on own transport. Move easy to Poperinghe where the road congestion was terrible with columns of M.T. coming and going in all directions. About ten trucks separated from convoy and directed to Dunkirk. Not seen again during operations. Unfortunately, these included two trucks on which all tools had been placed as well as Office trucks. In the hurry a separate route card had not been made out for each driver. Clearly this must be done whatever the circumstances.

The Bn. reached destination, woods 3 miles North of Poperinghe, about 0400 hours. Despite a trying time at Ypres the spirits of all ranks had materially improved due to their having worked under their own commanders as a unit and having seen enemy fall under their fire.

PERNOLLHOEK. May 29th.

A quiet day. 150 Brigade held Sector in front along Poperinghe Canal. Bn. in reserve to counter-attack or form defensive flank. Troops rehearsed on the ground during the afternoon.

ABOVE: *The Menin Gate and its bridge. The latter was blown by 2nd Lieutenant Smith on the afternoon of 27 May.*

RIGHT: *'Cameronians Drive' – the Canal towpath north of Houthem, now a cycle track. On the outskirts of Comines is another tribute by the town to the British defenders – a road named 'rue de la 143ème Brigade'.*

LEFT: *Sergeant Roby, of the Ox & Bucks, who held a position at Mai Cornet until relieved by the Engineers' and Lancers' counterattack on 27 May. He was painted by Eric Kennington.*

BELOW: *The inscription to the Comines' memorial.*

The memorial to the battle at Comines.

ABOVE: *Bedfordhouse Cemetery with Seaforth Highlanders' and Royal Scots Fusiliers' graves.*

BELOW: *Wreath to the Royal Scots Fusiliers in one of the old bunkers on Hill 60, photographed in August 2011. The inscription reads: 'The officers and men of the 2nd Bn. Royal Scots Fusiliers who did not take a step back on the fateful days of 26th–29th May 1940. You will not be forgotten.'*

was still holding out near the canal, the report was probably mainly referring to the aggressive patrols 1/7th Warwicks and 245th Field Company were carrying out about a mile back from the village centre. Similarly 1/7th Warwicks and 245th Field Company must have been the source of the flanking fire. The road they were on commanded the forward slopes of the Kaleute Ridge on their left, up the other side of which the Cameronians had counterattacked the evening before, as well as the countryside dropping down in front of them towards the canal. 245th Field Company's diary specifically referred to 'heavy casualties inflicted on the enemy on left flank with Bren fire . . .' [19]

Thus the 1/7th Warwicks and their supporting Royal Engineers were holding back elements of ID 61 on their right and of ID 31 on their left. By holding back ID 31 the Warwicks were protecting the area that the Sherwood Foresters later occupied and also shielding the Wiltshires. The Sherwood Foresters recorded no details of any fighting after they moved into position. They suffered eighteen casualties during the day, but some or perhaps all of these were caused by the air attack. The Wiltshires on 28 May merely recorded bouts of shelling and machine-gun fire, but no active fighting. They noted at one point effective British artillery retaliation by 9th Field. The Cameronians, by then on the left rear of the Wiltshires, had a similar experience. Shelling and mortaring began in the morning:

Shortly after the commencement of the [German] bombardment observers . . . saw large numbers of Germans forming up in a wood some 500 yards North East of their positions. Every available gun was directed on to the concentration, and the result was most gratifying. Germans were seen running in every direction, and great execution must have been done – not only by the accurate Artillery fire, but by small arms fire from the forward Infantry positions.

After this frustrated German attack there was little activity on this part of the front. [20]

By early morning of 28 May the northernmost battalion of 13 Brigade – the Inniskillings – was stationed on the St Eloi road near Oosttaverne, just north of the Cameronians. Some men from the Beds and Herts from 10 Brigade joined it and 'proved themselves of the greatest value'. Later in the day about sixty Inniskillings were sent up from the rear as reinforcements. They were ones who had 'got lost' the previous night – sometimes no doubt inadvertently, sometimes perhaps deliberately. [21]

The Germans pushed on to farms and other buildings that overlooked the Inniskillings' left flank, and the battalion proved it had considerable fight in it by reoccupying the nearest one, Nuyttens Farm. There followed a to-and-fro struggle involving this and adjacent farms. The Inniskillings had to evacuate it, and the Germans occupied it again: 'Shortly after this, heavy artillery fire from our own guns was brought down on the same farm . . . and after about 15 minutes of this, a German force of about a Company was seen to withdraw back to woods to the east.' This led to a heavy German bombardment of the road, during which 'many men were wounded'. Yet again the Inniskillings occupied the farm, led by Lieutenant Dane, who was later killed. The battalion aggressively used its carriers, pushing them forwards to attack another farm. They also had deterrent and supply functions: 'Time and time again they were sent forwards when attacks were threatened to patrol the road, they also proved invaluable for bringing up ammunition and carrying messages.'[22]

The Inniskillings were embroiled in rather heavier fighting than were the other battalions in 13 Brigade, but it was not on the scale of that endured by the Guards. The very fact that in their weakened state the Inniskillings could take the offensive suggests that the Germans did not attack in force on the 13 Brigade front.

ID 31's report sheds a little more light. On 27 May the plan was to make a concerted attack at 1400 the next day, but this seems to have been downplayed when the 28th dawned. Instead: 'The foremost sections of 17th and 82nd infantry regiments advanced at differing times without waiting for the order to attack, wherever a gap was noted in the enemy and it was possible to proceed.' At 0900 the III battalion of IR 17 reached the St Eloi-Warneton road. ID 31's diary stated that III/17 was on its right wing, and at some stage – from the placing of the entry it was probably the afternoon – 'the left wing of IR III/17 is attacked by the enemy co-operating with weak tank forces'. From the reference to 'tanks' and the likely timing this almost certainly referred to the Inniskillings' counterattacks with their Bren carriers in the vicinity of Nuyttens Farm. ID 31's diary continued: 'Because of increasing enemy resistance the division decides at 1700 to hold the line it has reached and to go over to defensive tactics.'[23]

Although localised attacks by the battalions of ID 31 had replaced the concerted attack originally planned for the afternoon, remnants of the original idea might be detected in the heavy shelling and bombing of Wytschaete during the morning and the afternoon, which is mentioned in various diaries. However, artillery bombardments that were not followed up by strong infantry attacks were not going to get very far and the division's decision to go on the defensive at 1700 was an admission of failure.[24]

The situation farther north, however, was very different. Here the remnants of the 2nd Northamptons and the 2nd RSF were isolated in forward positions to the east of St Eloi. Both battalions had been ordered by Stopford of 17 Brigade to hang on where they were in the hope that 10 Brigade would take over their positions early on 28 May. The reality on the morning of the 28th was that 10 Brigade was preoccupied in establishing itself a considerable way back, and there was no possibility of relief for these two battalions.

The Northamptons' CO, Major Wetherall, had set out to visit his right flank at 0700 and never returned. It was discovered later that he had been killed. Soon the battalion HQ, in a farm, was under attack and at 0900 the second-in-command, Major Watts, left to report the situation to brigade HQ. By the time he returned the position had been lost. The farm was in a slight depression and so initially out of sight of the advancing enemy, but as the forward companies crumbled it came under direct attack. According to the regimental history ammunition gave out and made surrender inevitable. Some troops from the forward companies made their way back and met Watts, who had returned to within 200 yards of the farm. They and the few other stragglers who were collected amounted to around forty men when they reached brigade HQ. The brigade war diary timed this at 1100; if accurate the Northamptons must have surrendered some time earlier.[25]

The RSF, even further forward, was probably surrounded when Stopford had made his way through to it at 0300 in the morning. As the Germans thickened up it was completely cut off, and at 0900 a carrier trying to get through from brigade was unable to get nearer than St Eloi. According to the war diary, however, this carrier found 160 men sheltering from enemy fire in a ditch near St Eloi. These must have been an amalgam of stragglers or support troops from the RSF and the Northamptons, plus the Seaforth Highlanders who had been positioned in the village. For some reason the Germans ceased firing and the men were able to withdraw. Meanwhile the RSF's forward companies and battalion HQ, located in a farm, kept fighting. Like the Northamptons they initially had some hope of being relieved but according to Lieutenant-Colonel Tod, the CO: 'The situation soon became quite hopeless. The Germans were still around, the barn was full of wounded and our ammunition was all but expended. Rightly or wrongly, I then surrendered' (at about 1100).[26]

The expectation that 10 Brigade could relieve the Northamptons and RSF was far too optimistic. Although Stopford could probably have preserved many men in the Northamptons and the RSF by pulling the battalions back late on 27 May, his decision to leave them forward may have been justified, even if it was a costly one. In the morning IR 54 had to overcome the two strong points, probably feeling that it could not leave British units where they could counterattack across its rear. In the meantime 10 Brigade was getting into position. The alternative scenario, in which Stopford pulled back the two battalions and re-formed roughly on the line Wytschaete–St Eloi and then northwards along the canal might have worked better – but it might not have done.

17 Brigade now had little to command except for the 6th Seaforths. The Seaforths had been a problem for Stopford on 27 May, retiring when they should not have done and finally being put into a reserve line in and around St Eloi. With the Germans behind the Northamptons and RSF by early on the 28th, St Eloi was now on the front line, and as early as 0600 the DCLI from 10 Brigade recorded troops from the Seaforths withdrawing through them. But the latter's war diary implied that they held on for a considerable time, with the Germans infiltrating around them. No doubt the reality is that some held on and others straggled back. According to 17 Brigade diary, at around 1015 Stopford met a major of the Seaforths, with about twenty-five men from it and the Northamptons, 'moving back towards Wytschaete'. Stopford 'collected' the men – the word implies that this was no kind of organised group – and ordered the major to take command and obtain ammunition, then take the men to a nearby hill where they could command the Wytschaete–St Eloi road. It is clear from the tone of the entry and from what happened after the battalion's return to Britain, which will be discussed in Chapter 11, that Stopford considered this retirement unauthorised. At some stage the reality that the Seaforths were in no state to resist was recognised, and their remnants retired to Wytschaete. They were completely disorganised by then and it took 'many hours' to collect stragglers and reorganise. Later Stopford sent the CO, Lieutenant-Colonel Reid, and some men to defend the Wytschaete–St Eloi road. Subsequently the CO of the Beds and Herts remembered the 'remnants of a badly cut-up and very shaky territorial battalion', in the vicinity – no doubt the Seaforths.[27]

Effectively the British defence in the northern sector now relied on 10 Brigade, although at daybreak only about half of each of its battalions had arrived. The DCLI had two companies – B and D – on a line extending roughly from St Eloi to Nuyttens Farm on the St Eloi–Oosttaverne road. There were a few Beds and Herts between the DCLI and the Inniskillings, who were contesting Nuyttens Farm with the Germans. The rest of 10 Brigade were in the Wytschaete area.[28]

After the DCLI noted Seaforths retiring through it, events moved quickly. At 0645 on 28 May a message was received from D Company that it had been overrun and soon after one from B Company, nearest St Eloi, reporting: 'The company commander, Major Phillippo, had been killed while rallying elements of the covering troops in front of his company, and placing them on his left.' These surely must also have been Seaforths. In spite of Phillippo's gallantry, German pressure was such that the company had to fall back. Then at 0745 Evelyn Barker, 10 Brigade's CO, arrived and ordered a counterattack, as the diary called it, by the battalion's carriers. In fact this seems to have been intended as a combined reconnaissance mission and demonstration of strength, not an attack to retake St Eloi. It was led by Captain Pine-Coffin, whose account is in the regimental history:[29]

> We encountered the Germans well before we got to St Eloi and found them in the village itself too. Fortunately they had only just got there and our appearance surprised and even scared them. They obviously thought we were tanks and ran about in all directions for cover. We took them on with our brens but were a bit inaccurate as the gunners had to stand up and fire from the shoulder. My own gun I remember chose this occasion to be difficult and refused to fire anything but single rounds which undoubtedly enabled many Germans to remain alive. One gunner put aside his Bren and instead tossed grenades amongst the Germans sheltering in the ditch beside the road. (This was Private Williams who lost an arm in the engagement and was awarded the Military Medal for his part in the action.) In all the platoon killed at least seventy that morning and our own casualties were one killed and three wounded.[30]

The number of German dead must be exaggerated but even so this is another example of how carriers, lightly armed and armoured though they were, caused havoc among the Germans who took them to be tanks. Their flimsiness is illustrated by the fact that of the seven carriers that set out, one failed to return because its steering was disabled by a collision with a cow. Three others were put out of action by the more conventional method of enemy fire.[31]

Meanwhile the DCLI's B and D Companies had fallen back, the latter suffering sixteen casualties while only about ten men from B (only a half company) returned, suggesting 30–40 casualties. DCLI's diary noted that their retirement was aided by the 'magnificent effort made by machine guns of the 1/7th Middlesex Regiment, who went into action in full view of the enemy near Wytschaete church, to stem the enemy's advance'. The 1/7th Middlesex was the battalion whose Sergeant Burford had captured the German orders three very long days ago; it had come up with the rest of 4th Division.[32]

With some stability returned to the southern sector after the counterattacks on 27 May, Franklyn could pay attention to the north. He set out at daybreak on the 28th to visit Barker, but there was still heavy congestion on the roads, which according to Franklyn were packed with refugees. It seems extraordinary that this was the case given the fighting going on in the near vicinity. As a result he took an hour to reach 10 Brigade HQ, which was at Kemmel. Barker was not there and there was no one to give Franklyn information. He could not afford to spare more time, so forewent his original intention to visit the other brigades and returned to Ploegsteert. Barker had, in fact, received orders earlier from Franklyn to move up to fill the gap between 5th and 50th Division. But on arriving at about 0920 at Dempsey and Stopford's joint HQ, an *estaminet* in Wytschaete, he found: 'The Boche had broken through east of Wytschaete and a nasty situation had arisen.' Barker, who was probably referring to the German breakthrough at St Eloi, concluded that it was best to stabilise the situation first before moving north.[33]

A number of things are interesting about all this. Franklyn was out of touch with the situation and remained so. In his memoir he implied that 10 Brigade did attack to the north and that 'by the early afternoon the gap had been sealed off'. But this was not the case, as will be seen. Although he could be criticised for his over-optimistic assessment of when 10 Brigade could deliver effective help to Stopford, Barker subsequently made some sensible decisions. The situation was difficult because he did not know where 17 Brigade troops were located – probably no one did. His order to send out the DCLI carriers was intended to remedy this lack of knowledge, although as it happened it also had the beneficial side-effect of shaking up the Germans. Then he went to see Stopford and Dempsey and took the decision to stay where he was. But Barker would have had to rely less on his own judgement if Franklyn, as he originally intended, had gone to 13 and 17 Brigades joint HQ in Wytschaete, only 2½ miles from Kemmel. If Franklyn had reached there, he would have had better information with which to make his dispositions. These might well have included a rationalisation of the command structure. 17 Brigade had ceased to exist as an effective fighting force by the morning of 28 May. Putting Barker in charge of the remnants would have ensured their more efficient use. Instead Stopford moved around collecting stragglers and setting up positions that might have had some value but would have had more if co-ordinated with 10 Brigade.[34]

Although Wytschaete was heavily bombed and shelled there seems to have been little in the way of direct attacks on British forces in and around the village after mid-morning on 28 May, apart from the intermittent fighting on the Inniskillings' front to the east of the village. The right wing of ID 31 may have penetrated beyond the

St Eloi–Wytschaete road when the DCLI fell back, but presumably the Inniskillings' attacks and the deterrent effect of the Middlesex's machine guns precluded any further penetration. By then 11 Brigade had also arrived in the Wytschaete area and 10 Brigade began its move northwards, as ordered earlier by 5th Division.

In the event two of the brigade's battalions – the Beds and Herts and the Surreys – experienced only localised fighting. The first had some men supporting the Inniskillings, and then late in the evening it was standing by for a counterattack on Voormezeele when orders were received to pull out. The radio was not working well – an indication that it was being used by the infantry at times – and a liaison officer got to the battalion only just in time to stop the attack. The CO, Lieutenant-Colonel J. C. Birch, had to run a mile over ploughed fields to battalion HQ to confirm the news and then a mile back to stop his companies. The Surreys actually occupied Voormezeele, which was under artillery fire from both sides, incurring some casualties in the process. But it was time to pull out, and further action was called off.[35]

The DCLI also moved north and at 1500 occupied a wood by the St Eloi–Voormezeele road, just 150 yards from the Germans – probably troops from ID 18 pushing west from St Eloi. In spite of the close proximity of the enemy there were few casualties in the DCLI advance: 'probably due to the fire support given by the R.A. who put down covering fire on the high ground occupied by the enemy'. The DCLI's forward position gave some protection to the northern flank, which had been exposed by the German advance along the canal. This was supplemented by 50th Division units stationed nearer Ypres, which are discussed in the next chapter.[36]

Farther south 11 Brigade got into position in the Wytschaete area during the morning of 28 May. The battalions experienced the heavy German shelling on and around Wytschaete, but it seems from the sparse records little else. 13 Brigade to the east was holding its positions and 10 Brigade provided a screen to the north, so the 11 Brigade did not get seriously involved. Two companies of 7th Cheshires, a machine-gun battalion, were also in defensive positions in the area but had little to do.[37]

Unfortunately ID 18's report is not as helpful as it might be in clarifying the details of the fighting in the north, since it is preoccupied with boasting about the division's 'difficult and self-sacrificing battle'. One of its regiments, IR 30, remained in reserve, where it endured 'heavy artillery fire' and 'continuous flanking [fire]'. So the attack was carried on, as it mostly seems to have been the day before, by IR 54. This was the only case where the Germans did not have a considerable numerical superiority. The three battalions of IR 54 faced the two-and-a-half of 17 Brigade (counting the weakened Northamptons as a half), although IR 30 was also involved in the initial attack on the 27th.[38]

On the 28th IR 54 started the day by knocking out the remains of the Northamptons and RSF – fifty-one prisoners from the former and thirty-nine from the latter were credited to the regiment. It also moved into and occupied St Eloi, where as has been seen the Seaforths quickly fell back. The DCLI's defensive action in the vicinity of St Eloi probably involved IR 54, although the DCLI may also have been fighting ID 31's right-hand battalion, IR III/17, which had reached the St Eloi–Warneton road at 0900.

German progress was then slower, however, as shown by the fact that they had not occupied Voormezeele by the afternoon. ID 18 had been occupied in an action with the 4th Green Howards, part of 50th Division, which is discussed in the next chapter, and this may have been one reason for their lack of progress.[39]

IR 54's performance was impressive, but the Germans may have missed an opportunity in the north. If IR 30 had been brought in and pressed vigorously westwards, the attack could have had a wider frontage and would have hampered the British efforts to use 50th Division to reinforce their front. The emphasis in ID 18's diary on the sealing off of Ypres suggests that fear of counterattack from the town – and of course the reality of flanking fire – was most likely the reason for keeping IR 30 in reserve.[40]

Another factor holding ID 18 back, of course, was the continued British artillery fire. 18th Field in the north was one of the British regiments involved in this sector. The regiment's diary stated that St Eloi was in the gap between 5th Division and 150 Brigade, belonging to 50th Division: 'Both units were trying to close it with men without success; it remained for the guns to close it with fire.' One of its batteries, 94/95, was covering the regiment's left-hand zone, which would probably have included St Eloi, and the battery was particularly active on 28 May. Although there seems to have been little German counter-battery fire, artillerymen were certainly not out of the danger zone, particularly the observers in or near the front line. Both 94/95's observers, Lieutenants Sambridge and Pollock, were wounded. 18th Field's other battery, 59/93, was supporting the Northamptons, but an officer sent out to liaise with them disappeared. Later another officer manned the battery's observation post and it 'joined in heartily'.[41]

18th Field's headquarters was positioned near Hollandscheschurr Farm, about 1,500 yards southwest of St Eloi and so close to the front line. The war diary recorded: 'Parties of dispirited infantry of the . . . and . . . Regiments [it coyly omitted their names] struggled past Regimental HQ "The enemy are through . . .

The Battalion is retreating . . . What is the way to safety." They were hungry and without leaders, but were quite easy to turn and start back with a hatful of hard-boiled eggs.' Hard-boiled eggs seem to have been a staple morale-raiser, since Gilmore had his Cameronians collect them the day before. If the infantry came from St Eloi they were likely to have been Seaforths with perhaps some stragglers from the Northamptons, RSF and DCLI. 'Were their own officers fit to rally them?' the diary asked rhetorically. The truth of the matter was that there were hardly any officers left in some of the battalions concerned. 18th Field, whose diarist was given to purple passages, concluded: 'No matter, the guns had the matter in hand for daylight, and orders were to retire at dusk.'[42]

The medium regiments too were still firing, if only to use up their ammunition. 216 Battery in 63rd Medium, for example, had run out of shells overnight and 214 Battery supplied them with 200 rounds. Then at 0855 an inventory recorded 420 rounds at 214's wagon lines, while 216's had none, so 214 handed over another 200 rounds. When at 1700 its observation post closed, 5th Medium ordered all remaining ammunition to be expended by 'shooting at likely targets off the map'.[43]

As the day wore on, 5th Division had solved some of its most pressing problems. There was still one – the gap that 18th Field hoped to close 'with fire' was simply too big. The Germans were not only in St Eloi but also along the line of the canal north and northwest of it. The DCLI history referred to its troops on higher ground seeing 'the close-ranked masses of the Germans pressing northwards with little to molest them . . .' But as already noted the Germans had failed to take initiative here in the morning, and by the evening it was too late to achieve a breakthrough.[44]

The overall impression of 28 May is that it was for the Germans a day of missed opportunities. To Franklyn this was because, by the early afternoon, 'the battle had been finally won'. This is an over-optimistic conclusion. The dogged resistance of the British was one important reason why most German units had ceased serious attacks by then or a bit later. But the Germans were still there, and both ID 31 and ID 18 had regiments in reserve, which had not been in the battle so far and could have been deployed in the attack the following day. Therefore the British would have had only a temporary reprieve – if they had stayed. Nevertheless the lack of effective German attacks on the 28th demands explanation.[45]

Some reasons are obvious. The British counterattacks of 27 May had a demoralising effect on ID 61 and ID 31. ID 61 was in a position to deploy a new regiment on the 28th, and this may account for the fact that its attacks on the Guards were renewed with vigour. But the German tactics, both against the

Guards and farther north against the Warwicks/Staffordshires line, were crude. As a result little progress was made. There was also a shortage of artillery ammunition in ID 61's sector. With horse-drawn transport, even the German army could not always keep itself supplied given the speed of its advance. In contrast the British artillery was still firing at full tilt.

ID 31 in the centre had other problems. It felt unable to deploy its reserve regiment, and its forward regiments had already taken considerable punishment. Even more important, the staunch defence of 1/7th Warwicks and 245th Field Company in a key position disrupted any hope of the division as a whole advancing in a concerted manner, while the Wiltshires' obduracy also impeded the advance. To these blocks was added the Inniskillings' aggressive tactics, which prevented IR 17 from making progress.

ID 18 in the north, facing the weakest opposition because of the Seaforths' collapse, made the best advances. But with its wide frontage, extending to the north of Ypres, it could attack 5th Division with only one regiment. Finally there was the rain. Most of the campaign before Dunkirk had been marked by fine weather, and it was fortuitous that there was a break on 28 May. Scattered references in war diaries suggested that rain extended over the whole front by mid-afternoon. The consequent mud must have impeded the attacker more than the defender. Flanders mud, usually in the First World War the bane of the British because they attacked more often, came to their aid in 1940.

In spite of these tangible reasons for the German failure, the strong impression remains that they could have tried harder. This was, after all, a remarkable army, which had already achieved extraordinary things. It seems likely that the German euphoria following the Belgian surrender led to some slackening of effort on the 28th. And with both Bock and Reichenau otherwise engaged on that day, there was no spur from higher up to drive IV Corps on.

As 5th Division successfully continued its resistance, the evacuation of BEF troops begun two days earlier was now well underway. Over 25,000 men had landed in England by midnight on 28 May. But the failure of the British and French to agree on policy meant that, as yet, Frenchmen were not among them. On the morning of that day Gort had had a difficult interview with Blanchard, who, having received no instructions from the French government, would still not agree to evacuate French troops. Furthermore General Prioux, commanding the French First Army in and around Lille, had declared that his men were too tired to pull back to the Lys. In spite of Gort's remonstrances Blanchard refused to order him to do so. Gort announced his intention of following the British plan whatever the French might do and pulling back that night from the Lys to the general line Cassel–Poperinghe–Ypres. The French First Army would soon be cut off.[46]

The pending split between the BEF and a large segment of the French forces was symbolic. On 28 May the British War Cabinet wound up its discussion of the French proposal that Mussolini should be asked to mediate. While Halifax continued to favour this, no one else did, and the proposal was turned down. It was a brave, critical and, most people would say, correct decision. Because of it Britain and the Empire would fight on, accepting that France might no longer be with them.[47]

10. Ypres and Withdrawal

O<small>N THE MORNING OF</small> 27 May 2nd Lieutenant Smith of 101st Field Company and his engineers were in Ypres with the intention of blowing bridges. On the previous day they had prepared the bridges to the east of the town for demolition, including the one immediately beyond the Menin Gate, where every year thousands attend the evening ceremony. By the 27th the Germans were shelling the town, and two direct hits were scored on the gate. Nevertheless the CO of the 4th East Yorkshire Regiment (East Yorks), which controlled that sector, refused to let Smith fire the charges in case the bridges were required for a counterattack. Smith clearly thought the idea was far-fetched, and his scepticism was confirmed when he returned to the bridge to find that a covering party of the East Yorks had withdrawn. The sole defenders were two of his trusty subordinates, Lance-Corporal Hourigan and Sapper Roach, both last encountered enjoying a festive lunch on 24 May. Enemy units were getting closer and at about 1600 the East Yorks CO either relented or was overruled and the Menin Gate bridge was blown. Smith recorded with satisfaction: 'This was done with complete success and without causing any structural damage to the gate but causing irreparable damage to the car of the Colonel East Yorks, the machine being completely wrecked by falling masonry.'[1]

50th Division, to which the East Yorks belonged, was unique among BEF divisions in that it had its own allocation of two troop-carrying companies – enough to carry its two brigades, 150th and 151st. Both consisted of north-country battalions and the division was designated 'Northumbrian'. The British army had a habit of naming its territorial divisions after ancient Saxon kingdoms and grouping the battalions in them accordingly, although regular divisions contained a geographical hotchpotch. 151 Brigade comprised the 6th, 8th and 9th Durham Light Infantry (DLI), the first two of which had taken part in the Arras counterattack. 150 Brigade comprised the 4th East Yorks and the 4th and 5th Battalions of the Green Howards, another Yorkshire regiment and the one Franklyn had joined as a subaltern before the First

World War. There was also a motorcycle battalion, the 4th Royal Northumberland Fusiliers, which was unique to the BEF. Thus, although the division was only two brigades strong, it was undoubtedly mobile.[2]

Ypres came within ID 18's area of operations, but the division did not attack the town directly with any force. Once they had established that it was strongly held, the Germans must have wanted to avoid getting tangled up in street fighting; a Sixth Army report of 28 May noted that house fighting was to be avoided because the English were very dangerous at it. (The fighting in and around Houthem may have been in their mind.) Instead the division's IR 51 was given the task of sealing the town off from the east – probably because of the fear of counterattack. Nevertheless 50th Division saw some action, especially to the north and south of the town.[3]

Initially only the division's 150 Brigade was released to Brooke on the morning of 26 May, and its battalions got into position in Ypres on the night of the 26th/27th. For the next two days, however, little happened to the East Yorks and the 5th Green Howards, both stationed in the town itself, except for shelling and the occasional German probe. Meanwhile 2nd Lieutenant Smith blew the other two bridges to the east of Ypres on the afternoon of 27 May and then departed northwards with his men. Their work was not yet done.[4]

150 Brigade had actually been preceded in Ypres by a pioneer battalion, the 1/6th South Staffordshires. Perhaps because of their lowly status, they did not get a mention in the official history, which seems tough as they played an active role in defending the town. Pioneer battalions were GHQ formations, tasked with construction, building defences and so forth. The battalion moved into the town at 1700 on 26 May, and when 150 Brigade arrived that night came under the command of its CO, Brigadier Haydon. On the 27th the South Staffords were 'mainly occupied in building tank blocks'. These testify to the BEF's continued concern with tank attack on this front, although, of course, it need not have worried. The battalion was in the south of the town and the CO, Lieutenant-Colonel W. E. Gibbons, recollected that in the afternoon of the 28th enemy pressure on troops holding the canal to his right seemed to increase. This probably relates to pressure on the 4th Green Howards mentioned below. However Bren gunners 'had a good long-range enfilade shoot' at Germans moving towards the canal. Most likely these were units of ID 18's IR 54. At about 1700 pressure on the South Staffords' right increased and the Lille Gate area was heavily mortared. Then the enemy advance guard approached the gate and, according to the battalion diary: 'C Company with in addition Bren guns of A.A. Platoon opened fire and advance easily stopped.' It added: 'Platoons were very steady . . .', but noted a tendency to open fire too early.

After half an hour the attack died away. It seems likely that, as the British units to the south of Ypres were forced back, the Germans gained in confidence and started pressing on the town itself, but firm resistance discouraged them.[5]

The 4th Green Howards originally guarded the southeast of Ypres, with the right-hand company on Zillebeke Lake. On 27 May the battalion was withdrawn westwards, probably to the canal where it turns northwards at the bend near Voormezeele, and the right of their line was reinforced by some troops from the 5th Green Howards. It was they who 'met the full force of an enemy attack launched at about midday on the 28th'. A platoon belonging to the 5th Battalion was overrun and their D Company forced to withdraw northwards. The German unit responsible must again have been IR 54 – the regiment that had earlier overcome the Northamptons and the RSF – as it recorded fourteen Green Howard prisoners. In spite of this German success the Green Howards' resistance seems to have discouraged any major incursion farther west by IR 54, since Voormezeele itself was not occupied (*see* Chapter 9).[6]

Also on the morning of 28 May Brooke told Haydon, 150 Brigade's CO, to send 4th Northumberland Fusiliers to clear up the German penetration in 17 Brigade's sector and fill the gap between 50th and 5th Divisions. The battalion moved southwest of Ypres, where it suffered some casualties from shelling even though it seems to have done no fighting. It recorded 'constant rumours of Germans having penetrated our left flank', which all proved to be false. This is further confirmation that ID 18's attack had run out of steam.[7]

To the north of the town the British defence was provided by 151 Brigade – 50th Division's other formation. On the morning of 26 May it had been supporting French troops at Carvin, and its diary then recorded a confused series of orders, which reflect the pressure on GHQ. It was initially directed to join 46th Division, which had been helping to hold the Canal Line facing southwest against the German panzer divisions. On the morning of the 27th the brigade moved up to Steenvoorde, west of Poperinghe, with its ultimate destination still undecided. Martel, 50th Division's CO, then intervened directly with GHQ and 151st moved in the afternoon over to the Ypres front, noting *en passant* 'no enemy air activity'. There the 6th DLI, which had been detached on 26 May before the brigade got involved at Carvin, rejoined them.[8]

Although technically 6th DLI had been released to Brooke in the late morning of the 26th, along with 150 Brigade, it had pursued a completely different path northwards. It is worth following this because the battalion's experience illustrates the communications difficulties that could affect the BEF. 6th DLI had initially been ordered to the Armentières area early on 26 May. The battalion made its way to Armentières, and it was only in the early hours of the 27th that it received news that it should remain in readiness to go to Ypres with 150 Brigade. The decision had taken twelve hours to reach them. This could well be an example of a battalion out of touch by radio where contact was maintained by liaison officers (motor contact officers, in BEF jargon). Perhaps in this case one of them had failed to find the DLI, or had himself been killed or injured. Liaison seems to have remained a problem, because it was not until 1100 on 27 May that the battalion received orders to move. Arriving at Vlamertinghe near Ypres at 1430, the men had a meal consisting of 'a few biscuits and some tinned fish'. Having rejoined 151 Brigade, 6th DLI got into line in the evening, taking over from the French 2nd DLM.[9]

German reconnaissance units had penetrated north of Ypres by the 27th, and that evening a mounted patrol crossed the Yser Canal, which unlike the Ypres–Comines Canal was a completed waterway and thus more of an obstacle. The patrol courageously swum it in the face of British troops but was then annihilated by the 12th Lancers, who were in the area. According to the Lancers: '. . . at the request of the Mayor of Woesten, the horses which survived were given to him to feed the civilian population which he said had been very short of meat, owing to the influx of refugees'. The incident is interesting as demonstrating the reliance of the Germans on horses even for reconnaissance. The ability to swim a water obstacle was a bonus, but, in terms of mobility and firepower, mounted patrols were hardly on a par with armoured cars.[10]

Once in position 151 Brigade held a line stretching from Ypres about three miles north along the Yser Canal to Boezinghe, the DLM still holding the canal from there northwards. 9th DLI was on the right of the brigade line, 6th on the left and 8th in reserve. At 0430 on 28 May the commander of 9 Brigade came in to report that he was taking over from the DLM. His formation was part of Montgomery's 3rd Division, which had evidently just completed the night march described in Chapter 9. Although Montgomery has often been criticised, the fact that one of his units could complete this march, find its position in the middle of the night and immediately take over the line helps to show why Brooke thought so highly of him.[11]

If Brooke's assessment of the DLM is correct, then it was lucky for the British that the Germans took until 28 May before they brought significant pressure to bear north of Ypres. In his memoirs Brooke described the French unit as 'more of an encumbrance than anything else', having lost all its tanks and possessing only a 'column of buses and workshops, with a certain number of men with rifles . . . Its fighting value was practically nil, whilst its power of blocking roads with its huge vehicles was unlimited.' In fact this assessment is not entirely fair or accurate. At 1300 on the 28th 151 Brigade recorded an offer of 'AFVs' (armoured fighting vehicles – i.e. tanks) from the DLM, 'to assist in clearing up the situation on the right flank' – that is, to help with 150 Brigade's problems south of Ypres. Thus the French clearly had some tanks, and were willing to use them to help the British.[12]

On 28 May there was some enemy pressure on 151 Brigade, but, as in Ypres itself, nothing very significant. In the morning the 6th DLI record using a 3-inch mortar against the enemy 'with considerable effect', noting also: 'H. E. [high explosive] ammunition had never been available for 2' mortars.' This is a rare mention of these small company weapons, and interestingly it is a negative one.

Later in the day there was some German pressure and two attempts at bridging on the brigade front, but British artillery and local counterattacks seem to have deterred them. It is likely that these attempted incursions were made by ID 254, which the map in Ellis showed as coming up to the Yser Canal by the evening of 28 May. This would be consistent with the lack of any mention of the attempts in ID 18's report, where it is implied that the function of IR 51, the northernmost regiment, was simply to guard the northern flank. The freeing up of other German divisions had been made possible, of course, by the Belgian surrender.[13]

The British artillery concentrations on this front were fired by 68th and 92nd Field Regiments, north and south of Vlamertinghe respectively. 68th Field had better luck with food supply than 6th DLI: 'Fresh milk, fresh cream, fresh fruit and fresh bread were obtainable from nearby farms.' On 28 May it established 'the best O.P.s [observation posts] for observed shooting that the Regiment had had since the beginning of the campaign . . .' 151 Brigade diary added: 'Throughout the day, co-operation with the artillery had been very good, and many calls for fire were quickly answered.'[14]

That evening, the short stretch of 50th Division line north of Ypres was the only part of the whole battlefront where the enemy was still fairly active. The lull was fortuitous, because for the troops of 5th and 50th Divisions and all their many ancillary units it was time to go home.

Brooke with his usual foresight had issued orders on 26 May that were for the next four days. They covered the withdrawal of 3rd Division to the north of Ypres on the night of the 27th/28th, as detailed in Chapter 8, and 4th Division's subsequent withdrawal that night to cover the Lys. Brooke originally ordered one brigade of 4th Division to hold the Ypres–Poperinghe line as a 'lay-back' position, so that 5th Division and the rest of 4th could retire through it on the night of 28/29 May. In the event, all of 4th Division became committed to the battle. More importantly, during 28 May Brooke received news that Nieuport was threatened by German columns, so 4th Division's next task was to move up to its defence. As a result 50th Division, which in the original plan was to go into reserve on the 29th, held the lay-back line along with 3rd Division.

Subsequent to 28/29 May Brooke's orders were, understandably, more sketchy as events would dictate them nearer the time. Nevertheless up to the latter date he was remarkably prescient. The orders foreshadowed pretty closely what actually happened, including the holding of the Ypres–Comines line and the position on the Lys, 3rd Division's leapfrog north, and the approximate position of the lay-back line on the 29th.[15]

Clearly some sort of march order had to be established for the swollen establishment of 5th Division. Including 12 Brigade in the south, which was still under the command of 4th Division, there were twenty-one battalions of infantry, three-and-a-half machine-gun battalions, six medium and heavy artillery regiments and six field regiments. There were other miscellaneous artillery detachments and a host of other units such as anti-tank and engineer companies, as well as the field ambulances, which received and treated the wounded after they had passed through the regimental aid posts. Of course a lot of them – the infantry battalions in particular – were severely denuded. Furthermore all but essential equipment was to be dumped or destroyed on the spot as units left. As a result many infantrymen were able to ride on their own battalion transport, usually devoted to supplies, or hitch a lift with gunners who had spare space.[16]

The medium artillery under Brigadier 'Ambrose' Pratt were the first major branch of the forces engaged to pull out. The first of their departing units was actually a field regiment, 115th.* With one battery engaged elsewhere, the regiment apparently only had four guns left and had been stationed on Mount Kemmel, giving it a 'grand view of the war E. and S. of Ypres'. It must have been the originator of the fire from Kemmel, which Brooke noticed when 3rd Division was journeying past his HQ near Ploegsteert on the night of 27/28 May. With such a small number of guns, 115th Field cannot have made much impact and departed at 1100 on the 28th. 65th Medium and 1st Heavy went in the early afternoon, and the others in the evening. They were firing almost up to the point of departure: '63rd Medium Regiment, as ever, being the last of the Corps artillery to fire in support of 5th

---

* Corps commanders medium artillery (CCMAs) usually had one or two field regiments under command.

Division.' This was at 1900 hours. Pratt, one of the most sympathetic characters among the senior commanders, ended his orders for withdrawal thus:

> The Corps Artillery had rendered invaluable assistance to many Divisions from the River Dyle area, the Escaut canal to the river Lys, and the C.C.M.A. thanks all ranks for their splendidly loyal response to all calls made on them. Travel hopefully.[17]

Pratt's HQMA diary gave the total of rounds fired by the medium artillery during the battle as 32,000. On first impression this is an astonishingly large total, the more so as the usual figure given is 5,000. The latter number was mentioned in Brooke's diary, reproduced in Bryant and has been frequently quoted since. In fact comparison puts the total into perspective. At Alamein three medium regiments with forty-eight guns fired 83,500 rounds during the twelve days of the battle (the 824 field guns in the same battle fired more than a million). Each medium gun averaged 145 rounds per day. At Ypres–Comines 69th Medium was only in action from the evening of 27 May, firing 1,200 rounds in total, and the four guns of 115th Field presumably fired a few hundred. Subtracting these leaves a total of 30,000 or so fired by four medium and one heavy regiments.

Most batteries started firing on the morning of 26 May, so about eighty guns fired for about two and a half days. The resulting average is 150 rounds per gun per day, or almost exactly the same as the Alamein figure, which was fired over a much longer period.[18]

In actuality 5,000 rounds would have been a very low total, given that there was no shortage of ammunition. The puzzle is how Brooke, an artilleryman by training, made the error. It is possible that someone gave him the approximate average fired by each regiment, and after a busy and stressful day he jotted this down as the total without giving it any thought.

No more rounds would be fired by the BEF medium artillery, however, because the guns would be left behind. Before the regiments left: 'All equipment likely to be of use to a pursuing enemy is to be put out of action, e.g. breach mechanism, spares, sights, telephone and R.T. [radio transmitters] removed.' Some of the unit war diaries detailed this process and the mechanics of pulling out. 20/21 Battery of 5th Medium noted: 'Guns rendered unserviceable and all instruments saved.'[19]

The regiments evacuated in stages, the wagon lines first and the gun groups last. Part of 63rd Medium's Regimental HQ actually pulled out on the evening of 27 May, with the regiment's 214 Battery firing 'overhead and across the Convoy'. Not surprisingly the diaries reported heavy congestion and enemy shelling on their journeys north. 20/21 Battery, for example, was heavily shelled on the last stages of its journey between Bergues and Cappell on the outskirts of Dunkirk. 5th Medium found the congestion so great that they abandoned their vehicles south of Bergues. 63rd Medium's HQ group left an account of its journey on the night of the 27th/28th as the battle continued to rage:

> Over on the right sky-line gun fire flashes, Verey lights and star shells were observed. Just before dawn a stationary convoy of ambulances drawn up on the left-hand side of the road was passed and a short distance further on a few enemy shells within a few hundred yards of the convoy – no damage resulting. The next village had been shelled but the convoy passed through without incident. At dawn little more than half the journey had been completed, as progress had been slow owing to heavy congestion on the road.[20]

The field artillery regiments, by contrast, for the most part kept their guns, although jettisoning other equipment. According to 5th Division's HQ Royal Artillery diary: 'During 28th orders were received to get rid of all possible transport and equipment less that required to fight guns in a last-ditch position at Dunkirk, prior to embarkation.' The exceptions were the 18-pounders, the First World War vintage guns, which were unmodernised apart from being fitted with rubber-tyred wheels. Like the medium guns they were destroyed *in situ*. 60th Field, whose Captain Derry has already been extensively quoted, had them as did an odd battery, 21/24th, which had been attached to 9th Field. The 4.5-inch howitzers, with which some territorial field batteries were equipped, also were discarded. According to the diary of 68th Field, whose 269 Battery had them, no more stocks of ammunition in that calibre were available. When the news for withdrawal was given to the regiment at midday, the battery was ordered to 'expend all its ammunition as effectively and rapidly as possible' before destroying its guns. But most field regiments went on firing later than the mediums. The Germans, after all, were not going to stop attacking in order to let the British pull out – rather the contrary, if they had known what was happening. Thus it was important to keep firing until the last moment, while such fire also covered the infantry, who were starting to thin out.[21]

The northern end of the front around St Eloi and Voormezeele had remained active until relatively late but even here, according to 18th Field: 'As the sun went down it began to be reasonably certain that the enemy had shot his bolt for the day; and eventually we pulled out into a reasonably quiet evening bound for the next position.' Nonetheless some batteries were firing until late. 9th Field in the centre recorded its last gun out of action at 2130. Between 2000 and 2130 it noted: 'Concentrations and harassing fire put down while troops withdrew in turn.'

97th Field in the south similarly withdrew its last gun at 2130. According to the HQMA war diary: 'The actual last shell to be fired over the Messines-Wytschaete ridge was loaded by 27 Army Field Regiment, near X-roads 570526.' This puts it near Spanbroekmolen, northwest of Messines. 27th Field Regiment only had one battery in action on the 5th Division front, 21. Unfortunately the regimental diary was very terse, and 21 Battery's – as with many other battery diaries – non-existent, so there are no further details.[22]

Like the medium regiments, the field artillery units experienced heavy congestion as they travelled, mainly via Poperinghe. It may have been worse by the time they went because by then the infantry was on the move, as well as numerous French units. Lushington of 97th Field recalled: 'Units were mixed up in inextricable confusion and to make matters worse large numbers of French soldiers on horseback and on foot kept crowding in among us and pushing their way past, making anything like continuous movement impossible.' The diaries suggested that this was not an exaggeration. According to 20/76 Battery of 9th Field there was: 'Very severe congestion on the Poperinghe–Proven road [i.e. the road towards Dunkirk] owing to French horsed units and lack of traffic control. One troop covered 17 miles in 10 hours.' 18th Field recorded conditions in Poperinghe:

> The night was as black as ink, Poperinghe a ghost like town with ruined houses here and there, nobody to direct traffic except one over wrought military policeman who knew nothing anyway. A high velocity gun was firing intermittently on the town, but I doubt whether anybody cared; this particular nightmare had ceased to be a nightmare by constant repetition.[23]

As with the artillery, a few of the infantry units pulled out early. First to go was 12 Brigade, guarding the Lys at the very southern end of the line. Fighting had died down there in the afternoon, and the brigade slipped away in the evening. It had an important task to fulfil. With the surrender of the Belgians, the Germans could now make for the coast.

Brooke in his constant movement that day had been to see Ronald Adam, now commanding the perimeter at Dunkirk and 'found Germans were already trying to force Nieuport [on the coast east of Dunkirk]. So had to alter orders to 4th Div to bring them into the perimeter defence to cover Furnes to Nieuport'. It was around thirty-five miles from Warneton to Nieuport via Poperinghe, so troop carriers were ordered – evidently some had been kept available for emergencies such as this. To forestall difficulties in liaison, according to 4th Division: 'A Staff Officer was actually sent to the HQ of Troop Carrying Company. He then returned through 12 Infantry Brigade HQ to make sure that the rendezvous was clearly understood.'[24]

12 Brigade was urgently needed. Nieuport–Furnes was manned by no more than scratch forces, some already familiar – the hard-working 12th Lancers, 4th Division engineer units and some artillerymen acting as infantry. The brigade left behind 6th Black Watch, which was so intermingled with other units that it was thought impossible to withdraw it separately. In spite of its early departure the rest of 12 Brigade was still near Poperinghe at 0500 the next morning, because there was so much congestion, but then got moving: 'The Brigade Commander was standing at the road junction for [the] turning to Dixmude directing the Brigade column to Furnes'; by 0700 it was at Nieuport.[25]

The remainder of 5th Division had less far to go. After the heavy losses of the last two days they were given a reserve line position behind 3rd Division and 50th Division. In several cases numbers in the battalions were so small that they rode on their own transport, having destroyed the bulk of the supplies it usually carried. The Cameronians did this, although they moved 'not in the "regulation" manner, but by putting men on the mudguards, radiators and roofs'. The 8th Warwicks, who had lost heavily, had space enough to pick up men from other units when they passed through Kemmel.[26]

17 Brigade went first, presumably because it was no longer playing an active part in the battle. Its attenuated numbers meant that the whole brigade moved in a column, departing at around 2030. Most of the other battalions started pulling out at 2030 to 2100 and finished around 2130. By then it would have been dark. As already noted some field gun batteries were still firing, and this would have covered the noise of lorries moving away.

The British were by now well versed in pulling out when the Germans were opposite them. They would have known that the Germans rarely fought at night and were unlikely to start significant attacks at nightfall. Fortunately this pattern continued. In the centre the Wiltshires noted: 'Rear parties withdrew from contact without disturbance from the enemy'. Nearby, the Inniskillings' carriers covered the withdrawal, but their diary reported: 'The enemy made no attempt to follow up and appeared to be unaware of our actions.' 10 Brigade in the north, however, stayed until later. This made sense because the Germans had been most active there and there was always a danger that they would cut in southwest of Ypres if the sector was left undefended. The DCLI and the Beds and Herts recorded their last movements away from their positions at midnight or later. They seem to have bypassed Poperinghe and went to reinforce 12 Brigade in the Furnes–Nieuport area.[27]

Although a few infantry diaries reported congestion on the roads, most said little about the journey. The officers who wrote them must have been exhausted or, if the diaries were written up later, a night in a lorry did not seem worth recording. A few battalions, for example the Sherwood Foresters, recorded the loss of detachments, usually around Poperinghe, where the congestion and the number of deviating roads cannot have helped. The North Staffordshires experienced heavy congestion after Neuve-Église – again, mainly French troops – and at Poperinghe. But they still reached their temporary destination at Stavele, a few miles north of Poperinghe, by 0600, where they had an improvised meal: 'The first of any consequence since the afternoon of the 26th.'[28]

50th Division in and around Ypres went later than the other units. They had only a short distance to travel, because they were headed for Brooke's lay-back line. His original order had suggested this would run from Poperinghe to Ypres, but in the event Ypres was abandoned and the line ran up from Poperinghe to Lizerne on the Yser Canal. 50th Division held from Poperinghe to Woesten and had to throw back a flank guard to Proven, northwest of Poperinghe, as I Corps, which was meant to hold this line, had come farther back than was planned.[29]

50th Division's battalions moved out of their positions in the early hours of 29 May. In most cases the division's own transport was able to carry them, although the 4th East Yorks 'proceeded by bicycles, civilian cars and on foot to Poperinghe'. The withdrawal was covered by 13th/18th Hussars, who earlier had helped with the first counterattack in the south. Their historian remembered enemy shelling and 'intense continuous air attack'. There was a curious coda involving a rare mention of radio in infantry battalions. At 1120 on the 29th, 8th DLI's wireless set (presumably in a truck) 'reported by radio that it was now located in position near Brielen, that there was heavy enemy shelling and that no British troops could be seen'. This was not surprising as the British front line was now two or three miles away and the truck was the wrong side of it. The unit was ordered to 'move immediately in a N.W. direction', and it rejoined 151 Brigade without further adventures. Thus the battalion's radio truck seems to have been the last to know of its unit's withdrawal – an indication of how little radio was used.[30]

5th and 50th Divisions had pulled out in their entirety, apart from a few stragglers, but there were still substantial remnants of the BEF left south of Poperinghe on 29 May. Most of these also got away, but more through luck than good judgement. Pownall's diary showed that GHQ by now was preoccupied with the evacuation. It relied on the corps to oversee the retreat, but was over-sanguine about their ability, with the exception of II Corps, to do this. Command and control had more or less broken down in III Corps, holding the Canal Line facing southwest. Its commander, General Wason, had been thrust into the position when Ronald Adam was appointed to organise the Dunkirk beachhead on the 26th. Wason seems to have found it difficult to get to grips with his command, which was spread out along the long Western Front. On 28 May part of the corps – 44th Division – was still in the Hazebrouck area. Some cover was provided by French III Corps, under General de la Laurencie, west of Armentières. III Corps was part of First Army commanded by General Prioux, who had earlier refused to move northwards, claiming his troops were too tired.[31]

Prioux seems to have changed his mind more than once but finally decided that most of his army would stay put. Only III Corps made its escape. De la Laurencie was given permission to move north, starting on 29 May, but when Major-General Osborne of 44th Division called on him late on the 28th he was informed that the French would pull out at 2300 hours that night. Apparently 'onze heures' was all Osborne could elicit from the French general. Presumably it was French III Corps' troops and horse-drawn wagons that impeded and infuriated 5th Division as they were moving through Poperinghe in the small hours of the 29th. However de la Laurencie would probably not have got out at all if he had left it any later. ID 7 was advancing south of the Lys and 'while it was still night time' captured the entire French 124th infantry regiment at Deulemont. This was farther east than were de la Laurencie's forces, but by 29 May all IV Corps' divisions were advancing rapidly westwards and would have cut right across the French line of retreat.[32]

De la Laurencie's move left Osborne isolated. His division had moved on the night of the 28th to the Mont des Cats, a few miles from Hazebrouck. Osborne's rationale was that the hill was 'tankproof', so the division would lie up during the day and break out overnight. But the Germans attacked early, casualties were mounting and the situation looked bleak. Osborne seems from Blaxland's account to have virtually given up until persuaded to pull out on the morning of 29 May. By this time the only other British force south of Poperinghe was the garrison of Cassel, farther west, who in a famous rearguard action fought on until the evening of that day. As Blaxland pointed out, 44th Division was wide open to German attack but nonetheless successfully retreated northwards. It must have steered a fortuitous path between the panzers advancing from the east and IV Corps from the west. Its troops seem to have got to Poperinghe, and the haven provided by II Corps, with only a few losses, although ID 18 took some 44th Division men prisoner on the

29th. The haul was not large – seventy-six in all including some stragglers from 48th Division. IDs 31 and 61 may have taken more, but nevertheless the decision to pull out was fully vindicated. If the division had stayed, many more of its men would surely have gone into captivity.[33]

11. Aftermath

E VEN AS THE BATTLE on the canal continued on 28 May, the Belgian ceasefire meant that German units that had been fighting on that front were free to turn west. The way was opened to attacks on the Allies anywhere between Ypres and the coast at Nieuport. In practice this mainly meant the British, as there were few French units in the area. The whole line northwards from Noordschote, where 3rd Division's defences ended, was now potentially vulnerable – and almost unguarded.

Bock, Army Group B's commander, had considered the implications of the cessation of hostilities with Belgium even before the ceasefire was implemented. On 27 May a Belgian emissary arrived to request terms, and Bock wrote:

> I am worried that the unavoidable negotiations with the Belgians will result in a halt of our forward movement which, abetted by the resulting tangle of German and Belgian troops, the English will be able to exploit for themselves. The Belgians were, therefore, told to stay off the roads in complete units under their officers until further orders came.

He also set the boundaries between Sixth and Eighteenth Armies at Dixmude, so there would be the minimum friction and delay between them. Bock continued to intervene on the 28th: 'Worry that the surrender of the Belgians will stop the advance of my armies won't let go of me. I, therefore, issued orders for motorised battalions to be driven forwards towards the Yser Canal between Nieuport and Ypres as powerfully and quickly as possible.'[1]

The threat faced by the British when the Belgians surrendered gave rise to some of the most exciting incidents of the campaign, as scattered British units raced to block the German advances. For a brief period the war became a *Boy's Own* adventure – or would have done if it had not been a matter of real life and death. Among the main participants in these adventures was Gort's trusty reconnaissance regiment – the 12th Lancers – with its invaluable detachment of engineers led by 2nd Lieutenant Smith.

According to the 12th Lancers' summary of events, their CO, Herbert Lumsden, had been convinced on 27 May that 'the Belgian army would not long be continuing the struggle'. It is not clear whether Lumsden actually knew early on the 28th that the Belgians had already agreed a ceasefire prior to their formal surrender later that morning. In any event, whether through knowledge of the ceasefire or through his own intuition, Lumsden sent Smith off to destroy the bridges north of Noordschote. On the way he blew up the bridges on 3rd Division's front, which had already been primed for demolition. Meanwhile Lumsden assigned his squadrons to cover the line extending from Noordschote to the sea at Nieuport – almost sixteen miles covered by a few armoured cars.[2]

The Lancers' summary continued: 'The first contact made with the enemy was at Dixmude where 2/Lieutenant E. C. Mann reported that a black Mercedes Benz open touring car carrying a white flag and four fully armed German officers had passed him travelling at high speed.' Mann had been busy discussing the blowing of the bridges with Smith and had, therefore, missed the car until it was too late. According to Smith, who thought there were three cars, refugee traffic prevented Mann's two armoured cars catching up with the Germans. The Lancers were now on the hunt for the staff car or cars, but it was no easy task given their other commitments: 'It was a case of "Calling all [armoured] cars, calling all cars, black car containing German Staff Officers last seen moving West from Dixmude expected to move North, stop it or shoot".' Three staff cars, no doubt the same ones, were next seen at Nieuport, where: 'the occupants were conversing with Belgian Staff Officers and what appeared to be French Officers'. The cars moved out again, and one car managed to recross the canal at Dixmude. This time 'the three officers in the back seat were hard hit'. Wounded or not, the Germans would have ascertained the lack of defences in the area and the fact that the bridges at Nieuport and Dixmude were still intact, although the Belgians had prepared the latter for demolition.[3]

Smith and Mann went on to Dixmude bridge, presumably after the Germans had recrossed. Mann had to draw his revolver to persuade a Belgian officer to press the demolition switch but either the charges had been tampered with or the fuse had failed. There followed a strange incident when a French major told Mann that he would take charge and Mann could forget about the bridge. Mann was soon convinced that the major was a German masquerading as a Frenchman, but by then he had disappeared. Were the French officers at Nieuport also Germans in disguise? Mann again 'persuaded' the Belgian to show Smith where the charges were laid, and Smith provided a new fuse. According to Smith two Belgian officers opposed the blowing of the bridge and they 'may even now be arguing about it, certain it was that there was no argument on the bridge'. The bridge was satisfactorily blown, Mann commenting: 'Belgian Engineers never stinted the amount of explosives in their demolition charges.'[4]

Then according to Smith: 'The destruction had only just been completed when German motor cyclists arrived at high speed closely followed by infantry in lorries and it seems certain that they hardly expected the kind of reception they received.' What kind of reception was amplified by the 12th Lancers' summary: 'Well directed machine gun fire of this troop [Mann's armoured cars] soon accounted for the motor cyclists and for many of the men in the leading lorries. Nothing stirred for half an hour when German ambulances arrived to remove their wounded.' But then other German troops arrived. Mann's armoured cars counted some 250 vehicles entering Dixmude and reported: 'The road from Dixmude to Roulers as far as they could see was a solid mass of enemy MT [motor transport]'.[5]

Mann's quick thinking and Smith's cool efficiency had prevented a dangerous German incursion. Whether it would have been disastrous to the British if the motorised battalion – as the force described above presumably was – had got across is an open question. Most of the German forces in Army Group B were not motorised and would have taken much longer to advance.

On the British side, 3rd Division's 7th Guards' Brigade was in reserve about ten miles east of Dixmude, while the same division's left brigade on the Yser line was about six miles away. The DLM, for what it was worth – which is difficult to tell – was also in the vicinity. But the situation would undoubtedly have been difficult. The blowing of the bridge prevented it even being that. After the initial firefight the 12th Lancers became preoccupied elsewhere, and engineers of 59th Field Company, having taken part only the day before in the Comines counterattack, arrived to guard against German attempts to construct a replacement bridge at Dixmude.[6]

Farther north the situation was also threatening. Another troop of the Lancers had arrived at Nieuport, to find two bridges intact. Here German forces from Eighteenth Army were advancing down the coast. First to arrive at around 1100 was a motorcycle patrol. There was a brief and bloody battle with the Lancers' armoured cars in which both sides suffered, but the Germans came off worse. Just before this the Lancers had encountered a number of Belgian officers who were:

> . . . discussing whether their King had, or had not, capitulated. Many of the better ones particularly those belonging to the Cavalry and Air Force seemed

to think that he had, and expressed their disgust very quickly. A number made enquiries as to how they could join the British army, as they obviously wished to continue their struggle against the Germans.[7]

Meanwhile Smith continued his work, destroying bridges north and south of Dixmude. One of these, a footbridge, had been set on fire by a troop of Lancers. It was, however, already primed for demolition by the Belgians. But they had 'very wisely', as Smith ironically put it, 'fixed the firing end of the charge on the enemy side of the bridge'. In his usual, low-key style Smith then described an act of considerable bravery by himself and Lance-Corporal Hourigan: 'While L/Cpl Hourigan used a sandbag to keep the flames away from part of the charge, 2/Lieutenant Smith crossed over the bridge and refixed the detonating charge and the bridge was destroyed without any more trouble.' After having dealt with this and other bridges around Dixmude, Smith went to Nieuport. By now heavy fighting was going on, and, while one bridge had been destroyed, it was impossible to deal with the other.[8]

The fighting in Nieuport eventually sucked in not just the Lancers but also a host of miscellaneous units drafted from anywhere within reach. There were two light tanks; 7th Field Company, another of the 4th Division engineer companies which had fought at Comines; gunners of 53rd Medium Regiment, one of II Corps' units which had destroyed its guns south of the Lys before pulling out; and other miscellaneous units, including a substantial contingent of RASC men from II Corps Ammunition Field Park. All were under Lieutenant-Colonel Brazier of 53rd Medium, who became in effect an infantry CO for twenty-four hours. Fortunately the main body of German troops did not start arriving until the afternoon of 28 May. They too had been impeded by refugees, as the British had so often – hence their slow progress. According to Blaxland they had been provided with enough lorries to lift most of the division. Bock's urgings had obviously had their effect, but, as at Dixmude, they were not quite effective enough. The scratch British forces, reinforced during the night of 28th/29th by 22nd Field Regiment with its full complement of guns, held the line, although the Germans gained control of the undestroyed bridge and pushed troops across it. 12 Brigade, which had been sent to Nieuport on the evening of 28 May from their defensive position on the Lys, arrived the next morning and took over during the day. Subsequently the rest of 4th Division arrived and held a line from Nieuport to Furnes. Nieuport, which was on the edge of the beaches stretching to Dunkirk, remained a lynchpin of the Allied defence and was held until late on 31 May.[9]

The German attack on Nieuport was even more of a threat than that on Dixmude, but the successful British defence put a final end to any chances the Germans had of quickly rolling up the Allied line on the eastern side of the corridor leading to Dunkirk. Thus it is a fitting conclusion to this account of the defence of that corridor, which started with IV Corps' preliminary attacks on the Ypres–Comines Canal in the afternoon of 26 May. There were some other German attacks on the eastern front on the 29th: 3rd Division fought a sharp rearguard action on the Yser line in the afternoon; 7th Guards' Brigade of the same division marched to defend Furnes, since the forward line between Nieuport and Dixmude had now been abandoned, and subsequently there was street fighting in and around the town. But both these actions point up the fact that, except at Nieuport, the Germans had needed a day or more after the Belgian ceasefire to bring up substantial forces including artillery. By that time many of the defenders of the line had fallen back inside the Dunkirk perimeter, and 3rd and 4th Divisions – both relatively unscathed by fighting so far – had taken over the defence in accordance with the plan Brooke drew up on the 26th.[10]

While the British were falling back on the night of 28/29 May, IV Corps on the Ypres–Comines line still thought it had a battle to fight. All the indications are that the Germans were oblivious of the British withdrawal. ID 61's history quoted elaborate orders in which IR 151 was to start the divisional attack, with its preliminary target Warneton. Then both forward regiments, IR 162 and IR 151, would continue in the direction of Neuve-Église. Instead: 'When infantry scouts investigated on the morning of 29th May, they came up against no resistance.' Apparently a few Grenadier Guards were taken prisoner at Warneton. They were described as 'weak enemy defenders', but were almost certainly stragglers. Then 'the division, in marching column, pushed westwards in sunny, windy weather'. Farther north ID 31 reached the Kemmel at 1300, forestalling the panzers coming from the west by two hours. Meanwhile officers from ID 18 had 'entered Ypres and hoisted the swastika on the towers of the cathedral and town hall'. ID 18's report recorded: 'Masses of abandoned ammunition, heavy guns, tanks, ack-ack guns and columns of lorries evidence the end of the war in Belgium and Northern France.'[11]

IV Corps might have foreseen the end of the war in the north, but the British had one more task, the most vital of all: to get away. Gort and Pownall had foreseen the possibility of evacuation as early as 19 May. As a preliminary measure, Gort had ordered that rear area troops and other surplus personnel should be sent back and almost 28,000 had arrived in England by the 26th. Just before 1900 on that day the formal order for the evacuation – Operation Dynamo – was given by the Admiralty. Thus the Battle of the Ypres–Comines Canal effectively commenced at much the same time as the evacuation of the BEF. On the first full day of Operation Dynamo heavy bombing quickly put the main port out of action. There was confusion, which led to ships heading for Dunkirk being sent back empty, and the smaller vessels needed to clear the beaches had not yet been sent over. As a result only 7,669 men were landed in England on the 27th. On 28 May, however, organisation improved, and the east mole – really just a long jetty demarcating the eastern edge of the harbour – began to be used for loading troops. By the end of the day 17,804 more had returned.[12]

This was also the day when the British units on the Ypres–Comines line began making their way towards Dunkirk. Most of the infantry formations still had fighting to do or, at least, defence lines to man. 3rd, 4th and 50th Division's roles have already been mentioned, and even the remnants of 5th Division occupied a reserve line on 29 May. The majority of the field artillery regiments retained their guns for further use, but for the medium artillery regiments and a few other units the campaign was effectively over.

Some troops involved in the battle had already started the journey home. These were the wounded. For the BEF as a whole there were around 14,000, apart from the many wounded who were captured.[13] Gilmore's memoir vividly described the stages of evacuation for stretcher cases such as himself. He was wounded in the stomach and leg on the evening of the 27th after leading the Cameronians' counterattack. His first memory was waking in an Advanced Dressing Station in a barn, he thought at Locre, a small village near Kemmel. The prewar British Army of horses, point-to-points and the heat and dust of India was briefly recreated when Gilmore woke to find Major Paddy Creagh of the RAMC tending his wound. Creagh had last been seen by Gilmore unconscious, after breaking his own collar bone in a fall at Lucknow races in 1928. Gilmore also mentioned the RAMC orderlies, London territorials, who 'could not have been more gentle and kind'. Then he was taken by an ambulance to a Main Dressing Station situated in a convent: 'There were scores and scores of other stretcher cases, many in a far worse plight than I was. The continual cry was for water. The RAMC orderlies did their best, but they were very few, and the only tea they had was from their own rations; this they gave until there was none left.' A convoy departed, which Gilmore almost missed, but an additional lorry was found. Later he learned that the dressing station was captured soon afterwards.

Then began an agonising journey lasting forty-eight hours, with frequent lengthy delays. Lack of support for his head was, he remembered, the worst problem. During this saga, Gilmore's lorry took numerous wrong turnings, and at one time its occupants heard the noise of approaching tank tracks, which the occupants thought were German but turned out to belong to the Fife and Forfar Yeomanry. The lorry finally reached Dunkirk: 'We arrived eventually near what must have been an inner basin of the harbour and there were stuck. It was a scene of desolation. Recent bomb damage everywhere; a tug [perhaps meaning an artillery tractor] halfway across the road; cars smash[ed] up; a searchlight unit burnt out and still smouldering.' Gilmore had met another acquaintance, Brigadier Parminter, earlier and the lorry driver, who faithfully stuck to his duty, set out to find him.[14] Finally the lorry was rescued and taken to Parminter's HQ. By now two of the six wounded in the lorry were dead, and two delirious – Gilmore did not think they survived. Only he and a private were conscious. Parminter gave them brandy and water and 'very yellow' NAAFI cake. 'True to form', this was 'so tasteless that in spite of the fact that I was desperately hungry I could not eat it. The brandy and water was a different matter.'

Gilmore was finally lifted from the mole onto the *Maid of Orleans*, one of the cross-Channel ferries which did invaluable work in the evacuation: 'A kindly steward brought me some bully beef sandwiches. I had never eaten anything so delicious in my life.' He was slung ashore by crane at Dover, perhaps a testament to his weight as much as to the severity of his wounds. The Casualty Clearing Station there was the old workhouse: 'From my stretcher I could see a very large hall with a number of operating tables with separate teams for each. Apparently all the big London hospitals had teams of surgeons etc. working.' Gilmore was operated on by a – female – gynaecologist from Guy's, he thought a Dr Moore. Hearing of her specialism and needing an operation on his stomach, he managed to joke that in spite of its size he had no need of a gynaecologist. She operated: 'What an excellent job she made.'[15]

Gilmore's saga was no doubt more difficult and painful than that of many casualties, but it illustrates the problems in evacuating the wounded in the midst of the dereliction of Dunkirk. It also illustrates the dedication of the medical professionals, whether regulars or volunteers such as those at Dover, and the medical auxiliaries.

By the time Gilmore got back on 30 May, some artillerymen had already arrived in Britain. Part of 63rd Medium's headquarters had left on the evening of the 27th. After slow progress that night, the next day they reached a point about ten miles from Dunkirk, where they abandoned their vehicles. Hundreds of others were parked there to be destroyed later: 'In one direction on the horizon was a large pall of smoke rising hundreds of feet into the air, and it was soon apparent that this lay in the direction of Dunkirk.' The party got split up on the approach to the town. One group ended up on the promenade and, as they marched towards the mole: 'Marines were placed at strategic points marshalling and assisting men of the BEF . . . The organisation and behaviour of the naval and marine forces was admirable.' The group had boarded by about 1600 hours on 28 May, the diary noting assistance from the low cloud and pall of smoke. There was time for an issue of tea to the thousand or so aboard the ship before arrival at Dover, where they disembarked at dawn on the 29th.[16]

The exploits of Captain Derry of 60th Field were recounted in Chapter 6. The remnants of his battery ended up in a reserve position in La Basse-Ville, west of Warneton, late on 27 May. But after the success of the counterattacks they were well behind the British lines and did not see further action. They destroyed their guns – unmodernised First World War 18-pounders – and pulled out at 2100 on the 28th, making their way by lorry to Izenberge, a little place south of Furnes. The next morning they trekked down to the beaches at La Panne. This was the first day that large-scale evacuation from the beaches took place, in most cases via the famous 'little ships' used as ferries to larger ones lying offshore. Derry, however, boarded the MV *Bullfinch*, a cargo ship that had been beached. MV *Bullfinch* had swung broadside on and become firmly grounded, while subject to German bombing and strafing. Eventually, as Derry recalled: 'After a very anxious time from 1730 to 1815 the vessel floated and proceeded towards England.' In fact she had been pulled off by a passenger vessel, MV *Royal Sovereign*. Some 1,500 men on board came back safely.[17]

In total, 47,310 men landed in England on 29 May, in spite of continual air attack and heavy losses in ships. It was almost as many as had been evacuated up to the day before. Equally importantly the ships were now taking off large numbers of fighting men in organised units such as 60th Field and 63rd Medium, as opposed to rear area troops and stragglers.[18]

Other medium regiments had to wait until 30 May before they embarked. 5th Medium, for example, had proceeded towards Bergues, but shelling was too heavy to allow them to go through the town. Abandoning their vehicles and splitting into different parties, they arrived on the beaches at various times on the 29th. Then: 'An uneventful afternoon and night was spent awaiting transport and watching the severe bombing attacks on naval vessels. Luckily the beaches were hardly attacked at all, and only two lightly wounded casualties were suffered before embarkation of unit personnel.' This was mainly carried out on the 30th, although some did not go until the 31st. Personnel of Pratt's HQMA also departed on 30 May, in their case from the east mole. Two of their number were killed in bombing attacks on the ships they embarked on, while other personnel were 'bombed off one destroyer and two merchant ships before being picked up by a third'.[19]

In spite of these experiences, 30 May was in general a day of restricted German air activity because of mist and low cloud. It also saw an invaluable innovation on the beaches – the building of jetties out of abandoned lorries. Whoever first thought of the idea – there is some dispute – it was quickly copied. Because of these factors loading rates increased still more, and by midnight on the 30th another 53,823 men had been landed in England. In total, Operation Dynamo had now brought back more than 125,000 troops.[20]

Almost inevitably, it seems, the 12th Lancers were involved as they seem to have been with almost anything important that occurred to the BEF. On 30 May they had been ordered to embark in the morning, but when they reached the beach at La Panne they discovered: 'The Regt. had been personally and directly ordered by the C-in-C to reorganise the embarkation beaches at La Panne.' By 1300 they had taken over and reorganised three embarkation points and then made a lorry jetty. They supervised embarkation there, which 'continued in perfect order and with unabated zeal throughout the night'. At one stage more than 3,000 men per hour were embarking – presumably just in their sector. Still there on the 31st, the Lancers observed that shelling was intermittent and not severe, while 'any plane venturing to fly over the beach was met by a veritable tornado of Bofors and machine gun fire'. The Lancers alone had some dozen guns mounted in the sand dunes. The above presents a very different picture to the chaos and low morale depicted by some commentators, although of course the presence of a well-organised unit such as the Lancers must have helped.[21]

The saga of the 12th Lancers continued with their own embarkation at Malo les Bains late on 31 May: 'chiefly on dredgers belonging to the Tilbury Construction and Dredging Company'. This was truly in the realms of 'little ships' crewed by civilians whose connection to the open sea might be quite remote. Their 'very charming' hosts had fifty years' experience, but in two cases had 'lost sight of the shores of Great Britain for the first time in their lives'.[22]

Another familiar unit involved in jetty building was 225th Field Company of Royal Engineers, who had taken part in the first Comines counterattack. They arrived at La Panne in the early hours of 31 May. Then they spent 'all day building piers out of motor vehicles'. At 2230 a pier had to be repaired, and it was for his involvement in this episode that my stepfather, Bill Hedley, won his MC. His citation read:

> After having worked for the previous 24 hours on the construction of piers he was in charge of boats on the night of embarkation. Under heavy fire he continued throughout the night to collect all available boats and to organise their loading and despatch. When one pier became damaged in spite of heavy fire he organised repair parties and by his own example kept them at work throughout heavy shelling.

Finally, the tide going out, the pier became useless and the company were taken off in a variety of boats further down the coast.[23]

The battered remnants of 5th Division's infantry battalions also started back on 31 May. They had done no further fighting in their reserve position between Stavele and the Ypres–Furnes road. The Northamptons' history recorded the battalion putting its vehicles out of action on the 30th by mixing sand with the engine oil and racing the engines. Then it marched back to the Dunkirk mole, meeting Dempsey and Stopford there on the 31st. The history paid tribute to Stopford, 'always calm and cheerful however black the situation', to whose foresight it attributed the smooth progress to the mole. The battalion finally left on the destroyer HMS *Malcolm*, arriving at Dover on 1 June. More than 68,000 men, the highest daily total, had been landed the day before, and more than 64,000 on that day. By now many French troops were among them, Weygand having finally authorised their withdrawal on 29 May.[24]

Among the last British troops to go were the pioneers of the 1/6th South Staffordshires, still attached to 150 Brigade. In spite of their position a long way down the military pecking order they seem to have retained both discipline and good spirits. At least their diarist thought so. Although he may have gilded the lily a bit it seems unlikely that he simply made up an account of the last days when there were plenty of other witnesses. On 2 June they reached Dunkirk town near the mole: 'Spirit and discipline of troops excellent. None left shelter areas without orders, but between raids and bombardments, paddled in the sea and practised trick riding on abandoned motorcycles, scene often resembling Blackpool beach on Bank Holiday.' At 2100: 'Portion of beach cut off by picquet with gate left, into which troops filed two deep . . . Discipline admirable. No attempt to hurry unduly. Column about 4000 strong all moving by 2140 hours. Not a shot fired as they proceeded along mole in orderly column of route.' Two destroyers and two cross-Channel packets took them off, and they landed at Folkestone at dawn the next day. The diarist noted that they had kept their Bren guns, as did many other units. The last British troops were actually taken off in the early hours of 3 June, although more than 50,000 French troops were evacuated the following night. In total, and including those evacuated pre-Dynamo, 224,230 British troops came back to England; 140,000 French were also evacuated.[25]

The group from 63rd Medium Regiment's HQ, who had landed early on 29 May, recorded their reception at Dover: 'On entering the dockside railway station a plentiful supply of sandwiches, chocolate and fruit was available for the men without charge.' (The last comment demonstrating a remarkable modesty – as if the writer expected that the men might have to pay for their railway refreshment room sandwich like any other passenger.) They then entrained for Winchester and arrived at 1030, picking up further supplies of food and tea *en route*.[26]

Like 63rd Medium, most units arrived split up on different ships. And similarly they boarded trains when they disembarked and were sent all over the country to temporary accommodation. 12th Lancers, for example, landed at Margate in four separate parties and ended up in Liverpool, Halifax and Rhyl in North Wales. Then between 4 and 6 June half of them rejoined the regiment at Brighton, while the other half were given leave. This was a quick regrouping judging by other units' experience, and possibly the War Office attached special priority to the Lancers, because of their value on the retreat.[27]

More typical were the 6th Seaforths, regrouping up in Turiff in northeast Scotland. On 2 June their strength was precisely two – the Orderly Room sergeant, who had not been involved in the campaign, and one other soldier. Other men then came in, initially a trickle swelling into a stream: nine on 3 June, forty-four on the 4th and so on until the peak of 105 returners on 10 June. Up to 27 June, men were still coming in, including eighteen from hospital. Some of these may have been cases of sickness rather than wounds, but presumably some had been lightly wounded in the campaign. In all 434 other ranks and sixteen officers returned. During the campaign there were sixteen officer and 320 other rank casualties (including missing).[28]

The Seaforths did not suffer as badly as the other two 17 Brigade battalions on 27 and 28 May. This must have been partly because the Seaforths 'came back' – retreated – early on the 27th and then went into reserve. They are the only example found where disciplinary action was taken after the campaign. One of the Seaforths' officers was seen by Stopford, the brigadier, falling back again on the morning of 28 May – the incident is described in Chapter 9. Subsequently on 14

June there was a Court of Inquiry on the officer's conduct at brigade HQ, although the results were not revealed. There was also a cryptic note in the brigade war diary about a consultation between the brigadier and the colonel-in-chief of the regiment – a largely honorary position but no doubt involved when a controversial personnel change occurred. Subsequently Lieutenant-Colonel Reid, the CO during the campaign, left the battalion, and it can be presumed that the two things were connected and that the Seaforths' relatively poor performance was the reason.[29]

Morale and its connection with fighting ability are discussed further in the conclusion. But it should be said that the Seaforths certainly cannot be accused collectively of giving up without a fight. Of their casualties during the campaign, 176 including nine officers were killed or wounded, and no doubt significant numbers of the 'missing' were also killed or, if prisoners of war, were wounded.[30]

A large majority of the BEF had returned to Britain to fight again. With them came their commanders, and many of those directly involved in the Battle of the Ypres–Comines Canal went on to play important roles in the years of fighting ahead.

The most important was Alan Brooke. Whatever Gort and Pownall's earlier reservations about his pessimism, his rock-like imperturbability and good judgement during the retreat enhanced his reputation – his leadership of II Corps during the battle being the highlight. It must have been one of the reasons why he was chosen to return to France after Dunkirk in order to command the large number of British troops still south of the Somme. There he had the moral courage and force of character to insist, against Churchill's urgings, that they should also be evacuated. Brooke told the prime minister on the crackly telephone line between Le Mans and London that 'the French army was, to all intents and purposes, dead'. To Churchill's remonstrance that Brooke had been sent to make the French feel that we were supporting them, Brooke retorted that 'it was impossible to make a corpse feel'. Churchill, to give him credit, did not hold this against Brooke, who was quickly made C-in-C of Home Forces. With the British believing that they were in imminent danger of invasion, this was the most important job in the army, after that of CIGS.

Then in December 1941 Brooke replaced Dill as CIGS. For three and a half years he then resisted Churchill's wilder schemes and pursued a steady course in which the opening of the Mediterranean and knocking out of Italy were seen as the first steps towards the eventual invasion of northwest Europe. This 'Mediterranean strategy' has been often criticised, but it had the merit of working, albeit slowly.

What alternatives such as an earlier invasion of northwest Europe might have achieved is unknowable.[31]

Brooke was a great supporter of Montgomery, one of his divisional commanders during the retreat. Montgomery's role in the Ypres–Comines battle was peripheral, but his handling of 3rd Division's march from south of the Lys to north of Ypres on the night of 27/28 May was critical to the wider manoeuvre that Brooke was executing, and its success must have enhanced his status further in Brooke's eyes. It was Brooke's advocacy that helped Montgomery get the job of commander of Eighth Army in 1942, after which his ascent was continuous.

Much less well known than Montgomery, but one of the most successful generals of the Second World War, was Miles Dempsey, commander of 13 Brigade in the central sector of the battle. Dempsey seems to have fought the battle well – 13 Brigade's war diary being cleverly constructed to bring that fact to the foreground.[*] In fairness to Dempsey, whose personal integrity was stressed by all who knew him, diaries were not usually written up by commanding officers, and so he may have had nothing to do with it. The diary was probably irrelevant to the fact that Dempsey's reputation was enhanced by his conduct during the retreat. He was then fortunate enough to miss the North African campaign – the graveyard of many British generals' careers – before becoming a corps commander in time for the invasion of Sicily and the Italian campaign. By now a protégé of Montgomery's, his upward ascent continued, and in 1944 he commanded the British Second Army during the invasion of Normandy and the eleven months of fighting, which followed. Opinions are divided as to how far Dempsey was essentially under Montgomery's shadow, and how far he was his own man.[†]

Montague Stopford of 17 Brigade also ended as an army commander, although of a less famous army in a less well-known theatre. From 1943 he was in Burma, commanding first a corps and then in 1945 Twelfth Army. He held various other senior posts in southeast Asia during the period of winding down after the war – briefly under the direction of Dempsey who had also been moved out there.

Alan Adair of 3rd Grenadier Guards had as rapid a rise as did Dempsey, although from a lower level – he was only a major in 1940. By 1942 he was a major general commanding the Guards Armoured Division, which then fought with Dempsey's Second Army through Normandy and beyond until the end of the war. Perhaps its most famous exploit was the hundred-mile dash in two-and-a-half days that

---

[*] See Appendix 1.

[†] Readers might like to consult Peter Rostron's recent biography, *The Life and Times of General Sir Miles Dempsey*, Barnsley, Pen & Sword, 2010.

culminated in the liberation of Brussels on 3 September 1944. It must have been satisfying for Adair to advance so quickly over the same terrain as had seen the BEF's bitter retreat in May 1940.

Donald Butterworth of the North Staffordshires also ended as a major general, although his future career did not take him outside the United Kingdom. In keeping with the modest and reticent character of his regiment, whose history is commemorated in just one slim volume, very little seems to be known about his life.

In contrast Herbert Lumsden, brilliantly successful as the CO of the 12th Lancers, continued in the limelight. He commanded X Corps in North Africa in September 1942, but then fell foul of Montgomery. Nick Smart believed his dismissal by the latter was a result of a personality clash as much as of any failure by Lumsden. Later he became the British representative on Douglas MacArthur's staff in the Pacific, where in January 1945 he was killed by a kamikaze attack on USS *New Mexico*.[32]

'Ambrose' Pratt, the CCMA in the battle, continued in similar roles at a slightly higher level in Tunisia, Sicily and Italy before retiring as a major general. After his obituary appeared in *The Times* in 1960, an 'other rank' at his HQ with V Corps in Tunisia, John Bone, wrote a letter of tribute:

> I best remember him wearing an army issue pullover with badges of rank sometimes obscured chatting to a motley collection of O.R.s outside the map room or tent and explaining the situation on the First Army front in North Africa. He made us all, cooks, drivers, batmen etc feel as if we were really doing something and that our small contribution was really very important.[33]

Pratt was also the recipient of a touching letter from his French liaison officer, Raymond Paikine, which showed something of one Frenchman's attitude to the British and the events of 1940. It was an attitude very different to Weygand's. Postmarked Montlucon, Allier, and dated 28 July 1940, it read:

> Dear Sir.
>
> I just learn that the mail is working again to Great Britain, and I won't wait any longer to try to give you some news.
>
> I have just been demobilised and have rejoined my family a few days ago somewhere in the centre of France, in a non-occupied town. And now that you know we are all safe, and if the censor will allow me to say so, let me tell you Sir, that I have lost my smile on the day of the armistice, and won't get it back before your victory. God may protect you and your

country. I don't dare to say what is in my heart, but you will understand that I have not changed, and am still very confident that you will have your way. Please Sir, do still believe in my friendship, and accept, my very heartiest wishes of health and victory.

Respectfully yours, (Sgd) PIKE.

It is nice to think that the BEF, that army of nicknames, also gave them to their French liaison officers.[34]

Henry Pownall never reached the heights but had a respectable future career. He was briefly vice CIGS under Dill and commanded in Northern Ireland for a while in 1940–1 – an important position given fears of invasion. Later he went east. Brooke considered him as supreme commander for southeast Asia in 1943, but in the end Mountbatten became supreme commander and Pownall his chief of staff. That Brooke even considered him in the role of commander suggests that he did not think badly of Pownall, in spite of their clashes in 1940, as does his comment on Pownall as Mountbatten's chief of staff: 'I had full confidence in his ability and considered he might counter some of Dickie's lack of balance and general ignorance in the handling of land forces'.[35]

By contrast Gort's career ran into the sand. Whether justified or not, the stigma of leading a defeated army stuck to him. In fact his later commands were perhaps more suitable for his pugnacious character and interest in detail: he was governor of Gibraltar in 1941–2 and then of Malta in 1942–4, both fulcrums of the British campaign in and around the Mediterranean. He finished as high commissioner in Palestine and Transjordan. What he would have made of the later stages of that thankless posting is not known, as at the end of 1945 he collapsed and was invalided home with cancer, dying in March 1946.[36]

Harold Franklyn continued to hold important positions, but, probably because of his age, was not subsequently posted abroad, so never again experienced an active operational command. This was ironic given that he had charge of two of the BEF's most successful actions: the Arras counterattack and the Battle of the Ypres–Comines Canal. He commanded VIII Corps in Britain in 1940–1. As with Pownall's Northern Ireland command, corps commands in Britain at that time were important because of the fear of invasion. Then Franklyn became GOC of British troops in Northern Ireland, and finally C-in-C Home Forces in 1943. By then this was essentially an administrative position, although presumably, given the large number of troops concerned, quite an important one. Brooke's occasional references to Franklyn in his diary are remarkable for the absence of any waspish comments. Even Dempsey, usually seen as a modest man, was described by Brooke on one occasion as 'suffering from a swollen head' and given a dressing down – this when he was a senior general.[37]

Many of the units that fought at Ypres–Comines prior to retreating from Dunkirk were able to gain their revenge later in the war. 5th Division travelled widely, participating in the capture of Madagascar from Vichy France before going to India and then Persia, when in 1942 that country briefly became the centre of British fears of a German breakthrough in the Caucasus. Then the division returned to Europe, fighting in Italy before finishing the war in northwest Europe.[38] 50th Division was in the D-day invasion spearhead, in June 1944, with some of its battalions the first to land. Montgomery's old command, 3rd Division, was also in the D-day landings. They were supported by the 13th/18th Hussars, who had taken part in the first Comines counterattack. On D-day they were piloting the amphibious tanks, which 'swum' ashore. Fortunately most of theirs survived the swim, in contrast to the Americans who suffered heavy losses.

What of the German units involved? All of them, as was practically inevitable, fought in Russia. ID 18 became a motorised division in 1941. It was almost destroyed in the Soviet summer offensive of 1944, but parts of the division fought on right up to the Battle of Berlin. For the personnel who survived all the way through to that spring of 1945, it must have seemed a long way from the heady summer of 1940. But they would have been few: the division's initial strength was about 18,000; its total casualties were 18,000 dead and missing and more than 60,000 wounded. Many of the casualties would have been the reinforcements constantly drafted in as the Russian front drained the Wehrmacht, but even so it can only have been a few lucky ones who came through the war from 1940 alive and without a serious wound, or without having been captured.[39]

ID 31, too, was destroyed by the Russians in the summer of 1944. Its remnants were used to form the basis of a Volksgrenadier division, which also finished the war in the Berlin area. Volksgrenadier divisions were one of Hitler's last-ditch expedients, formed with two regiments rather than three and with less artillery. ID 61 also became one in late 1944, after suffering heavy losses in Courland. The division staff were captured in Konigsberg in April 1945.

The German divisions' fate had been anticipated earlier in the war by Sixth Army, of which they were part during the Battle of the Ypres–Comines Canal: its final remnants surrendered at Stalingrad on 2 February 1943. Armies are HQ formations and their composition may change from time to time, so most of the units in Sixth Army in 1943 were different to those in 1940. Coincidentally IV Corps, although with a different divisional line-up, had been reallocated to the army a few months before, in time for the 1943 surrender.

With Sixth Army into captivity went its commanding officer, Friedrich Paulus. Hitler had made him a field marshal a few days earlier, hoping Paulus would commit suicide – apparently no German field marshal had ever been taken captive – and save some face for his master. Paulus resisted the temptation, and indeed later threw in his lot with the Soviets. His connection with the Ypres–Comines story is that he was chief of staff under Reichenau in 1940 and, as such, must have been ultimately responsible for the orders of 24 May, which were captured by Sergeant Burford.

The career of the officer who abandoned the orders when he ran for his life from Burford's revolver, Eberhard Kinzel, is equally remarkable in a different way. Kinzel seems not to have suffered at all from his – and the German army's – misfortune over the capture, rising to become lieutenant general and chief of staff of the German armies in northwest Europe at the end of the war. He was one of the four German officers who signed the surrender document at Lüneburg Heath on 4 May 1945. Subsequently Kinzel feared that he would face lengthy imprisonment and hence separation from his beloved mistress, Erika von Aschoff, and in a suicide pact he shot her and then himself. Ironically, since most generals escaped any significant punishment, Kinzel probably would have done too.[40]

As was seen in Chapters 3 and 4 Walther von Reichenau, the commander of Sixth Army in 1940, probably bore less responsibility for the battle than either Bock or Schwedler, the commander of IV Corps. But in spite of Bock's disparaging comment that he was a 'big kid', Reichenau seemed set for the highest ranks of German command until his career was cut short. A zealous Nazi and anti-Semite, he was one of Hitler's favourite generals. Yet, strangely, he remained on good terms with his sister-in-law Maria, who throughout the war sheltered Hans Hirsch, her Jewish lover, in her apartment. Reichenau continued with Sixth Army until late in 1941, when Hitler dismissed Rundstedt as head of Army Group South. Reichenau took over, but his triumph was short-lived as he suffered a cerebral haemorrhage followed by a fatal heart attack in January 1942.

Ironically, Reichenau was replaced by his former superior, Fedor von Bock, the commander of Army Group B in 1940. When the invasion of Russia was launched, Bock commanded Army Group Centre. The editor of Bock's diary, K. Gerbet, argued that in this position Bock, unlike Reichenau, did not act to accelerate the terror against Russian Jews behind the German lines. Bock's diary yields little evidence one way or another. When the Soviet winter offensive of 1941 began Bock was replaced. Although Evan Mawdsley is critical of his military judgement, Bock's diary suggested that he anticipated and warned against the over-extension of the German advance. It also suggested that health reasons as much as a loss of confidence by Hitler were behind his replacement. Certainly when Reichenau died only a month later, Bock retained enough standing to be appointed as his replacement. In July 1942 he was removed for the final time. Mawdsley suggested that the ostensible reason, a minor delay to one operation, was not the real one, which was Hitler's 'long-standing friction with the sexagenarian and aristocratic Prussian field marshal and [his] desire to assert his own authority'. Bock survived almost until the end of the war when his car was strafed by a British plane and he was killed.[41]

Bock has had little written about him by British historians, while Rundstedt has often received their plaudits. Yet Bock seems to have read the implications of the British retreat, and the situation prior to and during the Dunkirk evacuation, far better than Rundstedt.

The Germans who were involved in the Battle of the Ypres–Comines Canal were to go onto further triumphs, but, ultimately, their journey led to disaster and in many cases death. These they had already been brought to the inhabitants of the towns and villages on the Ypres–Comines line. Bourgeois described the scene around Comines:

> Everywhere, among the craters left by the shells (for example four hundred and forty-four on the twenty-four hectares cultivated by Emile Bonte at Mai Cornet) lay animals with their entrails torn out and stinking in pools of blood. Buildings, with shattered windows, their fronts riddled with shell splinters, likewise the burnt out ruins of Gerard Nuytten's, the Ghesquieres' and the Dekerle's farms and of the Cle des Champs, made the scene nightmarish right from the boundaries of Mai Cornet. Here and there, in the midst of the broken glass, the bits of broken tiles and the debris of all kinds, lay bodies from both armies.[42]

Many of the inhabitants of Comines and its immediate vicinity had little warning of the battle and, as several war diaries testified, remained throughout sheltering in cellars where possible. No doubt most of the inhabitants of the villages farther back removed themselves and constituted a large part of the refugees crowding the roads whom Franklyn came across on 28 May. In Ypres the inhabitants sheltered in cellars and in the ramparts, as this South Staffordshire diary entry of the 28th testified.

All refugees moved out of tunnels in the ramparts in our sector at dawn; a most unpleasant but necessary job.* Impossible to evacuate to civil hospitals whose cellars were full of aged people and cripples unable to move without transport. 62 dead civilians buried by 'A' Company from one hospital alone. Belgian nuns and red cross did wonderful work but the civil authorities had abandoned their posts and no arrangements had been made to feed these people many of whom were starving. This did not make the thought of a siege defence very cheerful.[43]

In the event the South Staffs moved out that night, distributing food that could not be carried 'around civil hospitals before the enemy could get at it'.[44]

---

* The diary does not explain why they were moved, but fear of fifth columnists in the immediate vicinity of British troops may have been the reason.

Conclusion

THE BATTLE OF THE Ypres–Comines Canal is one of those curious hybrids in military history: both sides could regard it as a success. To the German forces involved, it was an important step on the road to their eventual stunning victory. The lectures on German IV Corps' operations given soon after the campaign recorded that after the battle:

> . . . the ring is closed. Tens of thousands of French lay down their arms in the next few days around Lille and south of it . . . The march to the sea did not work in spite of British determination.* The divisions of IV AK [Armeekorps] had the lion's share of the victory. Hard to find words to describe these achievements.[1]

Tactically, too, the Germans seem to have had the best of the fray. Casualties on each side were comparable, but considerable numbers of British prisoners were taken (*see* Appendix 3). If they considered the battle more closely, however, thoughtful German observers might have been less optimistic about its course and outcome. As the lecturers themselves had noted a few pages earlier: 'The British are fighting [to allow] the retreat of their columns heading north in a continual stream . . .' And they were, of course, successful in that aim.[2]

After the battle, the British forces that had been south of the Lys were stationed between Ypres and the coast. The march to the sea had worked for them. On 27 and 28 May, while these troops escaped, the German divisions on the Ypres–Comines front were making limited progress against British forces, which at first were distinctly inferior in numbers. If the Germans inflicted greater losses, they did not achieve the much more important tactical success of breaking the British line on a permanent basis. In strategic terms, too, the British could view the battle with

---

* A true enough judgement if applied to French troops.

184

satisfaction. It was not exactly a victory – after all it was one stage of a retreat – but it was a vital building block in their successful withdrawal.

The survey of the battle in this book points to two lessons for students of military history in the Second World War. One is what the battle shows about the fighting ability of the BEF compared to the German army. The other lesson is its significance to the saving of the BEF.

Casualties are one macabre test of success or failure. Given that the Germans were attacking and the British defending, the higher total of British killed and captured seems to imply that the Germans fought more effectively. It is often suggested that casualties in defence are typically lower than those in attack, for the obvious reason that defenders have more opportunity to take shelter.

This is a simplistic perspective, however. The British had few of the usual advantages of the defence, having just a few hours to prepare along a line that offered little in the way of natural shelter. They were initially opposed by a much superior force. There were, most probably, twelve battalions in the front line of the German attack as against seven British, of which one – the 8th Warwicks – was seriously denuded.[3] In these circumstances it was likely that the British would eventually give way. When this happened on 27 May, the first day of the battle, it was inevitable that British troops in the front line, many of them by that time wounded, would be captured. It also occurred on the morning of the 28th in the north, when elements of the Northamptonshires and the RSF made their last stand. As Colonel Tod of the RSF said: 'The Germans were still around, the barn was full of wounded and our ammunition was all but expended. Rightly or wrongly, I then surrendered.' Most people would judge that Tod did the only thing possible. 'Fighting to the finish' is the stuff of heroics but not of modern Western warfare. Martin Middlebrook, drawing examples from the First World War and the Korean War, concluded: 'Men in Western armies do not normally fight on to certain death.'[4]

The idea that defenders incur fewer killed is also something of a myth. Everything depends on the circumstances of the battle. At Ypres–Comines, the British not only started with a mediocre defensive position and a considerable inferiority in numbers but also the knowledge that they must not lose too much ground. Hence it was essential to counterattack. Successful counterattacks regained ground and destabilised the enemy. A number of examples of this occurring were seen in earlier chapters. Counterattacks were, however, potentially expensive in lives. Not only did those participating have to leave the relative safety of their trenches or dugouts, but also such attacks had of necessity to be organised hastily and might lack artillery or machine-gun support. During the course of the battle there were frequent British counterattacks. They encompassed the two major ones in the south on 27 May, complemented by the Cameronians' costly attack in the centre, and numerous local attacks. The 1/7th Warwicks and their trusty helpers from 245th Field Company also mounted a whole series during the 27th. The Cameronians and the Inniskillings both mounted attacks on the morning of 27 May, too, and the latter continued on the 28th with the struggle for Nuyttens Farm, during which Lieutenant Dane was killed. Yest another counterattack on 27 May was by the RSF to cover their retreat from Hill 60, and both they and the Northamptons seem to have attempted counterattacks on the morning of the 28th, although by then both battalions were surrounded.

Thus, although the British lost more men killed and captured than did the Germans, that does not necessarily suggest inferior fighting ability. It may just have been an inevitable result of the way the battle had to be conducted. The more important indicators are the successes of the British in regaining ground on 27 May, when they brought reinforcements into the battle, and in holding their positions on the 28th after the initial German gains in the north.

This brief review brings us back to questions posed in the first chapter. How well trained and led was the BEF? How did its equipment compare to the Germans'? Did communication difficulties hinder it? How effective was the support given by the artillery?

The evidence provided by a close study of the Battle of the Ypres–Comines Canal is that in a number of key characteristics the BEF was much better prepared than it is sometimes given credit for. Its physical equipment was discussed in Chapter 1 and there is not much more to be said here. On the downside was the lack of mortars. That this had a real impact is shown by the frequency with which British war diaries ruefully described enemy mortar fire. They also referred to the value of their own mortars, but clearly if they had had larger numbers they could have done more damage with them. The alleged superiority of German machine guns, however, received no real attention in war diaries. British war diarists frequently mentioned enemy machine-gun fire, but they gave equal or more prominence to the value of their own machine guns, both Vickers and Brens. The enemy submachine guns were what really caught the attention of diarists. The most striking revelation in diaries – both British and German – was the value of the Bren carriers. To the German infantryman they had the same damaging psychological impact as did tanks, with which they were frequently confused. Therefore there seems no reason from a study of the battle to revise the earlier conclusion that both sides were fairly equally matched in terms of fighting equipment, each having some advantages over the other.

Questions of training, morale and leadership are harder to pin down. Undoubtedly the British found it hard to cope with some elements of German tactics, notably infiltration. There were only two solutions to this: one was impossible, and the other difficult. The first solution was to have a more solid front line, which was impossible because of lack of numbers. The second was for forward troops to stand firm, even if they thought they were surrounded, and to wait for friendly counterattacks. But this was psychologically difficult even if troops were prepared for it, while the paucity of British forces meant that it was hard to muster the troops to counterattack even though, as has been seen, a number were launched. If the Germans were held, however, they showed their own tactical limitations. As stated in a 1941 publication on the German army (whose comments on tactics went back to 1940), if infiltration failed 'the attacking force then advance in mass formation making little use of the ground'. At a number of points during the battle this was exactly illustrated. If the British then stood firm, as they usually did, the Germans suffered heavy casualties and made no progress.[5]

In general the Germans thought that British morale was high. After the campaign IV Corps compiled a report on the British army. This was no doubt based mainly on the Ypres–Comines battle, although the corps had fought a number of other times against British troops. On morale the report stated:

> The English* soldier was in excellent physical condition. He bore his own wounds with stoical calm. The losses of his own troops he discussed with complete equanimity. He did not complain of hardships. In battle he was tough and dogged. His conviction that England would conquer in the end was unshakable.[6]

Of course there were times when morale cracked and troops fell back. This happened most notably with the Seaforths, but the very number of survivors in even the most hard-hit battalions tells its own story. Some 401 officers and men of the RSF mustered when the battalion regrouped during June 1940, for example, and most battalions recorded numbers of 400–450. They might have included a few lightly wounded who had already returned to duty, but most were unwounded survivors. On the most lurid reports, the RSF had been surrounded and virtually wiped out. In actuality, it evidently had not.[7]

---

* The Germans tended to use 'English' to mean 'British'.

There were many good reasons why men returned safely to Britain. Some may have gone astray in the interminable journeys before the battle and eventually reached Dunkirk. Some were involved in transport and supply, and thereby missed the fighting. A few were detached as a 'cadre' echelon in case a battalion was completely wiped out and had to be re-formed. My father-in-law, Bob Thorne, was one such and, therefore, escaped the 1st East Lancashires' fighting retreat, during which Captain Ervine-Andrews won the Victoria Cross (VC). Other troops, however, as with the Seaforths, made unauthorised and sometimes disorganised withdrawals. Several entries in artillery war diaries noted this phenomenon and showed the artillery's value as a rallying point for stragglers. Even with such incidents, however, there are often good explanations. In such a scattered battle, detachments might get bypassed. Sarkar gave an example in the Escaut engagement, in which elements of a company in a forward position completely missed the battle, found their company commander killed and eventually pulled back. In other cases, withdrawal may have been a rational strategy. When soldiers from the Northamptons and the RSF pulled back on the morning of 28 May, as some undoubtedly did, it was almost certainly better for their country as well as them that they lived to fight again rather than took further part in futile resistance. Even if many British soldiers made unauthorised withdrawals at various times, the Germans were clear on the relative capacity of resistance of the British and their Allies: 'In defence the Englishman took any punishment that came his way. During the fighting IV Corps took relatively fewer English prisoners than in engagements with the French and Belgians. On the other hand, casualties on both sides were high.'[8]

Finally German troops were certainly not immune from panic. This was most notable in the collapse of IR 176 after the Guards' counterattack on 27 May, but there were other examples. A considerable number of German prisoners seem to have been taken by the 1/7th Warwicks, perhaps infiltrators who had been cut off and lost their nerve.[9]

Leadership is almost as intangible as morale. It is clear that British officers at the highest level were willing to operate well forward, either to see the situation for themselves or to exert direct control. Brooke himself came under shellfire when he reconnoitred the canal on 26 May. Not long afterwards Gilmore of the Cameronians encountered Franklyn chivvying his troops into position on the canal. On the 27th Brooke found Franklyn out visiting his brigades, and on the 28th Franklyn again set out to do this, although he did not succeed. The brigadiers, too, were decidedly hands-on, particularly Stopford who visited all his battalion HQs on the night of 27/28 May, even though at least one of them was probably surrounded by the enemy.

James Muirhead of 143 Brigade was less prominent than Dempsey or Stopford, although an eyewitness has him close to the action on one occasion. His apparently muted part in the battle may be due partly to Franklyn's personal involvement in organising the second counterattack on the 27th. However Peter Caddick-Adams suggested that Muirhead did not have a reputation as someone who led from the front, and his career petered out in 1941.[10]

Launching the second counterattack – that of the Guards and Staffordshires – was Franklyn's major contribution to the battle. He approved but evidently did not know much about the previous counterattack by the Engineers/Hussars/Black Watch. Of course he also made the initial dispositions, but it is difficult to see how anyone else would have done that very differently. Otherwise his scope to make decisions was limited by the fluidity of the battle. The movements of 10 Brigade on 28 May, for example, were largely decided by their brigadier, Evelyn Barker. Franklyn's other main achievement was to keep up morale by visiting his units and by remaining calm, to which there is universal testimony. With the reassurance of such a presence behind them, his brigadiers and battalion COs largely fought the battle out themselves, with the support of the artillery.

In the wider retirement of which Ypres–Comines formed a part, the other senior officers of the BEF seem to have functioned well collectively in spite of individual failures. One early decision, before retirement had been decided on, was to move I Corps' medium artillery to the Ploegsteert area to form a central reserve. It was to pay dividends in the days ahead. The subsequent moves of II Corps are sometimes represented as entirely the work of Brooke, but in fact they formed part of a larger manoeuvre that had been planned during conferences involving GHQ on 26 May. Subsequent to that, command and control tended to break down in I and III Corps, and so one of Brooke's many achievements was to have maintained firm control of II Corps, which was a lynchpin of the defence during the next two critical days.

In spite of problems at corps level, divisions largely held together and retreated successfully. Then on 28 May, as the Battle of the Ypres–Comines Canal was still being fought, the Belgians surrendered. It was at this vital time that the BEF operated particularly effectively. Brooke and Montgomery extended II Corps' line northwards, while Ronald Adam, who was in charge of the British perimeter around Dunkirk, and his CRA Brigadier Lawson energetically mobilised scratch forces to defend the eastern perimeter at Nieuport, with results described in Chapter 11. David French has suggested that the Germans 'outthought and out manoeuvred' the BEF, but between 26 and 29 May this was not the case.[11]

At the middle-ranking and junior officer level the only example of sustained weakness is among the Seaforths, and here their heavy officer casualties provides one explanation. What is remarkable otherwise is the way some units, such as the 8th Warwicks whose officer ranks had been brutally thinned before the battle even began, managed to keep functioning. The continued resistance by them and other units or small groups was partly a result of leadership by both commissioned and NCOs, and in some cases private soldiers. Many examples have been given in the previous chapters.

Leadership, morale and training are all relevant to an assessment of that vexed question – how did the territorial battalions perform compared with the regulars? The IV Corps report mentioned earlier thought that the 'territorial divisions are inferior to the regular troops in training, but where morale is concerned they are their equal'. If by 'divisions' it meant formations that IV Corps encountered, it may have had the Seaforths in mind, as ID 18 captured a number of soldiers from that battalion. Clearly it put up a less satisfactory performance than others, although there were factors beyond the Seaforths' control which contributed to that. Because of the attention given in Chapter 5 to the (territorial) 8th Warwicks, and to the criticism of them by the (regular) Ox and Bucks, it is possible to be more discriminating about other territorial units. Far from deserving the criticism, the 8th Warwicks actually put up a fine display in spite of their heavy prior losses. Major Kendal, their CO, admitted one detachment did retreat on two occasions, but this was no more than happened in other battalions such as the (regular) Cameronians on the morning of 27 May. In fact the weakest link in the southern sector was the Ox and Bucks, which withdrew farther than either of the Warwicks' battalions before the counterattacks re-established the situation. As with the Seaforths, there were legitimate reasons for this, the Ox and Bucks occupying a largely flat stretch of land bordering the Lys with few natural defensive positions (although the Guards managed to establish a defensive line along the river Kortekeer later on). One reason for the Ox and Bucks' withdrawal was that their reserve company was unaccountably – and it would seem inexcusably – out of touch and, therefore, not available to make a local counterattack.[12]

Finally on this subject perhaps the best single battalion performance in the whole battle was that of the 1/7th Warwicks – the other territorial battalion in 143 Brigade – together with their gallant helpers 245th Field Company of Royal Engineers, also territorials. Like all the other battalions in the southern sector the 1/7th Warwicks lost heavily in the initial German onrush, although the numerous officer casualties of the German regiment involved in the attack on Houthem,

IR 82, show that the Warwicks exacted a heavy toll. What is remarkable is the way the 1/7th Warwicks continued to make local counterattacks throughout 27 May and were still aggressively patrolling on the morning of the 28th. Chapters 8 and 9 described how the resistance of the 1/7th Warwicks and 245th Field Company hampered German progress throughout the entire central sector.

The first chapter of *The Road to Dunkirk* mentioned that the 1/7th had actively trained after its arrival in France in January. That training must have contributed to its success, but it is uncertain how typical this was. The achievements of the 1/7th Warwicks certainly suggest that the territorial battalions could perform as well as the regular battalions and that reservations by regulars about the territorials perhaps owed as much to prejudice as to objective assessment.

Whatever doubts have been expressed about the infantry, most commentators have been positive about the contribution of the Royal Artillery in both world wars. On the evidence of its performance in the Battle of the Ypres–Comines Canal, it deserves this praise. What is striking is that even those of its operational skills that have been questioned, in particular liaison with the infantry, in fact seem to have been carried out well. In spite of the lack of inter-arms training before the German attack, there never seems to have been any suggestion that the artillery pursued their own agenda. They were there to support the infantry.

The number of tributes paid to the field artillery, who were the branch of the artillery responsible for close infantry support, is striking: Sergeant Welburn of 60th Field and his detachment manhandling their 18-pounder forward to deal with enemy snipers and mortars 'with great skill and daring' (Chapter 6); a 25-pounder battery engaging an enemy mortar within a few minutes of receiving the map reference from the Northamptons (Chapter 8); and the effective covering fire provided by the artillery as the DCLI advanced near St Eloi (Chapter 9). These examples could be multiplied. Conversely the infantry diaries recorded a few instances where the artillery was firing on British troops, but in a battle with a constantly fluctuating front line it must have been difficult to avoid this without unduly restricting the artillery's fire.

Morale in the artillery seems to have remained high. Artillerymen had some inbuilt advantages over infantrymen, of course. The infantryman's lot in a defensive battle was to remain inactive for long periods, often in isolated positions, the target of enemy shells or mortar fire, possibly with enemy submachine-gunners infiltrating behind him with the noise of their fire stretching his nerves to breaking point. He might wait hours like this before even heavier shelling and machine-gun fire heralded an attack. Artillerymen by contrast had a defined job among a group of comrades, usually not far from other guns in the battery. For the most part the main danger was counter-battery fire, and there was relatively little of that in the battle. If they were firing frequently there was plenty of activity to take their mind off their fears.

In contrast to the tributes paid to the artillery, the RAF was the recipient of plenty of criticism during the campaign. The war diaries were full of comments about the presence of the Luftwaffe and the absence of the RAF. This was not, of course, the fault of the RAF pilots and men. Not only were they thinly stretched but also from 26 May onwards their main task was the defence of the Dunkirk area against enemy air attack. However, as shown in Appendix 2, in spite of the absence of the RAF the Luftwaffe was of little more than nuisance value to British troops, which is why it has rarely been mentioned in this book. Indeed when the Battle of the Ypres–Comines Canal started it was not even that, since attacks were rare. The heavy artillery bombardment of Wytschaete on 28 May was accompanied by air attacks, and earlier there had been a damaging attack on the Sherwood Foresters; but with a few such exceptions the Luftwaffe by then was mainly engaged in attacking targets nearer the coast.[13]

The BEF has been heavily criticised for its lack of effective communication. The absence of battlefield radios was noted in Chapter 1, but there is no evidence that the Germans had these or, if they did, that they worked well on the battlefield. The Germans seem to have mainly used rocket signals, but when the situation became chaotic, as it did for ID 31 after the various counterattacks on 27 May, then they found communication as difficult as did the British. Clearly technical difficulties hampered the use of the radios that existed in the BEF, in the artillery and at battalion HQs in the infantry. As was seen in Chapter 6 the artillery's radios did not always work. Communication problems for the infantry can be illustrated by the incident late in the battle when a liaison officer had to be sent to call off an attack by the Beds and Herts, when yet again the radio was not working. In general during the battle brigadiers seem to have communicated with battalions via liaison officers or personal visits, suggesting that radios were regarded as too unreliable (and perhaps too insecure). One striking example where effective radio communication might have been invaluable was during 6th DLI's erratic progress northwards, recounted in Chapter 10. They took well over twenty-four hours to arrive near Ypres, in spite of having their own transport. Most of that time had been spent waiting, and communication difficulties seem the most likely reason for these delays. Communications were sometimes very effective: for example, the 12th Lancers had radios in their armoured cars and used them to keep in touch with each other and with GHQ.

The verdict must be that more radios would have been better, but it is not clear that their relative paucity made any decisive difference. In sharp contrast to the lack of radios the BEF had the ability, denied to any other army, to move a large proportion of their units by lorry. The Germans clearly had some capacity to do this, even in the mainly horse-drawn divisions of Army Group B, as shown by Bock's orders to motorised units after the Belgian surrender to move towards the Yser Canal. But their capability was limited compared with the BEF. The author has found no survey that itemises all the key moves that the BEF units made and how they made them. But a cursory glance at the map suggests that the ability to switch several divisions from the eastern frontier line to the southwestern front on 23–24 May would simply not have been possible without motorisation. It would probably have been just possible to get 5th Division's units into position on the Ypres–Comines Canal by the 26th, by marching on foot. But the troops would have arrived exhausted and no doubt considerable numbers would have dropped out. The drawback to motorisation was that lorries were frequently late and, as was seen in Chapter 4, some 5th Division units waited many hours for them on 25 May. Presumably difficulties in locating units, in some cases accompanied by enemy air attacks, were the main reasons for delays. That the problem was systemic is suggested by an entry in the Ox and Bucks' diary for May 16th: '. . . after the customary long and tedious wait for troop-carrying vehicles'.[14]

Where units had their own vehicles progress was usually rapid. This was so with the artillery, where field regiments from all over got into position on the Ypres–Comines line early on 26 May having travelled overnight. 50th Division, who were motorised, also moved fast once they had their orders.

The BEF's ability to carry out complicated manoeuvres rapidly in order to shore up its threatened fronts gets remarkably little attention in the literature. Yet without the prewar investment in motorisation it would have been impossible. Such investment in motorisation was enhanced by the ability of the troop-carrying companies to move at night. Presumably they had been trained in this, and their expertise was particularly important, for example, on the night of 25/26 May. The 1/7th Warwicks' training itemised in Chapter 1 included several night exercises. In contrast a visit by British officers to the German army as late as August 1939 noted that the Germans were strongly averse to night operations: 'German officers who had carried out an attachment to the British army considered it remarkable that so much training was carried out by night.' Throughout the course of the battle the Germans tended to pack up at night, enabling the British to pull out unmolested on the night of the 28th. Therefore this was one area, and an important one, where British training was more thorough than German.[15]

Of course it would be naïve to portray the BEF as a perfect military organisation. As was seen in Chapter 1, in marked contrast to the Germans the British army in 1939–40 possessed no coherent doctrine of the offensive. This vacuum went back to the years between the wars when the idea that the army might once again fight on the Continent was anathema. As a result, at the beginning of the Second World War the British government – and the army high command too – was content for the BEF to remain as a junior partner to the French, whose doctrine was strictly defensive.

Some of the army's weaknesses were rectified after Dunkirk, but others were not. The Bartholomew Committee, set up to learn the lessons of the campaign, advocated increases in the number of heavy mortars and the issue of submachine guns, and both of these were done. Radios became more common. There were also tactical lessons learned: for example, in the use of infiltration techniques. Most importantly the army gradually evolved a doctrine of the offensive. This drew on a number of influences. One was the distaste felt by the generals of the Second World War for the butchery of the First, in which they had been junior officers. It dovetailed with Britain's limited manpower to produce a doctrine in which the deployment of massive firepower was central. This included lavish use of the artillery, which had already distinguished itself in 1940, as well as close air support, which from a British weakness became a strength.

Qualitatively the German army remained superior, if not in equipment then in training and doctrine, until much later in the Second World War. The British army was reluctant to change its basic operational procedures, which remained cumbersome and top-down. It was desperately slow in learning how to use tanks effectively. Peter Ewer has shown that Commonwealth – British, Australian and New Zealand – units in Greece in 1941 found it difficult to cope with even weak German tank attacks. This lack of understanding of tank tactics, both in defence and attack, continued to bedevil Commonwealth forces in North Africa until late 1942.[16]

The argument made here, however, is not that the British army was the equal of the German army in every respect in 1940. It is that that the BEF constituted an army capable of fighting a defensive battle with some skill and considerable tenacity, that it showed more flexibility and manoeuvrability than it is often credited with, and that morale remained surprisingly high in spite of constant retreat and dispiriting setbacks.

5th Division's night move to the Ypres–Comines front on 25–26 May raises the other central question of this book – indeed one of the central questions of the whole campaign. How critical to the success of the Dunkirk evacuation was the decision to move 5th Division and later 50th Division north, and how critical was the battle against German IV Corps which resulted? What would have happened if the two divisions had not moved north but had either carried out the attack south or taken some alternative course of action?

This can only be answered by looking at 'what-if' scenarios, or counterfactuals as some historians call them. Of course 'what-if' scenarios, being hypothetical, can only yield probabilities. It is not possible to say for certain what would have occurred if things had happened differently. Yet probabilities can be estimated, and they can be high or low, which means that the conclusions drawn are not necessarily hopelessly vague.

If Gort had not changed his mind on the evening of 25 May, 5th and 50th Divisions would have moved south to attack across the Canal de la Sensée on the 26th. Various scenarios might have persuaded Gort to stick with his original plan. The French might have made encouraging noises about the attack, or the Belgians might have seemed to be resisting better than they actually did. It is likely, in fact, that even if the information about Belgian weakness had not persuaded Gort to alter his plans, the capture of Sixth Army's operation orders would have done so. Brooke brought them to GHQ at about 1900, so Gort would still have had time to cancel the southern attack. Nevertheless the alternative scenario in which the British did move south, and launched their attack on the 26th, is worth a brief examination.

According to the German situation map of 24 May, and assuming that positional changes between then and the 26th were relatively minor, the Sensée between Douai and Valenciennes probably was the best point for an attack, in spite of Gilmore's reservations. On the 24th there was just one German division shown there, and that was resting. Maybe, however, the Germans screened the area so lightly because they reckoned it was as difficult to attack as Gilmore thought. Within fifteen miles or so there were four more infantry divisions, and those were only on the northern side of the corridor that the Germans had constructed from the Meuse to the coast. The corridor was now thirty miles or more wide, and more German infantry divisions were strung out facing the French in the south. No less than six were in the general vicinity Péronne–St Quentin, south of Douai. A motorised division was not far away, and the nearest panzer division was twenty-five miles or so from the attack area, not a great distance.[17]

It seems likely that Gilmore's reservations were correct. Even if the French had attacked with the three divisions originally promised, and the British with two, to advance thirty miles through the cluster of enemy divisions that would soon have formed would have been a Herculean task with limited possibility of success.

The fact that the Germans would have resisted, and had several options for the manner of their resistance, is another variable. Their attacks on the British southwestern front would probably have eased as the divisions taking part were diverted to seal off the Allied penetration. But Army Group B's – specifically IV Corps' – attack might well have stepped up a gear since the Germans would have been keen to take the pressure off their forces in the corridor.

The fact is, however, that this scenario did not come to pass. 5th and 50th Divisions went north, not south. According to Brian Bond, the military historian Basil Liddell Hart had yet another scenario, which took account of this: instead of moving up to the Ypres–Comines line, 5th and 50th Divisions could have counterattacked eastwards from the existing British line on the French frontier. German IV Corps, who at that point were attacking the Belgians, would themselves have been attacked from their left flank.[18]

During the German attacks on the Belgians around Courtrai from 24 May to 26 May, the British reaction was to write off the Belgians and assume that the BEF would have to make its own arrangements for defence. Might Liddell Hart's suggestion have been a better idea? Almost certainly not, because it would have occurred too late. Even if 5th and 50th Divisions had been moved up earlier on the 25th, they would probably have not been able to attack before 26 May, and by then the Belgians were retreating in disarray.

A more feasible possibility was for one or more of the existing four divisions on the frontier to have launched an immediate, if limited, attack eastwards, and the Belgians themselves requested such action.[19] The situation map showed that the Germans, with their customary willingness to take risks, had their side of the frontier defended by just one division, ID 7. A counterattack by the British might well have disturbed IV Corps enough for them to call off the attack on the Belgians.

The problem with this scenario is what is then likely to have occurred. The British were by then aware of potential problems with ammunition supply.[20] It had been fired off lavishly during Ypres–Comines as there was a finite end to the campaign, so stocks could be used up. An attack eastwards implied an open-ended demand at a time when the British supply lines were cut in two. Just as an attack on Army Group A would probably have led Army Group B to redouble its efforts, so the opposite might have occurred. The Germans could have called off the

Halt Order earlier than they did and unleashed the panzers against the vulnerable southwestern front.

Finally, is it really feasible that the Belgians, already severely weakened, would somehow have taken on a new lease of life as a result of a short respite on one front – remembering that they were simultaneously being attacked, and defeated, farther east by the German Eighteenth Army? The best guess is that they might have held out a few days longer if the British had launched a counterattack as requested.

The British certainly treated the Belgians badly. Pownall had little time for them, even before their final collapse, remarking on 23 May when the question of evacuating Belgian troops was raised: 'We don't care a bugger what happens to the Belgians.' If Gort had pursued his plan of 25 May to take the entire BEF south, the implication is that the Belgians would have been left in the lurch, with the BEF simply abandoning the Belgian right flank. Given the number of Belgian prisoners taken by the Germans in the fighting of 25–26 May, however, it is difficult to argue that the Belgians had much to offer militarily by that stage of the campaign. Nonetheless the country's military effort certainly deserves a more detailed study in English.[21]

This leaves us with what actually happened – the Battle of the Ypres–Comines Canal. If 5th Division had given way when it was attacked, and the Germans had penetrated west of the Messines–Wytschaete Ridge on 27 May, would British I and II Corps have been able to escape from their salient around Lille? It is difficult to see how. The Germans would have been to the north of them and would have had the Lys as a defensive line – a much more formidable one than the Ypres–Comines Canal. No doubt the British – like the French First Army, which fought on after Lille was cut off – would have hung on for as long as they could. But ultimately defeat and, for the majority, captivity seem by far the most likely outcome. Only the troops already in the Dunkirk perimeter and perhaps the remnants of the divisions on the southwestern front would have escaped. The larger part of the fighting troops in the BEF would have been lost.

Would such a loss have led to a successful German invasion of Britain? Probably not, because what deterred the Germans were the RAF and the Royal Navy. What would surely have happened was a serious weakening of Churchill's political position. The War Cabinet debate between Churchill and Halifax might not have been affected. Its conclusion, that Britain would have no part in any request to Mussolini to broker peace, was reached by 28 May; if Gort had taken some other course of action on the 25th the ultimate effect would probably not have been known within three days. But when the effect of not defending the Ypres–Comines line did become clear – and assuming as set out above that it would have been disastrous – then Halifax or others could have been emboldened enough to argue again for negotiation. It is quite incalculable as to whether such an argument would have gained enough political support, but it is a salutary thought that it might have done.

Gort has received much criticism over the years, although he has had his defenders too. Many of the criticisms may have been justified, but they seem to be beside the point. Nothing that he or the BEF could do was going to stop the Germans once they had broken through the French. If the latter with 117 divisions failed, how on earth could the British with thirteen succeed? Looking for explanations of the BEF's defeat in either its lack of equipment and training or in Gort's inadequacies are, therefore, futile exercises. The best trained and equipped small army in the world would not have stopped the Germans.

In reality, as has been seen, the BEF was on a par with the German army in terms of its equipment levels. If not as well trained, it was certainly able to fight defensive battles competently. Gort deserves the thanks of history if only for one decision: to call off the attack south and send 5th Division north on 25 May. It was a decision that he had the moral courage to make in the face of his instructions to follow French orders. Once Gort had decided, however, it was the men of 5th Division – the riflemen and Bren gunners, the signalmen and stretcher-bearers, RASC drivers, sappers and artillerymen – who had to act on his orders. It was they who ensured that the line was held and the rest of the BEF came home.

Appendices

Appendix 1.
Two Case Studies of Sources

T HE FOLLOWING TWO CASE studies show the problems that can arise when using war diaries and related material as sources.

Case Study 1: Withdrawals of the Inniskillings and Royal Scots Fusiliers

In Chapter 6 it was mentioned that two battalions – the Inniskillings of 13 Brigade in Hollebeke, the RSF in 17 Brigade just to the north – both thought that the other retreated first. All the diaries involved contain contradictions. This attempts to resolve them.

17 Brigade's diary recorded that at 1240 an artillery OP reported the enemy was in Hollebeke and the Inniskillings were retiring. Lieutenant-Colonel Tod of the Royal Scots confirmed this by phone. As a result of this alleged withdrawal of 13 Brigade, the RSF was withdrawn at 1300. The brief RSF diary merely noted that the withdrawal was 'to conform with the withdrawal of the 13th Infantry Brigade'. Since all diaries agreed that the RSF retired at 1300, this can stand as a firm fact. The time the Inniskillings actually retired is much less certain.[1]

13 Brigade's diary timed the Inniskillings' withdrawal at about 1500, the reason given being that the RSF had retired, thus enabling the Germans to direct enfilade fire on Hollebeke from the north. Thus there is a clear contradiction with 17 Brigade's evidence. Unfortunately the Inniskillings' diary does not clear matters up. It stated: 'At about 1300 hours the 17 Brigade was seen to be retiring', the inference being that the Inniskillings were not. It then continued: 'More determined attacks were made on B Company's front accompanied by heavy fire from their [i.e. the Germans'] guns – D Company also came in for some of this shellfire. At about 1300

hours B and D Companies [that is, the remaining forward companies] commenced withdrawing.' This appears to state that the withdrawal was at 1300 after all. They retired about two miles, or a bit less, and were re-formed at about 1600.

Although retirement would have been slow as it involved disengaging under fire and then going through extensive woods, it seems unlikely that it took three hours. Possibly the second '1300' is a slip of the pen. If an event is said to have occurred at 1300 hours and there follows descriptive material implying the passage of time, it seems likely that the next time recorded will be later, not the same. Thus the second '1300' might well have been intended to be '1500'. However, this must remain a supposition.[2]

There is still a lack of any firm third party evidence to back up the time of 1500 in 13 Brigade's diary for the Inniskillings' withdrawal, as well as flat disagreement between 13 Brigade and 17 Brigade. It is possible that 13 Brigade's diary has been sanitised and because of that an inconvenient event has been omitted, namely that the Inniskillings withdrew first. Of course all war diaries are to some extent artefacts, the product of bias and confusion and not just records of events 'as they actually happened'. But with many diaries the bias and confusion are immediately evident: two timings disagree because of genuine uncertainty, or some inter-battalion rivalry is obviously at work. 13 Brigade's diary is not like that. It seemed clear about timings. At no point was blame overtly put on another party: it nowhere hinted, for example, at the disarray among the Cameronians during the morning. Instead the action seemed to proceed smoothly with brigade HQ always being in control of the situation.

It seems highly likely, therefore, that 13 Brigade's diary was sanitised. It was written up later with a view to presenting a favourable account of the brigade's actions. In that it was no different from many other diaries. It just did it more cleverly. But, even granted that, it still seems highly unlikely that the diarist would actually have altered the times when the orders for withdrawal were issued. It is, of course, possible that the brigade's time of 1500 was a genuine error, or that a slip of the pen – or typewriter in this case – occurred here and not in the Inniskillings' diary. But this does not seem probable, because there is too much other evidence suggesting a later withdrawal time than 1300.

The Wiltshires' diary clearly indicated that Dempsey did not want the Cameronians, 13 Brigade's other forward battalion, to withdraw at that point, while the Cameronians' own diary gave their final time of withdrawal as 1600. Assuming that is roughly accurate, it seems unlikely that Dempsey would have left three hours between retiring his left and his right flank. Finally ID 31's diary stated that IR 17's attack on Hollebeke was stopped between 1400 and 1730, and the village was taken only when the attack was restarted. If the Inniskillings had withdrawn at 1300, then Hollebeke would presumably have been occupied soon afterwards. All the above offer strong circumstantial evidence for a later withdrawal time.[3]

Why, therefore, did the artillery officer who reported to 17 Brigade, and then Lieutenant-Colonel Tod of the Royal Scots himself, think that 13 Brigade was withdrawing at 1300? The answer surely is that, with some elements of both the Inniskillings and the Cameronians being pushed back, and considerable German penetration, it would be very easy to gain such an impression, just as the Ox and Bucks and the 1/7th Warwicks had gained it earlier. Like many other impressions, however, it was incorrect. The most likely conclusion, therefore, is that 13 Brigade's war diary described more or less what happened, although the numerous rough edges were considerably smoothed out.

Among those rough edges were the exact circumstances of the Inniskillings' withdrawal. The 13 Brigade diary, as usual, presented a clear and uncluttered account:

On the left 2 Innisks were also pressed, and had to carry out a most difficult withdrawal through thickly wooded country. Though the rifle companies successfully accomplished this, the whole of advanced Battalion HQ, including the Commanding Officer, who remained behind to control the withdrawal, was surrounded and captured.[4]

Now in fairness this is what brigade HQ, with many other things to worry about, may have thought at the time. But it is certainly not what actually happened.

The regimental history has the most detail, and is probably the best account because those captured at battalion HQ would have been able to contribute to it when it was compiled after the war. According to this a brigade liaison officer went direct to the forward companies, B and D (A having been forced back earlier). The liaison officer led the companies back through the thick woods between Hollebeke and the St Eloi–Warneton road. Battalion headquarters did not know this was happening – as usual the phone lines had been cut. Lefroy, the CO, then received a message, presumably verbal or written, from brigade ordering a withdrawal. Sending an officer forward to the companies, he was naturally surprised to find that they had disappeared. One can guess that Dempsey sent out two liaison officers to be on the safe side. One liaised successfully with the companies, and one with Lefroy, but unfortunately they did not liaise with each other.[5]

During the Inniskillings' retirement, according to the war diary: 'Many platoons and sections went back beyond the St Eloi road and were misdirected and never rejoined the battalion again.' At that point it was realised that the road itself was too far back. A brigade liaison officer had taken the troops there, so perhaps Dempsey was himself uncertain as to where he wanted the new line established. Alternatively the liaison officer had misunderstood his instructions or was incompetent. As a result the troops who had been collected on the road went forwards again to the eastern fringe of the woods and rejoined battalion headquarters, which had not moved. By 1800 the position had been stabilised with B Company on the right, C centre and D left: 'We were in touch with both flanks' – that is with the Royal Scots on the left and the Wiltshires, forming the centre of 13 Brigade's new line, on the right.[6] At this stage the companies had actually been reunited with battalion HQ. The whole process had involved a withdrawal and then a return over the same ground, during which many troops had got lost – or perhaps in some cases opted out of the battle. The HQ had not been captured – that occurred later (see Chapter 8).

The brigade account leaves most of this out. Instead there is a smooth narrative, which reflects well on everyone. Assuming that both the brigade's and the Inniskillings' war diaries were written up later, as seems likely, the writer of the former should have been able to establish more of the facts from the latter if he had tried. That Lefroy remained ignorant of the initial retreat may not have been known since he had been captured; but the fact that battalion HQ was actually captured later and only after it had been reunited with the companies was clear from the war diary.

Case Study 2: Timing of the First Counterattack in 143 Brigade's Sector, 27 May

In Chapter 7 the time of the first counterattack was given as 1900. In fact, there are two different times given and the discussion below explains why one was chosen.

When an initial account of the counterattack was put together, it was noticed that two of the Royal Engineer diaries said that the counterattack started at 1740, and one at 1900. A natural assumption was that the attack started at 1740 and the later time was an error. However the war diary of the Hussars recorded 1900, while the Black Watch did not give a time.

Suspicions were further aroused by two letters from Major R. R. Gillespie, commander of one of the engineer detachments – 7th Field Company. Gillespie had been put in charge of all three RE companies around midday on 27 May, when the threat to them had become evident. After the war he sent these letters to Major Joslen, Ellis' research assistant on the official history. From them it is evident that Gillespie was apt to misremember.

In his first letter to Joslen, Gillespie mentioned that he had come across a detachment of men from the Royal Norfolks, although he could not remember which battalion. Subsequently Joslen conducted a long epistolary hunt for these Royal Norfolks, and his letter book is littered with replies from various officers denying any knowledge of such troops in the Comines area. There seems little doubt that Gillespie misremembered 'Royal Warwicks' as 'Royal Norfolks'. He may even have met the stray detachment of men under a company sergeant major, which Kendal, the 8th Warwicks' CO, recorded as twice falling back without orders (*see* Chapter 5), since Gillespie noted in his letter that the detachment contained one NCO and no officers, but a considerable number of privates. Of course he might have misremembered this too, but it seems the sort of detail that, unlike a name or a time, would be recalled more accurately. Other examples of Gillespie's somewhat dogmatic beliefs in events that could not, in fact, have happened exactly as he thought are given in Chapter 7.[7]

The connection between Gillespie's shaky memory and the timing of the attack is also revealed in his letters to Joslen. He mentioned that, after Dunkirk, he had to 'remake the war diaries of 225 Field Company', as well as 'helping' with those of his own, 7th Field Company. It will be no surprise that the two diaries that timed the attack at 1740 were those of 225th Field Company and of 7th Field Company. Clearly the times given in these were not independent and were probably supplied by Gillespie. It was the other company, 59th Field Company, which said 1900 and 59th Field Company's diary seems likely to be contemporaneous because it referred to its commander, Major MacDonald, as missing. It was later learned that he was killed, and this was a correction that would no doubt have been made had the diary been written up afterwards. Further evidence for the later time came from Major Colvill, the Ox and Bucks commander, who also wrote to Joslen about the events of the afternoon. Colvill stated that he was in no doubt about the time of the counterattack, and this was because 'I was present at the orders for it given by [Carthew-Yorstoun] in the Railway Station at Warneton.' He also timed it at 1900.[8]

Appendix 2.   The Luftwaffe and the British Expeditionary Force

I MAGES OF DIVING STUKAS are a staple of documentary film footage of the German invasion of France and give the impression that the Luftwaffe was omnipresent. In fact, as John Buckley has shown, the Luftwaffe could not be everywhere. It had a devastating impact during the German crossing of the Meuse, but wear and tear and the necessity of covering an ever-widening area of fighting meant that Allied ground forces might be virtually untroubled for days on end. While BEF war diaries frequently recorded German air activity, often this consisted merely of planes flying overhead.[1]

For this book, the air activity recorded in the diaries of twenty-four British units were studied between 20 and 29 May inclusive. The dates only touched on the Dunkirk experience, as this was not central to this book. The units included many of those participating in the Ypres–Comines battle, omitting ones whose diaries were incomplete. There were thirteen infantry battalions from four different divisions, two machine-gun battalions, four medium and five field artillery regiments. Thus a variety of units covering a significant span of the campaign were in the sample.[2]

Diary references were divided into four categories: air activity with no impact on the unit (A); air attack with no or negligible casualties (up to three wounded) (B); attacks described as heavy but with no casualties stated (C); and attacks with significant casualties (D). In a few cases an attack was classified D if there was significant material damage, even if casualties were small.

The classification is crude. Category A, for example, encompasses anything from units recording heavy attacks on their neighbours to planes flying overhead. Units may not have bothered when nothing significant happened, so this category is no doubt incomplete. Nonetheless it is worth noting that on more than half (146) of the 240 'diary days' (24 units @ 10 days each) no air activity was registered. Units usually noted damage or casualties when they were shelled or engaged in infantry action, so it is reasonable to expect that they did the same with air attacks and, therefore, categories B to D do record the majority of serious attacks. By extension, some of the attacks in category C probably did not actually result in casualties, because otherwise they would have been mentioned.

Of the remaining 'diary days', forty-two were classified as A, twenty-six as B, twelve as C and fourteen as D. To give a flavour, A includes entries such as that of the 1/7th Warwicks on 23 May, when forty planes 'paid no attention to us though we must have been visible'. Category B includes one from the 2nd Inniskillings, on 20 May, who were machine-gunned by a low-flying plane 'but suffered no casualties' and that of the 91st Field, whose 'area [was] heavily bombed' on the 26th but suffered no damage or casualties. In fact, in all the raids thus classified precisely four wounded were mentioned. Category C (heavy attacks where casualties were not stated) includes entries such as that of the 2nd Beds and Herts and of the 2nd DCLI on 28 May, both of which mentioned 'heavy' or 'intensive' bombardment from artillery and the air. They were among units caught in the Wytschaete bombardment on that day.[3]

Entries classified as D (with significant casualties and/or material damage) include: one by the 1/7th Middlesex, who were also in the Wytschaete bombardment; one by the 2nd Wiltshires, on 20 May, when a petrol lorry was hit and several drivers wounded; and one by 9th Field, which had three wounded and several vehicles destroyed on 24 May. The last suffered two other category D attacks, losing several vehicles and a gun tractor on the 23rd and more gun tractors, as well as three killed and five wounded, when they came into action on the 26th. Two other units suffered attacks with significant casualties on three different days. One was the 1/7th Middlesex, the other the 6th Seaforths, their last such attack experienced when they were in the troop transport lorries on 26 May. Numbers of casualties were not given but must have been quite substantial over the three attacks.[4]

Outside those units, however, there were only a handful where there was definite evidence of heavy attacks that inflicted casualties. The RSF suffered dive bombing attacks on 23 May, which 'inflicted many casualties'. Two medium artillery units suffered losses from bombing on the beaches on the 29th. And as noted in Chapter 9 the 2nd Sherwood Foresters experienced an air attack that hindered their deployment on the morning of 28 May. They lost nine killed and nine wounded that day, although it is not clear whether all these were from the air attack. Excluding the attacks on the beaches, just six units out of the twenty-four experienced air attacks that definitely caused significant casualties or material damage. And even with these the casualties might be no more than those experienced in one moderate artillery bombardment.[5]

German air activity was no greater during the Battle of the Ypres–Comines Canal than at other times. One reason for this was that from 26 May onwards German air activity in the northern area was mainly devoted to Dunkirk and the beaches. Only the Seaforths and 9th Field record casualties on the 26th, and there was practically no air activity recorded on the 27th. On 28 May four units, three of them noted above, recorded that they were the targets of the heavy air attacks accompanying the artillery bombardment of Wytschaete.

Finally, because so far the RAF has mainly been mentioned in connection with its absence as perceived by the ground units, two successful Allied air attacks should be recorded. On 25 May units of ID 31 were crossing the temporary bridge at Marke on the Lys: 'At 1845 a flight of about thirty British bombers accompanied by fighter planes made an overhead attack causing losses to the division staff and the artillery unit crossing at the time of twenty dead and many injured.' This must have been the same as the attack by twenty-four Blenheims against pontoon bridges in the Courtrai area, which is recorded by Ellis. No British bombers were lost, but German losses were much greater than in most if not all of the attacks on British units. Then in the early morning of the 27th a bomb hit what seems, from the context, to have been IV Corps HQ in Courtrai, and again there were 'many dead'. The nationality of the aircraft was not recorded.[6]

Appendix 3.   Casualties

B RITISH CASUALTY FIGURES CANNOT be estimated from unit records with any certainty. War diaries are seriously incomplete, and it is impossible to know how many men were lost before the battle, went astray on the journey to Dunkirk and were subsequently killed or captured, or were killed at Dunkirk or crossing the Channel. However Bourgeois recorded the number of bodies found in the area, and these can be cross-checked against cemetery records. His sources were not given but it seems unlikely that he would give the precise figures he did without good reasons.

Bourgeois stated that 516 British bodies were found.[1] To these should be added:

- those whose bodies were found after his count or have never been found – but it seems improbable that there were many of these, because this is a well-populated and heavily cultivated region and the figure includes bodies found a considerable time afterwards;
- those killed in and around Ypres – the desultory fighting there suggests that these were few;
- those who died in British and German hospitals.

Any final figure is arbitrary because all these figures are guesses, but a final total of 600–650 seems about right.

According to Bourgeois, again, the British dead are buried in Comines, Warneton and Bas-Warneton municipal cemeteries; Oosttaverne and Bedfordhouse military cemeteries, both mainly for First World War dead; and Esquelmes, some distance away.[2] Walking around these cemeteries is, as always, a moving experience. The first three are mainly devoted to men from 143 Brigade along with Grenadier Guards, North Staffordshires and Black Watch, and a few Royal Engineers and Royal Fusiliers from 12 Brigade. Bedfordhouse in the north mainly has Seaforths and RSF, and Oosttaverne near St Eloi contains men from 13 Brigade, some Northamptonshires and a few from the DCLI and Royal Artillery. Esquelmes, which also has some dead from the Escaut battles, has bodies found in Houthem and Hollebeke – mainly Inniskillings, Cameronians, Warwickshires and North Staffordshires. In all there are 322 dead who were almost certainly victims of the battle.

To these should be added those whose bodies were unidentified or never found and who are listed on the memorial to the missing at Dunkirk. It is difficult to establish this number exactly, because the missing are recorded by regiment but not by unit; every individual would have to be checked to establish whether they were in a unit fighting at the canal. From regimental designations it can be established that no more than a hundred of the missing dead listed on 27 May could have been fighting at the canal.[3] Assuming around the same number on 28 May yields a similar figure to Bourgeois' 516. Again those buried around Ypres, and dying in hospitals away from the battlefield, need to be added on, but the same approximate total is reached.

There are precise German figures of British prisoners taken by ID 18: fifty-one Northamptons, twenty-seven Seaforths, forty-seven RSF, fourteen Green Howards and three RASC men.[4] It is likely that these figures include most of those captured from all the above infantry battalions, although ID 31 may have picked up a few. 13 Brigade would not have lost so heavily as 17 Brigade, because, apart from individuals left behind while withdrawing, only the Inniskillings' HQ was captured and it would not have had many personnel.

The biggest captures must have come in the south, where 143 Brigade's battalions all had front-line companies overrun. Even so, given that a number of men straggled back, it seems unlikely that more than a hundred men per battalion were captured. Allowing for those captured from the counterattacking units and miscellaneous others suggests a likely maximum of around 600 captives. Incidentally notes added by Kenneth Keens and Denis Dodd to Bourgeois' book suggest that captives were generally treated correctly, and Sean Longden's study of British prisoners taken during the campaign confirmed that this was usually the case immediately after capture. However once prisoners started the march east to prison camps, their treatment deteriorated sharply.[5]

Finally it is worth noting that most 5th Division battalions mustered 400–450 men in June, mainly unwounded returners.[6]

German casualties can be established much more accurately for the period 26–29 May. ID 18 and ID 31 figures come from archival sources, ID 61 from Muller-Nedebock cited in Bourgeois. Muller-Nedebock evidently used the same sources since he also gave figures for ID 31, which agree with the ones used in this book.[7] The figures given for 26 May have been halved since some of these casualties would have been incurred in the final Belgian fighting. Both ID 31 and ID 61 list considerable numbers killed on 29 May, but not ID 18. There is no evidence of significant fighting on that date, but, since the first two divisions had both suffered setbacks and disorganisation during the battle, it seems likely that they only accurately established their total dead on the 29th. ID 18 advanced steadily and would have been able to keep a running total. According to Muller-Nedebock, about 80 per cent of ID 61's missing rejoined their unit, and this figure has been used in this book, counting the others as dead (similarly with ID 18, but their missing total was very low). ID 31, however, only posted men missing on 29 May, and it has been inferred that these were all killed. Finally it has been assumed that 2 per cent of those wounded died of wounds at some later date, which adds about 6 per cent to the total of dead.

As with the British figures, the adjustments are somewhat arbitrary. The final figure is 582 dead with, not surprisingly, ID 61 and ID 31 suffering the most casualties; but it would be better expressed as 'about 600', or similar to the probable British figure.

German prisoners pose another problem. 1/7th Warwicks, in particular, reported taking prisoners and sending them back to 5th Division. But the division's provost company diary was missing and no other relevant material has been found in divisional records, nor anything reliable on whether any German prisoners from the campaign ended up in Britain. It seems most likely that they were left behind when the British pulled out. If any prisoners were retained, however, they should be subtracted from the total of deaths above, because they would be included in the German 'missing'.

Notes

Prologue

1   L. F. Ellis, *War in France and Flanders 1939–40,* London, Her Majesty's Stationery Office, 1953, pp. 194–6, 201–4; Battles Nomenclature Committee report, TNA WO 32/16347.

2   D. French, *Raising Churchill's Army: The British Army and the War against Germany 1919–1945,* Oxford, Oxford University Press, 2000, chapters 5 (the BEF), 8 and Conclusion.

Chapter 1

1   K.-H. Frieser, *The Blitzkrieg Legend: The 1940 Campaign in the West,* Annapolis, Naval Institute Press, 2005, p. 36.

2   C. More, *Britain in the Twentieth Century,* London, Pearson, 2007, pp. 73–5, 81.

3   R. Shay, *British Rearmament in the Thirties: Politics and Profit,* Princeton, NJ, Princeton University Press, 1977, p. 297; G. C. Peden, *Arms, Economics and British Strategy: From Dreadnoughts to Hydrogen Bombs,* Cambridge, Cambridge University Press, 2007, p. 127.

4   B. Bond, *Britain, France and Belgium 1939–40,* London, Brasseys, 1990, pp. 5, 12–13; N. Gibbs, *Grand Strategy: Rearmament Policy,* London, Her Majesty's Stationery Office, 1976, pp. 228, 460, 463, 466–8.

5   Ellis, pp. 358–67.

6   A. Brooke, *War Diaries, see* A. Danchev & D. Todman, *War Diaries 1939–45: Field Marshall Lord Alanbrooke,* London, Weidenfeld & Nicolson, 2001, p. 12 (1 Nov.); see also p. 20 (28 Nov.); French, pp. 161, 167–72, 179.

7   'Training, and quality of officers prewar' (TQO) (transcript in possession of author), pp. 4–5; 'Army 1938–9, Training, France 1940' (ARMY) (trancript in possession of author), pp. 7, 10–11; S. Bull, *World War 2 Infantry Tactics: Squad and Platoon,* Oxford, Osprey, 2004, pp. 18–19, for live fire exercises in the British Army post Dunkirk.

8   ARMY, p. 6; TQO, p. 6; French, pp. 49–50, 171.

9   TQO, p. 6.

10 Ellis, pp. 363–7; French, p. 172; TQO, p. 6.

11 French, p. 179; T. Harrison-Place, *Military Training in the British Army 1940–44*, London, Frank Cass, 2000, pp. 41, 43 (Pownall's diary comment); B. Bond, 'Introduction', in B. Bond & M. Taylor (eds), *Battle for France and Flanders*, London, Leo Cooper, 2001, pp. 6–7; Pownall, *Diaries, see* B. Bond (ed.), *Chief of Staff: The Diaries of Lieutenant-General Sir Henry Pownall*, vol. 1: 1933–40, London, Leo Cooper, 1972, pp. 248–9 (first quote), 251, 279 (second quote).

12 French, p 57 for Franklyn; TNA WO 167/244 December 1939 – May 1940; TNA WO 167/372 December 1939 – May 1940; 5th Division's diary recorded an exercise of 17 Brigade's, which was cancelled, but clearly it was reinstated as some of 13 Brigade's officers acted as umpires for it in late March.

13 TNA WO 167/840, dates as in text.

14 TNA WO 167/840.

15 French, pp. 161–8.

16 D. Edgerton, *Britain's War Machine: Weapons, Resources and Experts in the Second World War*, London, Allen Lane, 2001, pp. 61–3.

17 M. Farndale, *History of the Royal Regiment of Artillery: The Years of Defeat, Europe and North Africa, 1939–41*, London, Brasseys, 1996, p. 8; French, pp. 38, 86–8; *see* later chapters of this book for evidence about Bren carriers. They were also used for troop and store carrying, and their official title became 'universal carriers'; war diaries usually identify them simply as 'carriers'. For details on infantry weapons *see* D. Stone, *Hitler's Army 1939–45*, London, Conway, 2009; Bull, *Squad and Platoon*, pp. 27–8; www.bayonetstrength.150m.com and other websites such as Wikipedia.

18 www.bayonetstrength.150m.com.

19 www.bayonetstrength.150m.com; French, ch. 1; A. Jolly, *Blue Flash: The Story of an Armoured Regiment*, London, published by the author, 1952, pp 1–2.

20 Bull, *Squad and Platoon*, p. 24 for squad numbers; by 1944 the squad size was ten, the same as the Germans'. War diaries consulted: 2nd Cameronians; 2nd Wiltshires; 2nd Inniskillings; 6th Seaforths; 2nd Northants; 2nd Royal Scots Fusiliers; 2nd North Staffordshires; 2nd Sherwood Foresters; 1/7th Warwicks; 8th Warwicks; 4th Green Howards; 5th Green Howards; 4th East Yorks; 2nd Lancashire Fusiliers; 5th Northamptonshires; dates between mid-April and early May; the low figure for Sherwood Forester officers may reflect the fact that the last available roll was for 17 April. The reduction in the Inniskillings' numbers may have been connected with the plan to send 5th Division to Norway – one brigade had already been detached – which came to nothing.

21 French, pp. 27, 43; Ellis, Appendix 1, Order of Battle; Farndale, pp. 4, 9, 31–2; published sources are uncertain about territorial equipment, some implying that they only had 18-pounders, but 97th Field, a territorial unit, had '25 pounders' – presumably meaning 18/25-pounders (F. Lushington, *Yeoman Service: A Short History of the Kent Yeomanry 1939–1945*, London, Medici Society, 1947, p. 7); http://nigelef.tripod.com.

22 French, pp. 27, 43.

23 Brooke, *War Diaries*, *see* Danchev & Todman, pp. 34–5 (28 Jan).

24 Ellis, pp. 55–7; Brooke, *War Diaries*, *see* Danchev & Todman, pp. 34–5 (28 Jan); J. Buckley, 'The air war in France', in B. Bond & M. Taylor (eds), *The Battle for France and Flanders*, London, Leo Cooper, 2001, p. 123.

25 S. Bidwell & D. Graham, *Fire-Power: British Army Weapons and Theories of War 1904–1945*, London, Allen & Unwin, 1982, pp. 213, 262; Farndale, p. 32.

26 B. Montgomery, *Memoirs*, London, Collins, 1958, p. 50; Anon., *The Story of the Royal Army Service Corps 1939–1945*, London, Institution of the RASC and George Bell, 1955, p. 50.

27 P. Ventham, & D. Fletcher, *Moving the Guns: The Mechanisation of the Royal Artillery 1854–1939*, London, Her Majesty's Stationery Office, 1990, pp. 79, 81–2, 89–94, 106.

28 D. W. Boileau, *Supplies and Transport*, London: War Office, 1954, vol. II, pp. 307, 366–7. There are eleven troop-carrying companies' war diaries listed in The National Archives, although not all of them survive. This corresponds to Boileau's figures since apart from the original nine he noted two more sent out in June to the forces south of the Somme; TNA WO 167/1101 – TNA WO 167/1111; www.bayonetstrength.150m.com for battalion transport.

29 Ellis, p. 327; Frieser, pp. 29, 36.

30 Edgerton, pp. 28–31.

31 R. Overy, *The Dictators: Hitler's Germany and Stalin's Russia*, London, Penguin, 2005, pp. 444–5.

32 I. Kershaw, *Hitler 1889–1936: Hubris*, London, Allen Lane, 1998, pp. 550–1; Overy, p. 452; W. Deist et al., *Germany and the Second World War*, vol. 1, Oxford, Clarendon Press, 1990, pp. 406–7.

33 J. Bourne, *Britain and the Great War 1914–1918*, London, Edward Arnold, 1989, pp. 83–5, 97–9.

34 Frieser, pp. 4–5.

35 Frieser, pp. 28–33, 38–42 ('semi-modern' p. 31); L. Deighton, *Blitzkrieg*, London, Triad/Granada, 1981, pp. 203–4.

36 Stone, pp. 78–84, 86–9.

37 E. Mawdsley, *Thunder in the East: The Nazi-Soviet War 1941–1945*, London, Hodder Arnold, 2005, p. 20; Frieser, p. 24; S. Hart, R. Hart & M. Hughes, *The German Soldier in World War II*, Staplehurst, Spellmount, 2000, Chapter 2; 'Periodical notes on the German Army' TNA WO 208/2961 (a collection of notes issued from March 1940 onwards), *passim*.

38 Ages for all generals listed are at the beginning of the war.

39 French, p. 163.

40 J. Smyth, *Before the Dawn: A Story of Two Historic Retreats*, London, Cassell, 1957, p. 53.

41 Ellis, pp. 65–6.

42 Brooke, *War Diaries, see* Danchev & Todman, p. 18 (20 Nov. 1939); Pownall, *Diaries, see* Bond, *Chief of Staff*, pp. xxix (Introduction to Pownall), pp. 319, 339; E. Spears, *Assignment to Catastrophe: Prelude to Dunkirk*, London, Heinemann, 1954, p. 227 (Archdale quote); J. R. Colville, *Man of Valour: The Life of Field-Marshal the Viscount Gort*, London, Collins, 1972, p. 200 (Tong quote).

43 Bond, *Chief of Staff*, pp. xi–xxxii (quote p. xxix).

44 Danchev & Todman, p. xiv citing Anthony Powell, *The Military Philosophers*, London, Fontana, 1971, pp. 57–8.

45 Pownall, *Diaries, see* Bond, *Chief of Staff*, p. 243 (12 Oct. 1939).

46 W. S. Churchill, *The Second World War: The Fall of France*, London, Cassell, 1964.

47 A. Bryant, *The Turn of the Tide 1939–1943*, London, Collins, 1957.

48 Danchev & Todman, *passim*; A. Roberts, *Masters and Commanders*, London, Allen Lane, 2008.

49 H. Franklyn, *The Story of One Green Howard in the Dunkirk Campaign*, Richmond, Yorkshire, Green Howards, 1966, pp. 7–8.

50 Brooke, *War Diaries, see* Danchev & Todman, p. 29 (11 Jan. 1940); Franklyn, pp. 5, 18; P. Turnbull, *Dunkirk: Anatomy of a Disaster*, London, Batsford, 1978, p. 122.

51 Ellis, p. 11, citing Gort's instructions.

52 Bidwell & Graham, pp. 187–93.

53 Bidwell & Graham, pp. 22–4; M. S. Alexander, *The Republic in Danger: General Maurice Gamelin and the Politics of French Defence 1933–40*, Cambridge, Cambridge University Press, 1992, p. 200 for the deep-rooted French belief that the Germans would not advance through the Ardennes.

54 Bond, *Britain, France and Belgium*, pp. 26–7, 41, 52–3; Ellis, p. 24.

55 Bond, *Britain, France and Belgium*, pp. 27–9; Ellis, pp. 22–4.

56 Pownall, *Diaries, see* Bond, *Chief of Staff*, p. 255 (17 Nov. 1939); Brooke, *War Diaries, see* Danchev & Todman, p. 18 (19 Nov. 1939). In comments on the draft of the official history, Pownall said that he and Gort disapproved of the role of Seventh Army. This may be the case, but there is little at the time to bear it out, although a careful look at Gort's correspondence with the War Office or the BEF war diary in 1939/40 might turn something up; CAB 106/273, p. 193. *See also* Bond, *Britain, France and Belgium*, p. 28.

57 Brooke, War Diaries, *see* Danchev & Todman, p. 12 (3 Nov. 1939) and p. 55 (23 April 1940); Pownall, *Diaries, see* Bond, *Chief of Staff*, p. 277 (17 Jan 1940) and pp. 285–6 (22 Feb 1940); Bond, *Britain, France and Belgium*, pp. 44–5. (Georges didn't like his Christian name – apparently the intention was to call him Albert, but his father forgot and wrote down Alphonse; Colville, p. 167).

58 Pownall, *Diaries, see* Bond, *Chief of Staff*, p. 251 (4 Nov. 1939); Bryant, p. 71; Brooke, *War Diaries, see* Danchev & Todman, p. 13 (5 Nov. 1939), p. 35 (29 Jan. 1940), p. 37 (6 Feb. 1940).

59 Frieser, pp 61–8; I. Kershaw, I., *Hitler 1936–1945: Nemesis*, London, Allen Lane, 2000, pp 290–1.

60 Frieser, pp. 60, 65, 86; Kershaw, *Hitler 1936–1945*, p. 920, n. 43 discusses the derivation of 'Sickle Cut' – apparently Churchill's original usage was 'Scythe Cut'.

Chapter 2

1 Brooke, *War Diaries*, *see* Danchev & Todman, p. 59 (quote).
2 W. Murray & A. R. Millett, *A War to be Won: Fighting the Second World War*, Cambridge, MA, Belknapp Press of the Harvard University Press, 2000, pp. 59–60; Ellis, pp. 36, 49–50, 59.
3 Frieser, pp. 142–3; Murray & Millett, pp. 68–9.
4 J. Jackson, *The Fall of France: The Nazi Invasion of 1940*, Oxford, Oxford University Press, 2003, pp. 161–2; Ellis, pp. 49, 58–60; Bond, *Britain, France and Belgium*, p. 64. According to Frieser, pp. 241–3, French tank losses at the Battle of Hannut were heavy. G. Chapman, *Why France Collapsed*, London, Cassell, 1968, pp. 103–5, 164, agreed with this and stated that the French tanks subsequently withdrew, but also agreed with Jackson that the French then held their line successfully with infantry. The German tanks with Army Group B were sent south on the 16th (Chapman, p. 165).
5 Ellis, pp. 61, 68; Colville, p. 202 (quote): 'I am exhausted, and against the panzers I can do nothing.'
6 Ellis, pp. 69, 83–4; Pownall, *Diaries*, *see* Bond, *Chief of Staff*, pp. 321–3 (19 May), 323 (quotes).
7 Ellis, pp. 75–7, 81 (quote), 100–101; Murray & Millett, p. 76.
8 Ellis, pp. 75, 79.
9 Ellis, p. 119.
10 Ellis, pp. 117–18.
11 Ellis, pp. 128–30.
12 Ellis, pp. 73–4.
13 Ellis, pp. 68–9, 83–4.
14 Ellis, pp. 83, 87–95; Frieser, p. 283.
15 Ellis, p. 91; Frieser, pp. 275–7, 283–6.
16 Ellis, pp. 94, 96; Frieser, pp. 287–90.
17 Ellis, pp. 138–9; Frieser, pp. 291–5.
18 Ellis, p. 62 (quote), 138, 347–8; Frieser, pp. 292–9.
19 Halder, *War Diary*, *see* C. Burdick & H.-A. Jacobsen (eds), *The Halder War Diary 1939–42*, London, Greenhill, 1988, p. 165 (25 May); Kershaw, *Hitler 1936–1945*, pp. 295–6; Bond, *Britain, France and Belgium*, pp. 100 (Halder quote), 103–4.
20 Ellis, p. 138.
21 Frieser, pp. 309–14.
22 Ellis, pp. 121, 123, 136; Frieser, p. 300.
23 Ellis, pp. 154, 155, 157–8, 161–8.
24 Ellis, pp. 113–114, 135–6.
25 Bock, *War Diaries*, *see* K. Gerbet (ed.), *Generalfeldmarschall Fedor von Bock: The War Diary 1939–45*, Altglen, PA, Schiffer Military History, 1996, p. 9.

26 Bock, *War Diaries*, *see* Gerbet, p. 151 (24 May).

27 Ellis, pp. 130–2.

28 Ellis, p. 104; Jackson, pp. 58–9, 129–31.

29 Ellis, pp. 104–110.

30 Ellis, pp. 111–13; Jackson, p. 89.

31 Ellis, pp. 126, 142–3; Jackson, p. 91.

Chapter 3

1 G. H. Gilmore, 'The story of an eventful month', *Covenanter*, vol. XXXVII, no. 3, pp. 67–8.

2 Gilmore, *Covenanter*, no. 4, p. 78; Ellis, p. 141 for the plan of attack.

3 M. Weygand, *Recalled to Service*, London, Heinemann, 1952, pp. 64–5, 77–8, 80 (quote).

4 TNA CAB 44/67 'Draft history and narrative', p. 296 (27 May); Ellis, pp. 139–40.

5 Ellis, pp. 141, 147; Brooke, *War Diaries*, *see* Danchev & Todman, p. xxxix; Jackson, p. 88.

6 Ellis, pp. 147–8.

7 Brooke, *War Diaries*, *see* Danchev & Todman, 25 May, p. 69; Montgomery's diary for 25 May, IWM, BLM 19. Nigel Hamilton first spotted the reference in Montgomery's unpublished diary, before Brooke's diary was published; N. Hamilton, *Monty: Making of a General*, London, Hamish Hamilton, 1981, pp. 374–5.

8 TNA WO 167/190, 25 May.

9 Pownall, Diaries, *see* Bond, *Chief of Staff*, pp. 322–3 (19 May), and Brooke, *War Diaries*, *see* Danchev & Todman, p. 65 (19 May), for Brooke's plan; ironically, it was to establish the BEF's left – i.e. western – line of defence on the Ypres–Comines Canal and up to Dunkirk, while their right would be farther east.

10 TNA WO 167/300 & 167/372, 25 May.

11 Battalion diaries, TNA WO 167/758, 167/845, 167/721; HQ RA 5th Div. Diary, WO 167/246, 25 May; 9th Field Regt and 91st Field Regt, TNA WO 167/469 & 167/500, 25 May; the War Diaries of other units of 5th Division recorded no activity until the evening.

12 Archdale diary, IWM 78/52/1, p. 36 (25 May); on p. 1 of the diary it noted that up to the 22nd the diary was reconstructed from memory as his notes had been lost; this implies that the rest of it was contemporaneous, or at least based on contemporaneous notes; the timings are very precise, which suggests that they were accurate, but some of the entries – particularly the extensive passage cited below – give the feeling that they might have been written up later for dramatic effect. Churchill, pp. 70–1.

13 Ellis, p. 148; TNA WO 167/29/8; Archdale diary, IWM 78/52/1, p. 36 (25 May).

14 Archdale diary, IWM 78/52/1, pp. 37–8 (25 May).

15 Colville, p. 217. The printed edition of Pownall's diary said 5.00 p.m. (1700), but this is a misprint – the time in the manuscript was 6.00 p.m. (1800); Pownall, *Diaries*, *see* Bond, *Chief of Staff*, p. 340; LHCMA, Pownall diary.

16 Colville, p. 217; Ellis, p. 149.

17 Ellis, p. 176; 50th Division diary recorded that both its brigades spent the 24th reorganising, and there was no further comment on the 25th. The various moves in support of the French are itemised on the 26th (TNA WO 167/300 25–26 May).

18 Colville, pp. 215, 217.

19 'Lord Gort's despatches (France and Belgium, 1939–40)', TNA CAB 66/17/3, 25 May and 26–31 May.

20 II Corps WD, TNA WO 167/148/2 messages 0.272 (143 Brigade) and 0.273 (4th Gordons); transfer of the latter is also mentioned in CAB 44/67 as occurring at 1220; II Corps ordered it to report to 4th Division, which was then in charge of the Ypres–Comines sector.

21 G. Blaxland, *Destination Dunkirk*, London, William Kimber, 1973, p. 417.

22 Blaxland, pp 250–1 (quote p. 250); the 1/7th Middlesex diary (TNA WO 167/792) was muddled over dates and clearly written later; it adds nothing of value.

23 Bryant, p. 123.

24 Bryant, pp. 123–4.

25 Apparently much of Meinertzhagen's story is now known to be baseless. Details from Wikipedia (accessed 19 September 2010), which refers to biographies exposing Meinertzhagen as a fraud.

26 Bryant, p. 124.

27 Blaxland, p. 251.

28 TNA WO 167/29/7, 24 May, Appendix 13.

29 Bryant, p.125; diary extract also in Brooke, *War Diaries*, *see* Danchev & Todman, p. 69.

30 LHCMA, Brooke papers, 'Notes for my memoirs', 5/2/3.

31 Ellis, p. 148.

32 Bryant, p. 124; Ellis, p. 148; *Daily Mirror* cutting and comment on it in LHCMA, Brooke papers, 11/25b & 25c. Walter Lord (*Miracle of Dunkirk*, London, Wordsworth Editions, 1998, p. 23) and Maurice Piercy ('The manoeuvre that saved the field force', in B. Bond & M. Taylor (eds), *The Battle for France and Flanders*, London, Leo Cooper, 2001) are two authors who spotted that Brooke would have arrived too late for the plan to have affected Gort's decision, but neither discussed the timing in detail. On the other hand numerous authors apart from Ellis and Bryant have stressed the importance of the capture of German orders: for example, Major-General Mellenthin, writing from the German perspective, who relied on Ellis (F. W. Mellenthin, *Panzer Battles*, London, First Futura, 1977, p. 23); Blaxland himself; P. Warner, *The Battle for France 1940*, London, Cassell, 1990, pp. 136–7. Churchill, pp. 72–3, also mentioned the orders although left it open as to the part their capture played in Gort's decision.

33 Ellis, pp 135–6; 4th Division War Diary, 24 and 25 May, TNA WO 167/230 (quote); Brooke, *War Diaries*, *see* Danchev & Todman, p. 69.

34 TNA CAB 44/67, pp. 296–8.

35 Pownall, *Diaries*, *see* Bond, *Chief of Staff*, p. 340; Command Post War Diary message, 25 May, TNA WO 167/29/8.

36 TNA WO 167/452, 'Summary of events'.

37 Command Post War Diary 25 May, TNA WO 167/29; it is assumed that there was a few minutes' gap between the receipt of the messages by the signals officer and their transmission to Gort and Pownall.

38 Ellis, p. 149 and *see* earlier discussion in this chapter. Despite viewing numerous communications that Pownall had with the official historians, both while the history was being written and in comments on the draft, it has not been possible to locate written documentation of Gort's 'hunch'.

39 Franklyn, p. 28.

40 Franklyn, p. 28; TNA WO 167/845.

41 Sixth Army *Entwurf*, BA-MA Freiburg, RH 20–6/35, 25 May; TNA WO 167/29/7, 24 May, Appendix 13 (quote).

42 Ellis, p. 148 (he refers in error to VI Corps rather than IV); TNA WO 167/29/7, 24 May, Appendix 13 (quote).

43 6th Army *Kriegstagebuch Nr. 2*, 25 May, BA-MA Freiburg, RH 20–6/34A; Bock, *War Diaries, see* Gerbet, p. 152 (quote).

44 IWM, *IV Korps Vortraege und Ueberblick zum Westfeldzug 9–28.5.40*, p. 16; in the context, *Chef des Generalstabes* probably meant the corps chief of staff.

Chapter 4

1 Franklyn, p. 29; Ellis, p. 33.

2 No. 4 Company diary, relevant dates, TNA WO 167/1104; orders to lift 143 Brigade were received at 12.45; 48th Division diary TNA WO 167/289; TNA WO 167/805, 167/840, 167/841, 25–26 May.

3 TNA WO 167/821, 25–26 May; Ellis, pp. 181–2.

4 TNA 167/845, 25–26 May; Gilmore, *Covenanter*, no. 4, p. 78.

5 J. E. H. Neville (ed.), *The Oxfordshire and Buckinghamshire Light Infantry War Chronicle*, vol. 1, Aldershot, Gale & Polden, 1949, p. 119.

6 TNA WO 167/474, 25 May.

7 TNA WO 167/547, 24 May (quote). It was not possible to trace any other reference to the order.

8 Bidwell & Graham, p. 258, for the medium artillery command structure; I Corps MA diary, TNA WO 167/128, 25 May.

9 Bryant, p. 134; Brooke used the term 'heavy artillery', but technically it was the medium artillery, although Pratt had heavy batteries under his command. Brooke was no doubt unconsciously reverting to the simpler First World War distinction between 'field' and 'heavy', the term 'medium' being a later introduction.

10 LHCMA, Brooke papers, 5/1/2, ms. Brooke Diary, p. 40 (25 May). Neither the meeting with Pratt nor the reference to the German orders are reproduced in the published version of the Brooke diaries (Danchev & Todman), possibly because they were inserted out of sequence in the manuscript diary, at the top and bottom of the relevant page respectively. TNA WO 167/128, 25 May; TNA CAB 106/252 (Summary of II Corps' operations), p. 5. (The summary is dated 1942. Details in it are often inaccurate.)

11 TNA WO 167/538, 25 May (quotes).

12 TNA WO 167/128; WO 167/534; WO 167/538; WO 167/246, all 25 May.

13 *See* e.g. Mellenthin, p. 79.

14 Franklyn, p. 29; he estimated its length in this at 10,000 yards.

15 Franklyn, p. 29.

16 Franklyn, p. 29 (who estimated 143 Brigade's front at 5,000 yards, but 4,500 yards is more accurate); TNA WO 167/378 26 May.

17 TNA WO 167/840, 167/841, various dates; M. Cunliffe, *History of the Royal Warwickshire Regiment 1919–1955*, London, William Clowes, 1956, p. 43; WO 167/805, various dates.

18 TNA WO 167/821; WO 167/796, various dates.

19 TNA WO 167/845, 25 May; Giblett diary IWM 12200 P 233, pp. 15–21; TNA WO 167/721; WO 167/758; WO 167/845, 22–24 May.

20 www.gamber.net/cyclebel/comines.htm; posts entitled 'Lock numbers on Ypres–Comines Canal' in Ypres battlefields (battlefield sites) section of forum, July–August 2009; http://ypres1917.3.forumer.com; a post on this by Aurel Sercua references Lieven Stubbe, 'De Lijdensweg van een vermaade vaart Geschiedenis van het kanaal Ieper-Comen', *Westland Gidsenkroniek*, 43ste jaargang, no. 3, mai–june 2005, pp. 51–67. Websites accessed 23 October 2010. T. Weber, *Hitler's First War*, Oxford, Oxford University Press, 2010, Chapters 3 and 4 and p. 220. Hitler revisited Comines and other places in the vicinity in June 1940; P. Caddick-Adams, 'Exercise Macaw's Return: 143 Brigade and the Battle for Comines, 1940', *British Army Review*, No. 116 (August 1997), p. 54.

21 TNA WO 167/4 Memo to Billotte of 24 April.

22 Gilmore, *Covenanter*, no. 4, p. 78; the rise Gilmore described as steep is actually shallow, but there is a distinct slope; 13 and 17 Brigade diaries TNA WO 167/372 & WO 167/378, 26 May; Neville, p. 119.

23 Ellis, p. 173.

24 Ellis, pp. 172–3.

25 Bryant, pp. 130 (first quote), 131 (second and third quote); Brooke, *War Diaries, see* Danchev & Todman, p. 70 is briefer but confirms the main points.

26 TNA WO 167/919; WO 167/995 and 167/999, all 26 May.

27 D. A. Smith, 'Diary of detachment', TNA CAB 106/256, p. 8.

28 12th Lancers 'Summary of events', TNA WO 167/452, 26 May; Smith, 'Diary of detachment', TNA CAB 106/256, p. 9; Bourgeois, p. 4.

29 TNA WO 167/372; WO 167/378; WO 167/840; WO 167/841, all 26 May; Neville, pp. 119–20.

30 1/9th Manchester Regt diary, TNA WO 167/790, 25 May; 4th Gordons diary, TNA WO 167/745, 26 May; C. Miller, *History of the 13th/18th Hussars 1922–47*, London, Chisman, Bradshaw, 1949, p. 50 (quote).

31 Franklyn quote from an account by Gilmore of an anniversary memorial service in Comines in 1970, IWM 7506 75/100/1; the rest from Gilmore, *Covenanter*, no. 4, p. 78.

32 Gilmore, *Covenanter*, no. 4, p. 78.

33 TNA 167/841, 26 May (quote); Corporal Hawkins' account cited in D. Sarkar, *Guards V.C.: Blitzkrieg 1940*, 2nd edn, Worcester, Victory Books, 2006, p. 153. Corporal Hawkins identified the cemetery as British; in fact there were no British war cemeteries in Houthem that could be traced, but there was a German First World war cemetery, which does not now exist.

34 TNA WO 167/821; WO 167/816; WO 167/758; WO 167/721; WO 167/840; WO 167/841, 26 May; Gilmore, *Covenanter*, no. 4, p. 79; Hawkins from Sarkar, p. 153.

35 IWM, *Vortraege*, p. 18; BA-MA Freiburg, *Entwurf*, RH 20–6/35, p. 40; Bock, *War Diaries*, *see* Gerbet, p. 152.

36 6th Army *Kriegstagebuch* Nr. 2, BA-MA Freiburg, RH 20–6/34a, pp. 107–11; RH 20–6/35, *Entwurf*, pp. 41–2; Bock, *War Diaries*, *see* Gerbet, p. 157.

37 IWM, *Vortraege*, p. 20 (quote).

38 IWM, *Vortraege*, p. 20.

39 BA-MA Freiburg, ID 31 report, RH 26–31/6, 26 May (air attack) and 27 May (first two quotes); IWM, *Vortraege*, p. 20 (subsequent quotes).

40 H. Bourgeois, *The Battle of the Ypres–Comines Canal 1940*, Warwick, Royal Warwickshire Regiment Museum, 1991, Appendix II, p. 41.

41 Bourgeois, Appendix III, p. 45 (quotes).

42 IWM, *Vortraege*, p. 21 (quotes).

43 Ellis, pp. 174, 182, 197; Lord, p. 58.

44 J. Lukacs, *Five Days in London: May 1940*, London, Yale University Press, 1999, pp. 113 ff.; P. M. H. Bell, *A Certain Eventuality: Britain and the Fall of France*, Farnborough, Saxon House, 1975, pp. 40–2.

Chapter 5

1 Neville, pp. 120–1.

2 Axis History Factbook, www.axishistory.com; W. Hubatsch, *Die 61.Infanterie Division*, Eggolsheim, Dorfler, n.d.; IWM, *Vortraege*.

3 'The German Army 19 July 1940 – 19 Dec 1941', TNA WO 208/4324, Annexure 6, paras 31–7 (quotes).

4 'Periodical Notes on the German Army', TNA WO 208/2961, no. 30 onwards; also 'Notes on the German Army in War', TNA WO 208/2962, pp. 252–5 (Dec. 1940).

5 'Periodical notes', TNA WO 208/2961, March–May 1940; infiltration is first stressed in the August edn, no. 30, pp. 5–7.

6 TNA WO 167/840, 27 May; Cunliffe, p. 44; Neville, pp. 121–2, 188 (quote).

7 Caddick-Adams thinks that ID 61 was concentrated against 8th Warwicks and the Ox & Bucks, and 1/7th Warwicks lay entirely within ID 31's frontage; Caddick-Adams, 'Exercise Macaw's Return', p. 49.

8 TNA WO 167/840, 27 May; Cunliffe, p. 48; details of Wynne from Bourgeois, and Dodd papers, p. 4; TNA WO 167/397, 27 May.

9 TNA WO 167/995, 27 May.

10 'Kendal's account' (quote), in Kendal papers; Cunliffe, pp. 44–5.

11 Cunliffe, p. 45 (quote); 'Kendal's account', in Kendal papers, p. 1.

12 Cunliffe, p. 46.

13 Neville, pp. 122, 189.

14 Neville, p. 189; 'Charles' was Major Colvill; according to the Ox and Bucks chronicle (p. 122), it was actually Company Sergeant-Major Howland who was responsible for getting the mortars into action 'with commendable speed'. The 'storm troopers dressed in black' are a puzzle. SS troops wore field grey like the Wehrmacht, and anyway there were none in the vicinity. Only tank crews wore black, but again there were none in the area. Given that the troops were some distance away, perhaps it was just an optical illusion.

15 Neville, p. 190 (quote); Hubatsch, pp. 13–14.

16 Neville, pp. 154, 188 (quote).

17 Cunliffe, p. 44 for German prisoners.

18 TNA WO 167/502, 27 May (first quote); Lushington, pp. 20–1 (second quote); Neville, pp. 159–60, 188–9.

19 'Kendal's account', in Kendal papers, p. 1 (quote).

20 Piercy, pp. 55–6.

21 TNA WO 167/905 (quotes); 4th Division RE diary, WO 167/233, 27 May.

22 TNA WO 167/905 (quote); WO 167/921; WO 167/979, all 27 May.

23 Neville, p. 155.

24 'Kendal's account', in Kendal papers, in Kendal papers, pp. 1–2 ('dirty linen', p. 1); Cunliffe, pp. 45 (quote), 46.

25 Cunliffe, p. 43; Bourgeois, p. 11.

26 TNA WO 167/805, 20 May; Neville, p. 160.

27 Cunliffe, p. 46; TNA WO 167/840, 28 May (the 'had' is missing in the original).

28 Bourgeois, pp. 41, 45–6.

29 IWM, *Vortraege,* p. 22 for dead and wounded officers, supported by Sixth Army records (BA-MA Freiburg, Situation report West, RH 20–6/45a, p. 70; this records twenty-six officers dead and wounded); ID 31 report, RH 26–31/6, 28 May.

30 Bourgeois, pp. 45–6 (quotes).

31 Bourgeois, pp. 41, 45–6.

32 Lushington, p. 21; Lushington's account, written much later, may have got the times wrong, so it is not clear whether his message led to Major Brunker's visit from 5th Division mentioned earlier.

Chapter 6

1 C. N. Barclay, *The History of the Cameronians*, vol. III 1933–46, London, Sifton Praed, 1948, p. 37; Gilmore, *Covenanter*, no. 3, p. 68; 13 Brigade WD; length of front lines from contemporary British army maps.

2 The Cameronians' problems are mentioned in the diaries of the Inniskillings, Wiltshires and 1/7th Warwicks: TNA WO 167/758; WO 167/845; WO 167/840 (quote), all 27 May.

3 Gilmore, *Covenanter*, no. 5, p. 104.

4 The officer was 2nd Lieutenant Cholmondeley of the Royal Scots, mentioned by the brigade war diary on 26 May, but killed on the 27th; 17 Brigade diary TNA WO 167/378, 26 May; RSF diary WO 167/816, 27 May; J. C. Kemp, *The History of the Royal Scots Fusiliers 1919–1959*, Glasgow, The Royal Scots Fusiliers, 1963, p. 36.

5 TNA WO 167/378, 26 May; WO 167/796, 26 and 27 May; W. J. Jervois, *The History of the Northamptonshire Regiment 1934–1948*, London, Regimental History Committee, 1953, p. 62. The brigade war diary stated that the Northamptons were ordered to send two companies to the left of the Seaforths, but the brigade map and the Northamptons' history both say one.

6 TNA WO 167/378, 27 May.

7 TNA WO 167/474, 27 May (quotes); WO 167/378, 27 May (final quote).

8 TNA WO 167/821, 27 May.

9 TNA WO 167/816, 27 May; Kemp, pp. 35–6; Hill 60 details from the Wikipedia entry 'Hill 60 Ypres' accessed 14 December 2010.

10 TNA WO 167/816, 27 May.

11 TNA WO 167/378, 27 May; WO 167/796, 27 May; and Jervois, p. 65; TNA WO 167/816, 27 May and Kemp, pp. 35 (quote), 36.

12 TNA WO 167/816; WO 167/378; WO 167/845, 27 May. *See* Appendix 1 for further discussion of the Inniskillings' withdrawal.

13 TNA WO 167/721; C. N. Barclay, 'The action of the 2nd Cameronians (Scottish Rifles) on the 27 May', *Covenanter*, vol. XXXVII, no. 2 (July 1957); Gilmore, *Covenanter*, no 5.

14 TNA WO 167/372, 26 May; 60th Field diary, Report of Captain Derry, TNA WO 167/487.

15 Gilmore, *Covenanter*, no. 5, p. 104 (quote); TNA WO 167/372 and WO 167/721 (second quote), 27 May.

16 BA-MA Freiburg, RH 26–31/6, 28 May.

17 BA-MA Freiburg, RH 26–18/3, 27 May.

18 TNA WO 167/378, 26 May.

19 BA-MA Freiburg, RH 26–18/3, 27 May.

20 BA-MA Freiburg, RH 26–18/3, 27 May.

21 I Corps MA diary, TNA WO 167/128, 26 and 27 May; it stated 144 Brigade but obviously meant 143 Brigade; it is confused about the infantry brigades it was supporting in the north, so information here has been taken from the target areas given the regiments. For Messines Ridge *see* 5th Medium diary TNA WO 167/538, 25 May, cited in Chapter 4. 1st Heavy diary ammunition return, TNA WO 167/559. CAB 106/268 for total equipment levels in the BEF. For further artillery details *see* Chapter 1 and – a good website – http://nigelef.tripod.com/.

22 TNA WO 167/128, 26 and 27 May; WO 167/538, 25 May (part of entry related to morning of 26th); 5th Heavy Battery diary, WO 167/566; 63rd Medium diary, 26 May, WO 167/547.

23 TNA WO 167/559, 27 May (quote).

24 Other sources suggest that shrapnel was obsolete and not used by 1940 except perhaps in East Africa and the Far East, where there would also have been old First World War 18-pounders. Derry can hardly have been mistaken, however, so presumably some stocks were issued to the 18-pounder batteries in France.

25 This and previous paragraphs from Captain Derry's report in lieu of lost 60th Field Regiment diary, TNA WO 167/487.

26 Barclay, *The History of the Cameronians*, p. 38.

27 TNA WO 167/502, 26 and 27 May (first quote); WO 167/500 27 May (subsequent quotes). 'Counter-preparation' – breaking up enemy troop concentrations etc. – was so similar to 'defensive fire' that it was later abolished as a separate instruction (http://nigelef.tripod.com).

28 9th Field Regiment diary, TNA WO 167/469, 26 and 27 May; 20/76 Battery diary WO 167/513, 26 and 27 May.

29 TNA WO 167/246, 26 May.

30 TNA WO 167/474, 25 and 26 May. This diary is certainly not original – at the end it is dated 20 June 1940 and signed by the commanding officer.

31 TNA WO 167/474, 25 and 26 May, Appendix D

32 Stone, p. 130.

33 TNA CAB 106/268 for BEF equipment; WO 167/734, 28 May; BA-MA Freiburg RH 26–18/3, 27 May.

34 IWM, *Vortraege*, pp. 19, 23 for artillery units (*Abteilung*) allocated to IV Corps; totals are theoretical maxima and no doubt there were slightly fewer guns in practice: for example, 69th Medium, the British regiment deployed late on the 27th, had fifteen, not sixteen, guns (TNA WO 167/128, 27 May).

35 Five mentions of British artillery being shelled have been traced: once on the wagon lines (1st Medium); twice on the batteries – or regimental HQ, it is not clear – (3rd Medium and 91st Field); and twice on OPs (63rd Medium, 18th Field). The last may well have resulted from general enemy shelling of a locality, and the middle two instances were described as 'slight' and 'intermittent' respectively. Also 20/76 Field Battery's OP was once shelled – by British mediums! No diary mentions significant damage caused by such counter-battery fire as there was.

36 Brooke, *War Diaries, see* Danchev & Tolman, p. 71 (27 May, quote); Pownall, *Diaries, see* Bond, *Chief of Staff*, p. 344 (27 May); Ellis, p. 204.

37 Brooke, *War Diaries, see* Danchev & Todman, pp. 70, 71 (26 and 27 May); Bryant, p. 131 (quote); Pownall, *Diaries, see* Bond, *Chief of Staff*, p. 342 (26 May). Barker is sometimes said to have had a breakdown (e.g. French, p. 183), but he continued to function as a corps commander, if not very effectively.

38 Franklyn, p. 29.

39 Three paragraphs above based on Brooke, *War Diaries, see* Danchev & Todman, 27 May supplemented by Bryant, pp. 135–7; first quote from Danchev & Todman, p. 70, others from Brooke's memoir in Bryant, pp. 136–7.

40 4th and 7th RTR WDs (they had been formed into a composite battalion on 25 May), TNA WO 167/459 and 167/460, relevant dates. No unit diary during the Ypres–Comines battle mentioned infantry tanks.

41 Franklyn, pp. 30–2.

42 Lukacs, pp. 146 ff.; Bell, pp. 42–5.

Chapter 7

1 TNA WO 167/702, 26 May.

2 Franklyn, p. 32; 6th Black Watch diary, TNA WO 167/712, 25–26 May; 4th Division's diary is garbled, suggesting that 11 Brigade was put on this front, when in fact it was 12 Brigade, of which the Black Watch was part (TNA WO 167/230 and WO 167/370).

3 TNA WO 167/712, 27 May.

4 TNA WO 167/502; WO 167/905, 13th/18th Hussars diary WO 167/453 (a full-strength squadron would have about 145 men), all 27 May.

5 N. Nicolson & P. Forbes, *The Grenadier Guards in the War of 1939–1945*, Aldershot, Gale & Polden, 1949, map facing p. 36, has the engineers south of the railway only, but this is clearly wrong; engineers' diaries TNA WO 167/905; WO 167/921; WO 167/979, all 27 May 27; Miller, p. 51.

6 'Kendal's account', Royal Warwicks' Museum, p. 2; Denis Dodd's marginal notes to this itemised some of Kendal's mistakes.

7 Bourgeois, pp. 16–17, also map in Bourgeois for details of attack; TNA WO 167/905, 27 May; Miller, p. 51 (quote); Neville, p. 155. The time the attack started is discussed in Appendix 1.

8 TNA WO 167/502 (first quote); WO 167/547 (second quote); WO 167/128; WO 167/453, all 27 May. R. B. Pakenham-Walsh, *History of the Corps of Royal Engineers*, vol. VIII, Chatham, Institution of Royal Engineers, 1958, p. 36 claimed that 5th Division artillery in the rear of the attack – presumably 97th Field – were not allowed to fire in support, because of lack of ammunition. This gets no backing from the 97th Field diary or Lushington, *Yeoman Service*.

9 TNA WO 167/905; WO 167/921, 27 May; Pakenham-Walsh, p. 37. Unfortunately Pakenham-Walsh cited no sources; his account contained detail not found elsewhere, and it may have relied on yet another version by Gillespie (see Appendix 1).

10 Miller, p. 51; the Hussars' war diary contained less detail. There were three tanks in a troop.

11 Casualties from TNA WO 167/453; WO 167/905; WO 167/921; WO 167/979; WO 167/712, all 27 May.

12 Guards diary TNA WO 167/702, 27 May; North Staffs' 'Summary', attached to their diary, TNA WO 167/830.

13 There is an entry in the North Staffs' 'Summary' that suggests this.

14 TNA WO 167/702; WO 167/830, both 27 May; Thorne's quote cited in H. Sebag-Montefiore, *Dunkirk: Fight to the Last Man*, London, Viking, 2006, pp. 328–9 and *see also* Sarkar, p. 152.

15 Franklyn, pp. 32–3.

16 Franklyn, p. 33 put the time at 1930; the North Staffs' war diary (TNA WO 167/830, 27 May) implied a slightly earlier time, and the final time of the attack suggested the same. Adair in his much later memoirs (*see* O. Lindsey (ed.), *The Memoirs of Major-General Sir Allan Adair*, London, Hamish Hamilton, 1996) stated 1730, but there is no other support for such an early time. The North Staffs diary, although it was probably typed up later, contained numerous precise map references, which suggest that it was based on a contemporaneous draft.

17 Franklyn, pp. 29, 33.

18 Franklyn, p. 33.

19 TNA WO 167/702 and WO 167/830, both 26–27 May (Guards' diary 23 May for casualties).

20 Lushington, pp. 21 (first quote), 22 (second quote). Lushington's timing is awry: he put Adair's visit at 1800 and the Guards did not advance until around 2030. He probably mistimed the visit to much earlier than it actually was – it would make more sense if Adair visited him after the latter had had his orders from Franklyn, and while the Guards were marching to the start line.

21 TNA WO 167/128, Appendix G.

22 TNA WO 167/702; WO 167/830, both 27 May.

23 TNA WO 167/830, 27 May (quotes); Cunliffe, p. 47 for Gibbsforce; Bourgeois, p. 18 for the fighting beyond the Kortekeer.

24 TNA WO 167/995, 27 May (quotes).

25 TNA WO 167/830, 27 May (diary and 'Summary'); H. C. B. Cook, *The North Staffordshire Regiment*, London, Leo Cooper, 1970.

26 TNA WO 167/830, 27 May (diary and 'Summary').

27 TNA WO 167/840; Sebag-Montefiore, pp. 330–1 (quote); Bourgeois, p. 18; Miller, p. 51.

28 Adair, *Memoirs, see* Lindsey, pp. 117–18; Nicolson & Forbes, p. 35 and map p. 36.

29 TNA CAB 106/289, p. 142; *see* also Appendix 1.

30 By that time only one Highland battalion – the Queen's Own Cameron Highlanders – wore the kilt in action, so this was not a means of identification!

31 Nicolson & Forbes, pp. 33–4, seem to have originated the Black Watch story, which can then be found elsewhere; Adair, *Memoirs, see* Lindsey, p. 117.

32 Bourgeois, Appendix II, p. 41 (quotes) and Appendix III, p. 46 (final quote).

33 Bourgeois, Appendix III, p. 46 (quote).

34 TNA WO 167/979.

Chapter 8

1 TNA WO 167/721; Gilmore, *Covenanter*, no. 5, p. 105; according to Gilmore his memoir was compiled from extensive notes he made in hospital after he was wounded (*Covenanter*, no. 6 (March 1958), p. 136); Barclay, *The History of the Cameronians*, p. 39.

2 Gilmore, *Covenanter*, no. 5, p. 105; Barclay, *The History of the Cameronians*, p. 39. The casualty figure may refer to the Cameronians' total casualties that day; but the attack was obviously costly.

3 Gilmore, *Covenanter*, no. 5, p. 106 (quotes); Franklyn, p. 31 (quote).

4 Gilmore, *Covenanter*, no. 5, p. 106 (quotes).

5 TNA WO 167/845; WO 167/721, both 27 May; WO 167/372, 26 May.

6 TNA WO 167/758, 27–28 May (quote); Kemp, p. 36. The confusion in various accounts over what happened to the Inniskillings is discussed in Appendix 1. There is also some discussion about where they ended up. The Inniskillings' diary stated they reached the 'Oosttaverne crossroads' but that was the new location of the Cameronians. There is another crossroads about half a mile up the road towards St Eloi, and it seems likely that the Inniskillings were there on 28 May, since they were involved in fighting at Nuyttens Farm nearby.

7 BA-MA Freiburg, RH 26–31/6, 28 May.

8 TNA WO 167/721; WO 167/845, both 27 May, for time of British attack. *See* Glossary for time differences.

9 TNA WO 167/995 and WO 167/840 (quote), 27 May.

10 TNA WO 167/845 (quote), 27 May.

11 BA-MA Freiburg, RH 26–31/6, 28 May.

12 Barclay, *Action of the 2nd Cameronians*, p. 28; BA-MA Freiburg, RH 26–31/6, 28 May (quotes).

13 TNA WO 167/378, 28 May; WO 167/821 and WO 167/796, 27 May; Kemp, pp. 36–7 (quotes) for details of Tod's alternative replies. The RSF war diary actually gave his reply in the War Office wording, but the diary was written later and may have picked this up from the publicity given to it.

14 TNA WO 167/796, 27 May; Jervois, pp. 64–5 (quotes).

15 TNA WO 167/378 and WO 167/796, both 28 May.

16 TNA WO 167/378, 27 May (initial quotes), 28 May (final two quotes).

17 BA-MA Freiburg, RH 26–18/3, 27 May.

18 Jervois, p. 63.

19 TNA WO 167/513, 27 May.

20 TNA WO 167/500 (first two and final quotes); WO 167/246 (third quote), both 27 May; the 9th Manchester's (a machine-gun regiment) diary (WO 167/790) was very terse and shed no light. It is assumed that 'Gun Control' means that each gun fired over open sights on its own targets.

21 TNA WO 167/128, 27 May and Appendix J; WO 167/538, 27 May.

22 Chapter 6 for Brooke's instructions to Johnson; Joslen letter book, CAB 106/289, p. 166. 10 Brigade's war diary has no details – hence Joslen's request to Barker for further information. According to 17 Brigade's diary the two brigades co-located their HQs at 1445 on the 27th (TNA WO 167/378, 27 May).

23 TNA WO 167/378, 27 May.

24 TNA WO 167/734, 27–28 May for transport difficulties.

25 TNA WO 167/734; WO 167/828; WO 167/708, 27–28 May; the Surreys' WD is supplemented by Kingsford-Lethbridge's letter in Joslen.

26 Franklyn, p. 31.

27 TNA WO 167/796, 27 May; Kemp, p. 37.

28 Franklyn, pp. 33–4 (quote); Brooke, *War Diaries*, *see* Danchev & Todman, p. 71 (28 May).

29 Franklyn, p. 34 (quote); LHCMA, Brooke papers, 11/5, notes on interviews (Franklyn); Brooke's memoir is consistent as it had him visiting 5th Division HQ three times on the 27th, at one of which Franklyn was noted as absent (Bryant, pp. 136, 140).

30 The withdrawal of II Corps is fully described in Piercy, *passim*.

31 Bryant, pp. 141–2.

32 Brooke, *War Diaries*, *see* Danchev & Todman, pp. 71–2.

33 1st and 42nd Division diaries, TNA WO 167/190 and 167/266, 27–28 May; Ellis, p. 210 and map between p. 214 and p. 215; Blaxland, pp. 268, 279–90.

34 Ellis, pp. 198–9; Bond, *Britain, France and Belgium* for a sympathetic view of the Belgian dilemma, *see* in particular Chapter 4 for details of the surrender.

35 *IWM, Vortraege*, p. 23; IWM AL 710/3, pp. 375–9. The Belgian army was originally larger than the BEF in numbers, although probably inferior in equipment.

Chapter 9

1 TNA WO 167/370, 28 May.

2 Sarkar, p. 155.

3 TNA WO 167/840, 28 May.

4 TNA WO 167/995 (first quote and artillery quote); WO 167/840 (remaining quotes), 28 May. There were two parties of the 245th Field Company's men in the front line: the right-hand one had been heavily involved in the Staffordshires' counterattack on 27 May; the other, commanded by Lieutenant Evans, was on the far left of the 1/7th line.

5 TNA WO 167/830 and WO 167/841, 28 May; Cunliffe, pp. 50–3; Nicolson & Forbes, p. 35.

6 Cunliffe, pp. 50–1.

7 Adair, *Memoirs, see* Lindsey, p. 119.

8 Adair, *Memoirs, see* Lindsey, p. 119 (quote).

9 Nicolson & Forbes, pp. 35–6; TNA WO 167/702, 28 May.

10 Cited in Sarkar, p. 157.

11 Sarkar, pp. 157–8.

12 Sarkar, Appendix 1; about 30 per cent of those killed died of wounds. Soldiers who died of wounds may, of course, have incurred those wounds earlier, so the figures for each day are not exact. For comparison, according to the Guards' diary (TNA WO 167/702, 23 May) there were 186 casualties and missing in the action of 21/22 May at Esquelmes on the Escaut; Sarkar's list shows fifty killed on those two dates, and there were twenty prisoners, some of whom would have been wounded. So the dead were around 30 per cent of total casualties.

13 Bourgeois, pp. 41–2. (The 08/15 was a portable version of the standard German First World War machine gun. 'Tank strap' must refer to some component related to the water-cooling jacket.)

14 TNA WO 167/453, 28 May; WO 167/841 28 May; WO 167/840 27–28 May; WO 167/830 'Summary'; WO 167/702 28 May.

15 Bourgeois, p. 41 (first quote); TNA WO 167/830, 28 May (second quote); WO 167/502, 28 May (final quote); Adair, *Memoirs, see* Lindsey, p. 119.

16 TNA WO 167/370 28 May (quote); unlike 10 and 11 Brigades, 12 Brigade remained under 4th Division on 28 May, so the Warneton–Comines railway formed the divisional demarcation line (TNA WO 167/230, 27 May; TNA WO 167/244 Appendix 17 message 28 May); South Lancashire diary WO 167/784, 28 May.

17 TNA WO 167/712, Royal Fusiliers diary WO 167/739, 28 May; BA-MA Freiburg, *Kriegstagebuch Nr.2*, RH 20–6/34a, p. 121.

18 TNA WO 167/823; WO 167/845, 28 May. Orders were only given to the Sherwood Foresters at 0600 on 28 May, and 13 Brigade diary does not shed any light on why it took so long to order the Sherwood Foresters to move.

19 BA-MA Freiburg, RH 26–31/6, 29 May (quotes); TMA WO 167/995, 28 May (final quote); details of Warwicks' field of fire from personal observation.

20 TNA WO 167/840; WO 167/823; WO 167/845; WO 167/721, all 28 May; Barclay, *The History of the Cameronians*, p. 41 (quote).

21 TNA WO 167/758, 28 May (quotes, including 'got lost').

22 TNA WO 167/372; WO 167/758, 28 May (quotes).

23 BA-MA Freiburg, RH 26–31/6, 29 May.

24 TNA WO 167/378; WO 167/827; WO 167/845, 28 May.

25 TNA WO 167/796, 28 May; Jervois, pp. 56–7; TNA WO 167/378 28 May (17 Brigade diary stated that about twenty men arrived at brigade HQ).

26 TNA WO 167/816, 28 May; Kemp, pp. 37–9 (quote pp. 38–9).

27 TNA WO 167/734; WO 167/378 (quotes); WO 167/821 (quote 'many hours'), all 28 May; CAB 106/251 (final quote).

28 TNA WO 167/734; WO 167/708; WO 167/758, all 28 May; Kingsford-Lethbridge's letter in TNA CAB 106/289, p. 139. The DCLI thought there were two companies of the Beds and Herts on their right, the Inniskillings one platoon on their left. The Beds and Herts' diary was vague, but later the CO thought one company was involved (CAB 106/251).

29 TNA WO 167/734, 28 May; E. G. Godfrey, *The Duke of Cornwall's Light Infantry 1939–1945*, Upton-upon-Severn, Images Publishing, 1994, p. 73.

30 Godfrey, pp. 73–4; the diary stated two British were killed.

31 TNA WO 167/734, 28 May; the history stated ten carriers set out.

32 TNA WO 167/734, 28 May.

33 Franklyn, p. 35; letter from Barker in TNA CAB 106/289, p. 166; letter from and Kingsford-Lethbridge (Barker's brigade major) in CAB 106/289, p. 139; WO 167/378, 28 May for time.

34 Franklyn, p. 35.

35 TNA WO 167/378; WO 167/708; WO 167/828, 28 May; D. S. Daniell, *The History of the East Surrey Regiment*, vol. IV, London, Benn, 1957, p. 82; Lethbridge in CAB 106/289, p. 139; Birch in CAB 106/251. The Beds and Herts diary referred to an attack on St Eloi being cancelled at 2100, but Lethbridge stated the planned attack was on Voormezeele. Geographically this makes better sense, and Lethbridge seems reliable.

36 TNA WO 167/734, 28 May (quotes).

37 TNA WO 167/368; WO 167/778; WO 167/797; WO 167/827, all 28 May.

38 BA-MA Freiburg, RH 26–18/3, 28–29 May.

39 BA-MA Freiburg, prisoner reports, RH 26–18/53.

40 BA-MA Freiburg, RH 26–18/3, 28–29 May. IR 54's achievement was the greater as it had suffered significant casualties a few days earlier on the Escaut, when its opponents were the 8th Warwicks; Caddick-Adams, 'Exercise Macaw's Return', p. 47.

41 TNA WO 167/474 (quotes), all 28 May.

42 TNA WO 167/474 (quotes), all 28 May.

43 TNA WO 167/547; WO 167/538 (quote), 28 May.

44 Godfrey, p. 73.

45 Franklyn, p. 35.

46 Ellis, pp. 209, 213.

47 Bell, pp. 45–7.

Chapter 10

1 Smith, 'diary of detachment', TNA CAB 106/256 (quote); WO 167/851 27 May.

2 Ellis, pp. 365–6; E. W. Clay, *The Path of the 50th*, Aldershot, Gale & Polden, 1950, pp. 5–6; the division briefly had another brigade attached, but it was detached again on 17 May (Clay, pp. 8, 10).

3 BA-MA Freiburg, Sixth Army report, RH 20–6/45b, p. 16.

4 TNA WO 167/300, 26 May; WO 167/851 27–28 May; WO 167/750 27–28 May; CAB 106/256.

5 Gibbons' letter in TNA CAB 106/289, p. 99A (initial quotes); WO 167/831 28 May (later quotes). Gibbons' memory seems reliable, as details in his letter correspond to the war diary entry.

6 Movements pieced together from 50th Division's and 4th Green Howards' diaries, TNA WO 167/749, 27 May; WO 167/300, 28 May; W. A. T. Synge, *The Story of the Green Howards 1939–1945*, Richmond, Yorkshire, Green Howards, 1952, pp. 49–50 (quote p. 50); for prisoners, BA-MA Freiburg, RH 26–18/53.

7 Brooke, *War Diaries, see* Danchev & Todman, p. 71 (28 May); TNA WO 167/800, 26–28 May (quote 28th); WO 167/300, 28 May.

8 TNA WO 167/404, 26–27 May (quote 27th).

9 TNA WO 167/300; WO 167/729, 26–28 May (quote); WO 167/404, 28 May; Ellis, p. 201.

10 TNA WO 167/452, 27 May. Presumably the patrol was from IR 51, ID 18's northernmost regiment.

11 TNA WO 167/404, 27–28 May.

12 Bryant, p. 146 (first quotes); TNA WO 167/404, 28 May (final quote).

13 6th DLI and 151 Brigade diaries, TNA WO 167/729, 28 May (quotes); WO 167/404, 28 May; Ellis, map facing p. 214; BA-MA Freiburg, RH 26–18/3, 27–28 May.

14 TNA WO 167/490, 27–28 May (quotes); WO 167/404, 28 May (final quote). TNA WO 167/501 (92nd Field) whose exploits were commemorated in Gun Buster, *Return via Dunkirk*, London, Hodder & Stoughton, 1940; the book's brief reference to its involvement at Ypres is inaccurate in detail, although as a whole it gives an interesting insight into an artillery officer's life.

15 'Second Corps operation instruction no. 30', TNA CAB 106/249; according to this, the orders had been issued verbally on 26 May; Piercy, *passim*, discusses them.

16 Medium and heavy regiments: 1st Heavy; 1st, 5th, 63rd, 65th and 69th Medium. Field regiments: 9th, 18th, 27th, 60th, 91st, 97th (plus 115th mentioned below, which had only four guns).

17 115th Field diary, TNA WO 167/505; WO 167/128 (quotes; final quote, Appendix J); WO 167/505, both 28 May. Timing of 65th Medium's departure from HQMA diary (WO 167/128).

18 TNA WO 167/128, 28 May (also 27 May for 69th Medium's total); Brooke, *War Diaries*, *see* Danchev & Todman, p. 72 (28 May); Bryant, p. 144; Bidwell & Graham, p. 279. No figures have been found for field artillery rounds fired in the Ypres–Comines battle.

19 TNA WO 167/128 (first quote); WO 167/554 (quote), both 28 May

20 WO 167/538; WO 167/547 (quotes), both 28 May.

21 TNA WO 167/246, 28 May (first quote); WO 167/490, 28 May (second quote).

22 TNA WO 167/474 (first quote); WO 167/469 (second quote); WO 167/128 (third quote); WO 167/502; WO 167/479, all 28 May.

23 Lushington, p. 22; TNA WO 167/513, 28 May (first quote); WO 167/474, night 28/29 May (second quote).

24 TNA WO 167/739, 28/29 May; Brooke, *War Diaries*, *see* Danchev & Todman, p. 284 (28 May quote); TNA WO 167/230, 28 May (quote).

25 TNA WO 167/370, 29 May (quote); WO 167/739, 28/29 May.

26 Piercy, p. 65; TNA WO 167/721, 28 May (quote); WO 167/841, 28 May.

27 TNA WO 167/378; WO 167/821; WO 167/816, all 28 May; for the rest of 5th Division, diaries recording times between 2030 and 2130 included the Black Watch, Sherwood Foresters, Wiltshires and Inniskillings; the North Staffs stated 2000 and the Grenadier Guards 2200, but it is not clear whether these are starting or finishing times. *See also* DCLI and Beds and Herts diaries, 28 May.

28 TNA WO 167/823; WO 167/830 'Summary' (quote), both 29 May.

29 Ellis, pp. 205, 216.

30 TNA WO 167/85 (first quote); WO 167/729; WO 167/731; WO 167/749, all 29 May; Miller, p. 53 (quote); TNA WO 167/404, 29 May (final quote).

31 Ellis, pp. 175, 215.

32 Ellis, pp. 209–10; Blaxland, pp. 295 ('*onze heures*'); IWM, *Ueberblick*, p. 23 (quote).

33 Osborne's 'Narrative of events', TNA WO 197/99 (quote); S. Longden, *Dunkirk: The Men They Left Behind*, London, Constable, 2008, pp. 40–5; Blaxland, pp. 295–301; BA-MA Freiburg, prisoner reports, RH 26–18/53.

Chapter 11

1 Bock, *War Diaries*, 27–28 May, *see* Gerbet.

2 TNA WO 167/452, 'Summary', p. 24; CAB 106/256, 'Diary of detachment', p. 10; Blaxland, p. 272. (Blaxland thought Lumsden did not know. The 12th Lancers' account did not say that they were unaware of the ceasefire, although it could be read that way.)

3 TNA WO 167/452, 'Summary', p. 25.

4 TNA WO 167/452, p. 26 ('persuaded' and quotes as attributed), CAB 106/256, 'Diary of detachment', p. 11.

5 TNA WO 167/452, p. 11; WO 167/452, 'Summary', pp. 27–8 (quote p. 27).

6 Blaxland, pp. 270 (map showing disposition of forces in the area), 273; 59th Field Company diary, TNA WO 167/921 WD, 29 May.

7 TNA WO 167/452, 'Summary', p. 28.

8 CAB 106/256, 'Diary of detachment', p. 10.

9 Blaxland, pp. 312–14.

10 Blaxland, pp. 277, 314; Chapter 10 above for Brooke's plan.

11 Bourgeois, Appendix 2, p. 42 (quotes up to 'sunny, windy weather'); IWM, *Ueberblick*, ('entered Ypres'); BA-MA Freiburg, RH 26–18/3, 28–29 May (final quote).

12 Ellis, pp. 178–82, 212–13.

13 Casualties from TNA WO 162/179.

14 Gilmore spells his name Parmentier, but he must mean Brigadier R. H. R. Parminter from Gort's staff, who played an important role in organising the evacuation (Lord, p. 95).

15 Gilmore, *Covenanter*, no. 4, pp. 135–6 for above three paragraphs.

16 TNA WO 167/547, relevant dates, details of evacuation.

17 'Report of Captain Derry', TNA WO 167/487; details of *Bullfinch* in T. Mogg, 'Dunkirk and the General Steam Navigation Company', *Greenwich Industrial History*, vol. 10, no. 1 (April 2006).

18 Ellis, p. 233.

19 TNA WO 167/538, 28–30 May; WO 167/128, 30 May.

20 Ellis, pp 231–2; Lord, pp. 264–6.

21 TNA WO 167/452 'Summary', 30–31 May.

22 TNA WO 167/452, 31 May.

23 TNA WO 167/979, 31 May and 1 June (first quote); citation, Major C. S. Hedley, *London Gazette*, 20 December 1940.

24 Jervois, p. 68; Ellis, pp. 219, 237, 244.

25 TNA WO 167/831, 2–3 June; Ellis, pp. 245, 248.

26 TNA WO 167/547, 29 May.

27 TNA WO 167/452, 'Summary', June.

28 TNA WO 167/821, June. The Seaforths and other units distinguished returners from the BEF and newly drafted troops, so it is possible to calculate numbers reasonably accurately; in the Seaforths' case they also gave the number of casualties.

29 TNA WO 167/378, June.

30 TNA WO 167/821, June.

31 Brooke, *War Diaries*, *see* Danchev & Todman, p. 81 (the quotations are from the later 'Notes on my life' in Bryant, p. 172).

32 N. Smart, *Biographical Details of British Generals of the Second World War*, Barnsley, Pen & Sword, 2005, *passim*; *see also* N. Barr, *Pendulum of War: Three Battles at El Alamein*, London, Jonathan Cape, 2004, for Lumsden.

33 *The Times*, 28 April 1960 (obituary) and 5 May 1960 (letter).

34 TNA WO 167/128, Appendix K.

35 Brooke, *War Diaries*, *see* Danchev & Todman, pp. 74, 429, 451 (quote, which is from Brooke's later memoir); Smart, p. 255.

36 Smart, pp. 123–4.

37 Smart, p. 107; Brooke, *War Diaries*, *see* Danchev & Todman, p. 702 (4 July) for Dempsey.

38 G. Aris, *The Fifth British Division 1939 to 1945*, London, Fifth Division Benevolent Fund, 1959.

39 J. Engelmann, *Die 18 Infanterie und Panzergrenadier Division*, Eggolsheim, Dorfler, n.d, p. 4 (casualties); Stone, p. 130 (divisional strength); other sources for this and subsequent paragraphs on the German army are mainly standard internet sources such as Axis History Factbook (www.axishistory.com) and Wikipedia.

40 LHCMA, Brooke papers, 11/25c, document of 28 August issued by the deputy director military intelligence; TNA WO 205/1226, 'Report on the death of General Kinzel'.

41 Mawdsley, pp. 110–11, 163 (quote); Gerbet, pp. 22–3 (Bock biographical note).

42 Bourgeois, p. 35.

43 TNA WO 167/831, 28 May.

44 TNA WO 167/831, 28 May.

Conclusion

1 IWM, *Vortraege*, p. 25.

2 IWM, *Vortraege*, p. 21.

3 ID 61 and ID 31 almost certainly attacked with four battalions each. ID 18 attacked initially with two regiments, which implies four battalions, although one of those regiments subsequently went into reserve; *see* Chapters 5 and 6.

4 Kemp, pp. 38–9; M. Middlebrook, *The Kaiser's Battle*, London, Penguin, 1983, p. 335.

5 'The German Army 19 July 1940 – 19 December 1941', TNA WO 208/4324, Annexure 6, para 34.

6 Ellis, p. 326 – notes from which this was taken are in TNA CAB 146/456; Sarkar, *passim*, for the Escaut battle.

7 Battalion returns from June war diaries; they exclude new drafts.

8 ARMY, pp. 16–17; Sarkar, p. 129; Ellis, p. 326 (quote). There is a discussion of BEF morale in M. Connolly & W. Miller, 'The BEF and the issue of surrender on the Western Front in 1940', *War in History*, vol. 11, no. 4 (2004), pp. 424–41, which concluded that, in spite of the number of BEF prisoners (more than 40,000) – for which there were several good reasons – morale remained reasonably high. See also Caddick-Adams, 'Exercise Macaw's Return', p. 53, who noted the cohesion maintained by the badly battered 143 Brigade.

9 TNA WO 167/840, 27–28 May.

10 Gillespie of 7th Field Company said that he talked to Muirhead on the 27th, TNA CAB 106/289, p. 135; P. Caddick-Adams, *By God They Can Fight: A History of the 143rd Infantry Brigade 1908–1995*, Shrewsbury, 143rd West Midlands Brigade, 1995, p. 200.

11 Chapter 4 for the medium artillery; 'Lord Gort's despatches', TNA CAB 66/17.3, sections 44, 47, 48; Blaxland, pp. 310–14; French, p. 156.

12 Ellis, p. 326 (quote); Neville, p. 188.

13 Ellis, pp. 181–2.

14 TNA WO 167/805, 16 May.

15 'Periodical notes on the German army', no. 1 (March 1940), p. 7, TNA WO 208/2961.

16 'Bartholomew report', pp. 11, 22–3, TNA CAB 106/220; French, pp. 189–98; S. Bull, *World War 2 Infantry Tactics: Company and Battalion*, Oxford, Osprey, 2005, p. 9; Bidwell & Graham, Chapters 13–15; P. Ewer, 'The British campaign in Greece 1941: Assumptions about the operational art and their influence on strategy', *Journal of Military History*, vol. 76, no. 3 (2012), pp. 727–46.

17 The map can be found at the back of Ellis.

18 Bond, *Britain, France and Belgium*, pp. 85–7.

19 Ellis, pp. 176–7.

20 Ellis, p. 176.

21 Bond, *Britain, France and Belgium*, p. 92 (Pownall quote). Bond's invaluable book is mainly about the strategic and political sides of the Allied relationship.

Appendix 1

1 TNA WO 167/378; WO 167/816 (quote), 27 May.

2 TNA WO 167/372; WO 167/758 (quote), 27 May.

3 Wiltshires diary, TNA WO 167/845; Cameronians diary, WO 167/721; BA-MA Freiburg, RH 26–31/6, 28 May

4 TNA WO 167/372, 27 May.

5 F. Fox, *The Royal Inniskilling Fusiliers in the Second World War*, Aldershot, Gale & Polden, 1951, pp. 32–3.

6 TNA WO 167/758, 27 May (quotes); Fox, pp. 32–3.

7 7th, 59th and 225th Field Company diaries, TNA WO 167/905; WO 167/921; WO 167/979, all 27 May; 13th/18th Hussars' diary, WO 167/453, 27 May; Joslen letter book, CAB 106/289, pp. 135, 142.

8 TNA CAB 106/289, pp. 142 (Gillespie), 272 (Colvill – quote).

Appendix 2

1   Buckley, *passim*.
2   1/7th Warwicks; 8th Warwicks; 2nd Cameronians; 2nd Wiltshires; 2nd Inniskillings; 6th Seaforths; 2nd Northants; 2nd Royal Scots Fusiliers; 2nd North Staffordshires; 3rd Guards; 2nd Sherwood Foresters; 2nd Beds and Herts; 2nd Duke of Cornwall's Light Infantry; 1/7th Middlesex; 4th Gordons; 9th, 18th, 91st, 92nd and 97th Field Regiments; 1st, 3rd, 5th and 63rd Medium Regiments.
3   TNA WO 167/840 (first quote); WO 167/758 (second quote); WO 167/500 (third quote); WO 167/708; WO 167/734.
4   TNA WO 167/792; WO 167/845; WO 167/469; WO 167/821.
5   TNA WO 167/816 (quote); WO 167/823.
6   ID 31 report, BA-MA Freiburg, RH 26–31/6, 26 May; IWM, *Vortraege*, p. 22; Ellis, p. 147.

Appendix 3

1   Bourgeois, p. 35.
2   Bourgeois, p. 35.
3   Burials in the cemeteries before 26 May were not counted. Commonwealth War Graves Commission website: www.cwgc.org/.
4   BA-MA Freiburg, prisoner reports, RH 26–18/53.
5   Bourgeois, pp. 49, 52; Longden, pp. 79–80, Chapter 8.
6   From battalion war diaries.
7   BA-MA Freiburg, RH 26–18/3 Bd. 2; RH 26–31/9 Bd. 3, relevant dates; Bourgeois, p. 37.

Sources and Bibliography

T HE MAIN PRIMARY SOURCES used are the war diaries of units engaged in the Battle of the Ypres–Comines Canal. The limitations of these are discussed in Chapter 5. The narrative diaries are supplemented by messages, orders, personnel lists etc. which are usually attached as appendices to unit diaries. The following have also been studied while reconstructing the sequence of events.

Personal Diaries

Apart from personal biases, the main problem with these is that ignorance of the wider context can lead to unjustified inferences being drawn. A classic example is Alan Brooke's visit to GHQ on 27 May, when he found that they had departed 'without saying where they were going'. In fact messages were sent to corps HQs giving the new location, but for reasons explained in Chapter 6 it took almost a day to arrange this.

Memoirs and Autobiographies

Some of these were written very soon after the events. In fact they are almost equivalent to war diaries, some of which were also written up later. Notable are the accounts by 2nd Lieutenant Smith and Captain Derry, and Lieutenant-Colonel Gilmore's memoir, which, although published in the 1950s, was apparently based on notes made soon after the events. Where details can be cross-checked all the above seem pretty reliable. Unfortunately the same cannot be said of later memoirs, which are often extremely inaccurate about the sequence of events, although they may have some value as testimonies to feelings and experiences. Franklyn's is a classic example. His account of his meeting with Gort on 25 May, discussed in Chapter 3, contained a mass of inaccuracies and misrepresentations. Interviews such as with Captain Robert Thorne, used in Chapter 1, repeat some of the same drawbacks as a memoir, but they are useful in shedding light primarily about the workings of the army, and thus have a fair evidential value.

Alan Brooke's memoir, sections of which are reproduced in Arthur Bryant's *Turn of the Tide*, is different again. Insofar as it is based on the diary it seems usually to be reasonably reliable, where it can be cross-checked, about the sequence of events. However, as the editors of Brooke's diary pointed out (Danchev and Todman, 'Note on the Text', pp. xxxi–xxxiv), Bryant was a sloppy editor. Therefore on occasion Brooke's original 'Notes for my memoirs' in the Liddell Hart Centre for Military Archives has been used to check the wording.

Regimental Histories

These written up to the 1950s may often be based in part on personal testimonies or written statements by personnel who were present during the events, although the failure of most histories to give sources means that this has to be inferred. Insofar as the use of different sources meant accounts could be cross-checked, such histories may actually be of more value than many memoirs. The Ox and Bucks 'Chronicle' was different again, being based on an account compiled quite soon after Dunkirk and preserved with the battalion war diary. The publication rather than the diary has been cited for convenience.

One other useful British primary source has been the letter book of Major Joslen, the official 'narrator' – effectively, research assistant – for the official history written by L. F. Ellis. As the letters, mainly from officers in answer to queries from him, are post war, they pose the same hazards as do memoirs.

An unusual secondary source is the history of the battle by Henri Bourgeois, a native of Comines. The Royal Warwickshire Regiment published an English-language translation, and the copy held in the regimental museum archives has been used for this book. In part this relies on British sources such as regimental histories, but much of it evidently comes from Belgian reminiscences. It also contains a memoir by Feldwebel Muller-Nedebock and a translated excerpt from an unnamed German history of ID 61. Much of this is identical to the history by W. Hubatsch listed in the bibliography, but it also contains material not in the Hubatsch book. It appears to be based on an earlier history of the division also by Hubatsch published in 1961, some of which is repeated in the later book.

Other German sources are cited below. The *Vortraege* (lectures) and *Ueberblick* (overview) relating to IV Corps were evidently written quite soon after the campaign. A translation of the war diary of Army Group B is in the Imperial War

Museum, and Bock's diary has been published. Sources from the Bundesarchiv Militaerarchiv Freiburg comprise the diaries of Sixth Army and 18 ID and 31 ID.

Unpublished Primary Sources

The National Archives, Kew (TNA)

Departmental Papers

Cabinet (CAB): 44/67; 66/17/3; 106/249; Papers in series 106; 146/546

War Office (WO): 32/16347; 162/179; Papers in series 167 and 197; 205/1226; 208/2961/2, 208/4324. Papers in series WO 167 comprise war diaries of the following units: GHQ; Command Post/Advanced GHQ; I, II and III Corps; 1st, 4th, 5th and 50th Divisions; 10th, 12th, 13th, 17th, 143rd and 150 Brigades; HQ I Corps Medium Artillery; HQ 5th Division Royal Artillery; HQ 4th Division Royal Engineers; 1st Heavy Artillery Regiment; 5th Heavy Battery; 1st, 5th, and 63rd Medium Artillery Regiments; 20/21st Medium Battery; 9th, 18th, 60th, 68th, 91st, 92nd and 97th Field Artillery Regiments; 19/28 and 20/76 Field Batteries; 4th and 7th Royal Tank Regiment; 12th Royal Lancers; 13/18th Royal Hussars; 3rd Grenadier Guards; 2nd North Staffordshire Regiment; 2nd Sherwood Foresters; 2nd DCLI; 1/6th East Surrey Regiment; 2nd Bedfordshire & Hertfordshire Regiment; 2nd Lancashire Fusiliers; 1st East Surrey Regiment; 6th Black Watch; 2nd Royal Fusiliers; 1st South Lancashire Regiment; 2nd Cameronians (Scottish Rifles); 2nd Royal Inniskilling Fusiliers; 2nd Wiltshire Regiment; 2nd Royal Scots Fusiliers; 2nd Northamptonshire Regiment; 6th Seaforth Highlanders; 1st Oxfordshire & Buckinghamshire Light Infantry; 1/7th and 8th Royal Warwickshire Regiment; 4th East Yorkshire Regiment; 4th and 5th Green Howards; 6th, 8th and 9th DLI; 1/7th Middlesex Regiment; 1/9th Manchester Regiment; 4th Gordon Highlanders; 7th Cheshire Regiment; 2nd and 4th Northumberland Fusiliers; 1/6th South Staffordshire Regiment; 7th, 59th, 225th, 245th (Welsh), 252nd Field Companies; 4th Troop Carrying Company

Bundesarchiv Militaerarchiv Freiburg (BA-MA Freiburg)

Papers in series RH 20 and RH 26

Imperial War Museum Department of Documents (IWM)

Archdale diary
Army Group B diary
Giblett memoir

Gilmore memoir
Montgomery diary
IV Korps Vortraege und Ueberblick zum Westfeldzug 9–28.5.40

Liddell Hart Centre for Military Archives (LHCMA)

Brooke papers
Pownall diary

Royal Regiment of Fusiliers (Warwickshire) Museum

Dodd papers
Kendal papers

Papers in Possession of Author

Interviews with Captain Robert Thorne
'Training, and quality of officers prewar' (TQO)
'Army 1938–9, Training, France 1940' (ARMY)]

Other Sources

Boileau, D. W., *Supplies and Transport*, vols 1 and II, London, War Office, 1954
(found in WO 277/26)

Published Primary Sources

Diaries and Memoirs

Adair, A., *Memoirs* (*see* Lindsey, O.)
Bock, F. von, *War Diaries* (*see* Gerbet, K.)
Bond, B. (ed.), *Chief of Staff: The Diaries of Lieutenant-General Sir Henry Pownall*,
        vol. 1: 1933–40, London, Leo Cooper, 1972
Brooke, A., *War Diaries* (*see* Danchev, A. & Todman, D.)
Burdick, C. & Jacobsen, H.-A. (eds), *The Halder War Diary 1939–42,* London,
        Greenhill, 1988
Danchev, A. & Todman, D., *War Diaries 1939–45: Field Marshal Lord Alanbrooke,*
        London, Weidenfeld & Nicolson, 2001
Franklyn, H., *The Story of One Green Howard in the Dunkirk Campaign,*
        Richmond, Yorkshire, Green Howards, 1966
Gerbet, K. (ed.), *Generalfeldmarschall Fedor von Bock: The War Diary 1939–45,*
        Altglen, PA, Schiffer Military History, 1996

Gilmore, G. H., 'The story of an eventful month', parts 1–IV, *Covenanter*, vol. XXXVII, nos 3–6, September & November 1957, January & March 1958

Gun Buster, *Return via Dunkirk*, London, Hodder & Stoughton, 1940

Halder, F., *War Diary* (*see* Burdick, C. & Jacobsen, H.-A.)

Lindsey, O. (ed.), *The Memoirs of Major-General Sir Allan Adair*, London, Hamish Hamilton, 1996

Mellenthin, F. W., *Panzer Battles*, London, First Futura, 1977

Montgomery, B., *Memoirs*, London, Collins, 1958

Pownall, H., *Diaries* (*see* Bond, B.)

Roberts, A., *Masters and Commanders*, London, Allen Lane, 2008

Smyth, J., *Before the Dawn: A Story of Two Historic Retreats*, London, Cassell, 1957

Spears, E., *Assignment to Catastrophe: Prelude to Dunkirk*, London, Heinemann, 1954

Weygand, M., *Recalled to Service*, London, Heinemann, 1952

Published Secondary Sources

General Texts

Alexander, M. S., *The Republic in Danger: General Maurice Gamelin and the Politics of French Defence 1933–40*, Cambridge, Cambridge University Press, 1992

Barr, N., *Pendulum of War: Three Battles at El Alamein*, London, Jonathan Cape, 2004

Bell, P. M. H., *A Certain Eventuality: Britain and the Fall of France*, Farnborough, Saxon House, 1975

Bidwell, S. & Graham, D., *Fire-Power: British Army Weapons and Theories of War 1904–1945*, London, Allen & Unwin, 1982

Blaxland, G., *Destination Dunkirk*, London, William Kimber, 1973

Bond, B., *Britain, France and Belgium 1939–40*, London, Brasseys, 1990

Bond, B. & Taylor, M. (eds), *The Battle for France and Flanders*, London, Leo Cooper, 2001

Bourgeois, H., *The Battle of the Ypres–Comines Canal 1940*, Warwick, Royal Warwickshire Regiment Museum, 1991

Bourne, J., *Britain and the Great War 1914–1918*, London, Edward Arnold, 1989

Bryant, A., *The Turn of the Tide 1939–1943*, London, Collins, 1957

Buckley, J., 'The air war in France', in B. Bond & M. Taylor (eds), *The Battle for France and Flanders*, London, Leo Cooper, 2001

Bull, S., *World War 2 Infantry Tactics: Company and Battalion,* Oxford, Osprey, 2005

Bull, S., *World War 2 Infantry Tactics: Squad and Platoon,* Oxford, Osprey, 2004

Chapman, G., *Why France Collapsed,* London, Cassell, 1968

Churchill, W. S., *The Second World War: The Fall of France,* London, Cassell, 1964 (1st edn 1948)

Colville, J. R., *Man of Valour: The Life of Field-Marshal the Viscount Gort,* London, Collins, 1972

Connolly, M. & Miller, W., 'The BEF and the issue of surrender on the Western Front in 1940', *War in History,* vol. 11, no. 4 (2004), pp. 424–41

Deighton, L., *Blitzkrieg,* London, Triad/Granada, 1981

Deist, W. et al., *Germany and the Second World War,* vol. 1, Oxford, Clarendon Press, 1990

Edgerton, D., *Britain's War Machine: Weapons, Resources and Experts in the Second World War,* London, Allen Lane, 2011

Ellis, L. F., *The War in France and Flanders 1939–40,* London, Her Majesty's Stationery Office, 1953

Ewer, P., 'The British campaign in Greece 1941: Assumptions about the operational art and their influence on strategy', *Journal of Military History,* vol. 76, no. 3 (2012), pp. 727–46

French, D., *Raising Churchill's Army: The British Army and the War against Germany 1919–1945,* Oxford, Oxford University Press, 2000

Frieser, K.-H., *The Blitzkrieg Legend: The 1940 Campaign in the West,* Annapolis, Naval Institute Press, 2005 (original German edn 1996)

Gibbs, N., *Grand Strategy: Rearmament Policy,* London, Her Majesty's Stationery Office, 1976

Hamilton, N., *Monty: Making of a General,* London, Hamish Hamilton, 1981

Harrison-Place, T., *Military Training in the British Army 1940–44,* London, Frank Cass, 2000

Hart, S., Hart R. & Hughes, M., *The German Soldier in World War II,* Staplehurst, Spellmount, 2000

Jackson, J., *The Fall of France: The Nazi Invasion of 1940,* Oxford, Oxford University Press, 2003

Kershaw, I., *Hitler 1889–1936: Hubris,* London, Allen Lane, 1998

Kershaw, I., *Hitler 1936–1945: Nemesis,* London, Allen Lane, 2000

Longden, S., *Dunkirk: The Men They Left Behind,* London, Constable, 2008

Lord, W., *The Miracle of Dunkirk,* London, Wordsworth Editions, 1998

Lukacs, J., *Five Days in London: May 1940,* London, Yale University Press, 1999

Mawdsley, E., *Thunder in the East: The Nazi-Soviet War 1941–1945,* London, Hodder Arnold, 2005

May, E., *Strange Victory: Hitler's Conquest of France,* London, Tauris, 2000

Middlebrook, M., *The Kaiser's Battle,* London, Penguin, 1983

Mogg, T., 'Dunkirk and the General Steam Navigation Company', *Greenwich Industrial History,* vol. 10, no. 1 (April 2006)

More, C., *Britain in the Twentieth Century,* London, Pearson, 2007

Murray, W. & Millett, A. R., *A War to be Won: Fighting the Second World War,* Cambridge, MA, Belknapp Press of the Harvard University Press, 2000

Overy, R., *The Dictators: Hitler's Germany and Stalin's Russia,* London, Penguin, 2005

Peden, G. C., *Arms, Economics and British Strategy: From Dreadnoughts to Hydrogen Bombs,* Cambridge, Cambridge University Press, 2007

Piercy, M., 'The manoeuvre that saved the field force', in B. Bond & M. Taylor (eds), *The Battle for France and Flanders,* London, Leo Cooper, 2001

Rostron, P., *The Life and Times of General Sir Miles Dempsey,* Barnsley, Pen & Sword, 2010

Sebag-Montefiore, H., *Dunkirk: Fight to the Last Man,* London, Viking, 2006

Shay, R., *British Rearmament in the Thirties: Politics and Profit,* Princeton, NJ, Princeton University Press, 1977

Smart, N., *Biographical Details of British Generals of the Second World War,* Barnsley, Pen & Sword, 2005

Stone, D., *Hitler's Army 1939–45,* London, Conway, 2009

Turnbull, P., *Dunkirk: Anatomy of a Disaster,* London, Batsford, 1978

Ventham, P. & Fletcher, D., *Moving the Guns: The Mechanisation of the Royal Artillery 1854–1939,* London, Her Majesty's Stationery Office, 1990

Warner, P., *The Battle for France 1940,* London, Cassell, 1990

Weber, T., *Hitler's First War,* Oxford, Oxford University Press, 2010

Regimental and Unit Histories

Anon., *The Story of the Royal Army Service Corps 1939–1945,* London, Institution of the RASC and George Bell, 1955

Aris, G., *The Fifth British Division 1939 to 1945,* London, Fifth Division Benevolent Fund, 1959

Barclay, C. N., 'The action of the 2nd Cameronians (Scottish Rifles) on the 27 May', *Covenanter,* vol. XXXVII, no. 2 (July 1957)

Barclay, C. N., *The History of the Cameronians*, vol. III 1933–46, London, Sifton Praed, 1948

Barclay, C. N., *The History of the Sherwood Foresters 1919–1957*, London, William Clowes, 1959

Caddick-Adams, P., 'Exercise Macaw's Return: 143 Brigade and the Battle for Comines, 1940', *British Army Review*, No. 116 (August 1997)

Caddick-Adams, P., *By God They Can Fight: A History of the 143rd Infantry Brigade 1908–1995*, Shrewsbury, 143rd West Midlands Brigade, 1995

Clay, E. W., *The Path of the 50th*, Aldershot, Gale & Polden, 1950

Cook, H. C. B., *The North Staffordshire Regiment*, London, Leo Cooper, 1970

Cunliffe, M., *History of the Royal Warwickshire Regiment 1919–1955*, London, William Clowes, 1956

Daniell, D. S., *The History of the East Surrey Regiment*, vol. IV, London, Benn, 1957

Delaforce, P., *Monty's Northern Legions*, Stroud, The History Press, 2004

Engelmann, J., *Die 18 Infanterie und Panzergrenadier Division*, Eggolsheim, Dorfler, n.d.

Farndale, M., *History of the Royal Regiment of Artillery: The Years of Defeat, Europe and North Africa, 1939–41*, London, Brasseys, 1996

Fox, F., *The Royal Inniskilling Fusiliers in the Second World War*, Aldershot, Gale & Polden, 1951

Godfrey, E. G., *The Duke of Cornwall's Light Infantry 1939–1945*, Upton-upon-Severn, Images Publishing, 1994

Hubatsch, W., *Die 61.Infanterie Division*, Eggolsheim, Dorfler, n.d.

Kemp, J. C., *The History of the Royal Scots Fusiliers 1919–1959*, Glasgow, The Royal Scots Fusiliers, 1963

Jervois, W. J., *The History of the Northamptonshire Regiment 1934–1948*, London, Regimental History Committee, 1953

Jolly, A., *Blue Flash: The Story of an Armoured Regiment*, London, published by the author, 1952

Lushington, F., *Yeoman Service: A Short History of the Kent Yeomanry 1939–1945*, London, Medici Society, 1947

Miller, C., *History of the 13th/18th Hussars 1922–47*, London, Chisman, Bradshaw, 1949

Neville, J. E. H. (ed.), *The Oxfordshire and Buckinghamshire Light Infantry War Chronicle*, vol. 1, Aldershot, Gale & Polden, 1949

Nicolson, N. & Forbes, P., *The Grenadier Guards in the War of 1939–1945*, Gale & Polden, Aldershot, 1949

Pakenham-Walsh, R. B., *History of the Corps of Royal Engineers*, vol. VIII, Chatham, Institution of Royal Engineers, 1958

Sarkar, D., *Guards V.C.: Blitzkrieg 1940,* 2nd edn, Worcester, Victory Books, 2006

Synge, W. A. T., *The Story of the Green Howards 1939–1945,* Richmond, Yorkshire, Green Howards, 1952

Websites

Axis History Factbook, www.axishistory.com

Battalion organisation during the Second World War, www.bayonetstrength.150m.com

British artillery in the Second World War, http://nigelef.tripod.com

Commonwealth War Graves Commission website, www.cwgc.org

Information on Ypres–Comines Canal, www.gamber.net

Ypres battlefields forum, http://ypres1917.3.forumer.com

Index